Black-maned lion – icon of the Kgalagadi

Kgalagadi thunderstorms often arrive with fierce winds, lifting the loose sand into towering dust clouds

KGALAGADI SELF-DRIVE

Routes, Roads & Ratings

Text by **Ingrid van den Berg**

Photos by **Philip & Ingrid van den Berg Heinrich van den Berg & invited contributors**

Published by **HPH Publishing**

Geo Jooste

The lioness cools down on a dune crest after a hot summer's day

Contents

Typical Kgalagadi scene with red and white sand dunes, a dry riverbed, a lone lion and a brewing storm in the distance

Gate hours

The main entrance gate at Twee Rivieren is open from 7:30 to camp gate closing times. The main entrance gate at Mata-Mata is open from 8:00 to 16:30.

Camp gates:

• January	05:30 – 19:30
• February	06:00 – 19:30
• March	06:30 – 19:00
• April	07:00 – 18:30
• May	07:00 – 18:00
• June and July	07:30 – 18:00
• August	07:00 – 18:30
• September	06:30 – 18:30
• October	06:00 – 19:00
• November and December	05:30 – 19:30

Travelling distances to the park

- Upington to Twee Rivieren: 265 km
- Kuruman to Twee Rivieren: 383 km
- Kimberley to Twee Rivieren: 650 km
- Cape Town to Twee Rivieren: 1 076 km
- Johannesburg to Twee Rivieren: 1 090 km
- Durban to Twee Rivieren: 1 463 km
- Mata-Mata to Keetmanshoop: 280 km
- Kaa Gate to Maun: 797 km
- Mabuasehube Gate to Gaborone: 533 km
- Mabuasehube Gate to Maun: 787 km
- Mabuasehube Gate to Tsabong: 115 km
- Two Rivers to Gaborone: 810 km
- Two Rivers to Tsabong: 310 km

Travelling times within the park

Distances in the park are deceptive. It is more accurate to look at travelling time, taking game viewing into account. The following travelling times are the averages from Twee Rivieren to other camps:

- Twee Rivieren – Nossob: 4.5 hours
- Twee Rivieren – Mata-Mata: 3.5 hours
- Twee Rivieren – Kalahari Tented Camp: 3.5 hours
- Twee Rivieren – Grootkolk: 7.5 hours
- Twee Rivieren – Urikaruus: 2.5 hours
- Twee Rivieren – Kieliekrankie: 1.5 hours
- Nossob – Union's End: 4 hours
- Nossob – Mata-Mata: 4.5 hours
- Nossob – Bitterpan: 3.5 hours
- Nossob – Grootkolk: 3 hours
- Nossob – Gharagab entrance route: 3.5 hours

Recommended

Closed shoes to prevent scorpion stings in the evenings, a 10-litre emergency supply of drinking water in the vehicle, and remain with your vehicle in the event of a breakdown.

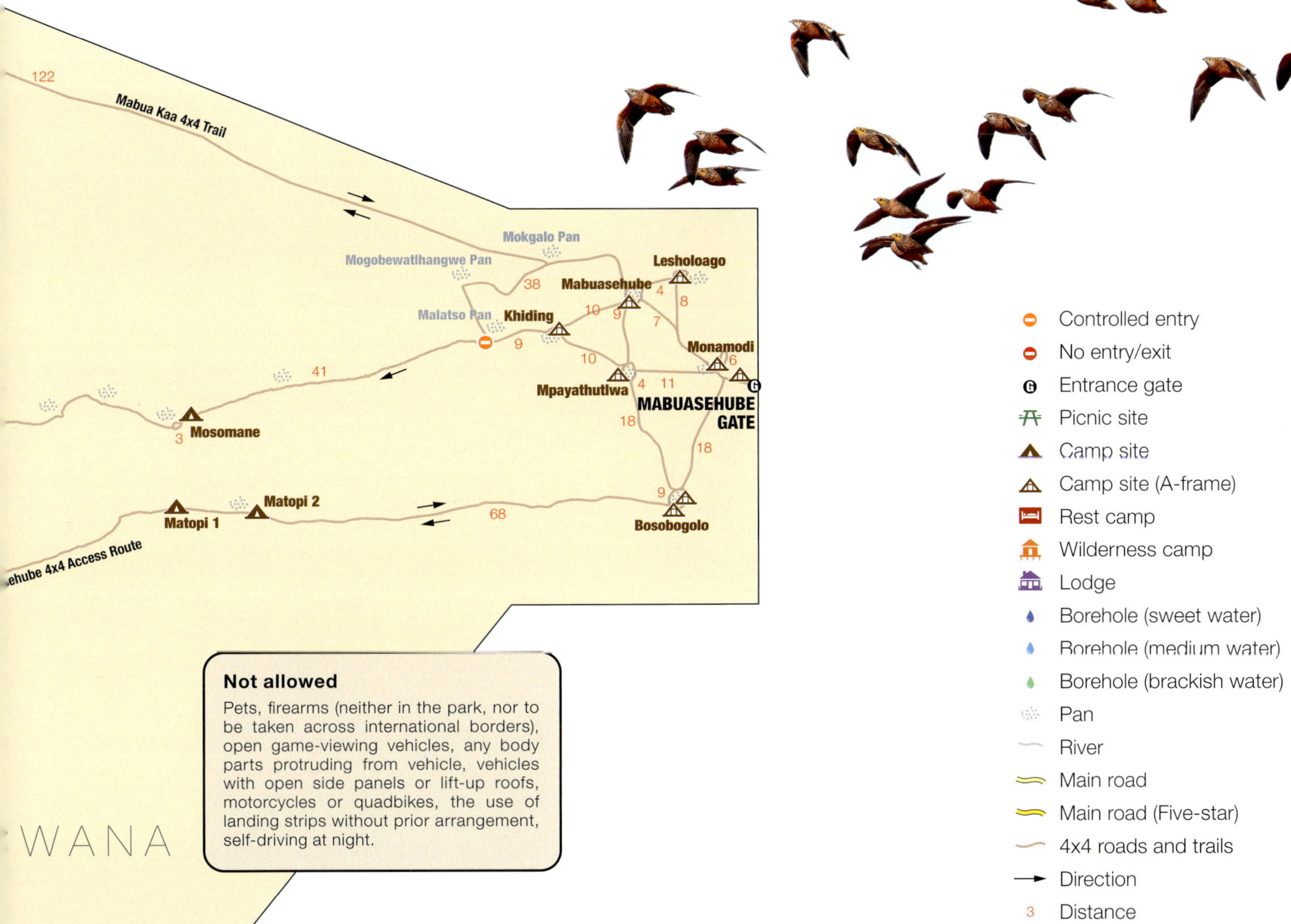

Not allowed

Pets, firearms (neither in the park, nor to be taken across international borders), open game-viewing vehicles, any body parts protruding from vehicle, vehicles with open side panels or lift-up roofs, motorcycles or quadbikes, the use of landing strips without prior arrangement, self-driving at night.

WANA

The Kgalagadi Transfrontier Park

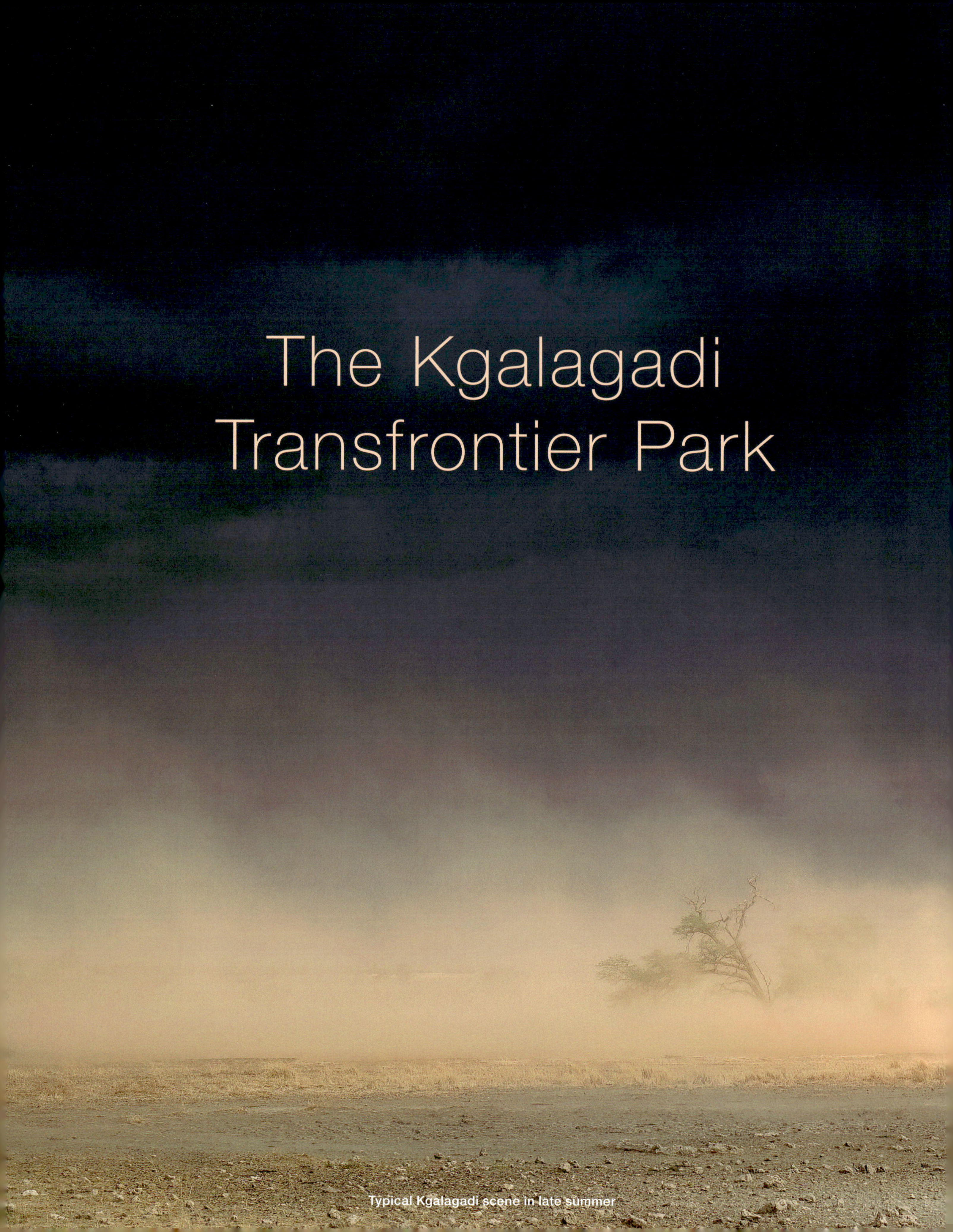

Typical Kgalagadi scene in late summer

Geo Jooste

Introduction

The **Kgalagadi Transfrontier Park** is one of Africa's great wildernesses. A vast, shared conservation area straddling the borders of **South Africa and Botswana**. Covering nearly **38000 km²**, it protects a landscape both harsh and fragile, where life endures through resilience and rhythm. Here, rolling dunes, dry riverbeds and endless horizons form a world of raw beauty and deep silence.

This is the realm of **lion**, **cheetah** and **leopard**, of **gemsbok**, **springbok** and **ostrich**, of mirages and starlit nights. Yet beyond its wildlife, the Kgalagadi speaks of something deeper: of solitude, timelessness and the delicate balance between survival and resilience.

This book is both a **practical guide and a journey**, leading you through its **camps**, **routes**, **wildlife** and **stories**. Whether you come to photograph, to explore or simply to listen to the desert breathe, the Kgalagadi will change the way you see wilderness and perhaps, the way you see yourself.

The **Kgalagadi Transfrontier Park** was born from a visionary idea, that wildlife knows no borders. Today, it stands as one of the world's great conservation success stories, a vast

wilderness jointly protected by **South Africa** and **Botswana**.

Its roots reach back almost a century. In **1931**, the **Kalahari Gemsbok National Park** was proclaimed on the South African side, largely through the efforts of conservation pioneers such as **Col. J. Stevenson-Hamilton** and **Joep le Riche**, the park's first warden. Its purpose was to protect the region's dwindling populations of **gemsbok** and **springbok**, threatened by hunting and drought. On the opposite side of the border, **Botswana** declared the **Gemsbok National Park** in **1938**, creating a parallel sanctuary across the dry riverbeds of the **Nossob** and **Auob**.

For decades, the two parks operated separately but shared the same vision. Rangers from both sides co-operated informally, allowing wildlife to move freely across the unfenced border, an early example of ecological partnership in Africa.

The dream of a single, unified conservation area finally came true on **12 May 2000**, when the two governments signed an agreement creating the **Kgalagadi Transfrontier Park**, the **first formally declared peace park in Africa**. Covering nearly 38 000 square kilometres, it symbolises not only ecological unity, but also cross-border co-operation and peace between nations.

Today, the Kgalagadi remains a model of transfrontier conservation. Wildlife roams unhindered across dunes and fossil riverbeds, and visitors can cross from one country to the other within the park itself.

Late summer rain

DISCOVERING THE SUBTLE BEAUTY OF THE KALAHARI

The park is an **off-the-beaten-track** destination with exceptional wilderness appeal. **Game-viewing** opportunities are excellent, **birding** is rewarding and **sightings of raptors** are often outstanding. The combination of striking scenery and abundant wildlife also makes the Kgalagadi a **paradise for photographers**.

It is worth remembering, however, that from the game-drive roads we see just a fraction of what happens in the field. **What we observe depends on many factors**: the time of day, the animals' natural movements and even what we ourselves are looking for. Our expectations usually shape what we notice.

The **roads and their verges** play a surprisingly important role in viewing experiences. **Predators** are frequently seen walking along the roads, leaving clear spoor and other signs such as resting marks or play tracks. **Clues to the smaller, hidden world** are also found here; tracks and sightings of beetles, rodents, millipedes, snakes and birds, as well as antelope and other large mammals. **After rain**, a host of species from brown hyena to mongoose, and from raptors to butterflies, **visit puddles in the road** to drink. When open water is scarce, **butterflies** and other insects can frequently be seen absorbing moisture from fresh dung.

Ant heaps appear overnight as colonies clear their tunnels of sand, debris and dead ants. These little mounds attract **chats and finches** searching for the rich pickings within. **Female agamas** dig nesting burrows in the compact soil of the roads or verges, carefully covering their eggs with sand. **Ground squirrels** and even **aardvarks** sometimes dig in the road too, though with far more disruptive results.

The **road verges** themselves can be a blessing and a frustration. Because of regular grading, the edges build up over time, forming high, soft banks that can obscure views. Yet, these sandy verges also nurture a profusion of seeds and plants, providing food and cover for rodents, reptiles and insects, as well as nesting sites for small birds and hiding places for stalking predators.

Birdlife along the roadsides is equally rewarding. Swallow-tailed bee-eaters, flycatchers, familiar chats, crimson-breasted shrikes and southern yellow-billed hornbills all use roadside perches to hunt. Fiscal shrikes – also called butcher birds – adopt the same technique, but take care not to confuse them with the similar-looking fiscal flycatcher, which hunts in much the same style and habitat.

Hennie Blignaut

Beauty lies in the eye of the beholder – whether a magnificent leopard, a humble carpenter bee, or the delicate yellow mouse-whiskers flower

THE SHAPING HAND OF GEOLOGY

The story of the Kgalagadi is written in **sand and silence**, its landscape sculpted over millions of years by shifting winds and ancient rivers. Beneath the red dunes and dry riverbeds lies a deep geological history that has given the park its distinctive character.

Life in the dunes and ancient riverbeds exists in a delicate balance. The geology not only defines the scenery, but also determines where plants grow and animals can exist.

The **Kalahari Sand Basin** is the largest continuous sheet of sand on Earth. It stretches from the **Gariep (Orange) River** in South Africa northward across **eastern Namibia**, **most of Botswana**, **western Zimbabwe**, and reaches into **Angola**, **Zambia**, **Gabon** and the **Democratic Republic of the Congo**.

Although it does not always resemble a true desert, the region's **sandy, porous soils**, **erratic rainfall**, and **almost total absence of surface water** make it a vast, semi-arid wilderness. Vegetation is sparse, summers blisteringly hot, and life depends on ingenious strategies of survival.

To understand the Kalahari landscape, we must look back to the **last Ice Age**, which ended around 10 000 years ago. Cooler global temperatures brought arid conditions to southern Africa. Rainfall decreased, vegetation thinned and huge dune fields developed across the interior. These became the **Kalahari Sand Beds**. Powerful winds sculpted the sands into long parallel ridges – some stretching hundreds of kilometres – depositing layers several hundred metres deep. What we see today is merely the vegetated remnant of that ancient desert.

In the **Kgalagadi Transfrontier Park**, the dunes form rhythmic rows separated by **dune streets** and occasional **pans**. Unlike the shifting **barchan dunes** of the Namib, these are fossil dunes, anchored by plants and long since stabilised. Their rich red and ochre hues come from a microscopic coating of **iron oxide** on each grain of sand. In places the dunes rise 10–20 m above the intervening plains. Beneath them lie the **Karoo sedimentary beds**, formed in the age of dinosaurs, the hidden foundation of this timeless landscape.

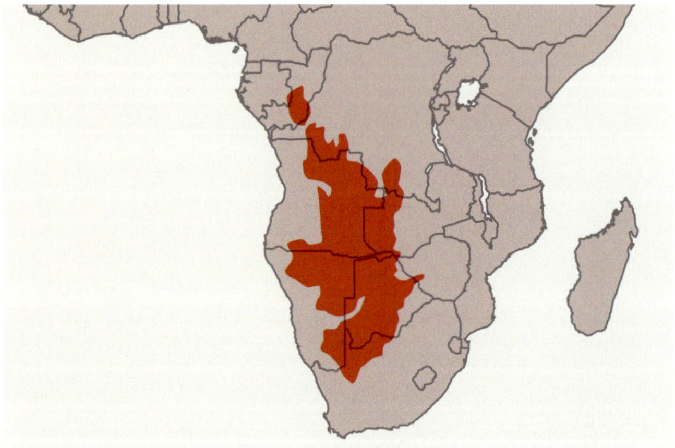

Distribution and extent of Kalahari sand

Crags and cavities in the calcrete cliffs and white ridges lining the dry riverbeds are home to a variety of wildlife

FACES OF THE KGALAGADI

Long before the modern desert formed, the Nossob and Auob Rivers were tributaries of the ancient Kalahari River, flowing during a wetter climatic period millions of years ago. Both originate in Namibia – the Nossob entering the park near Union's End, and the Auob at Mata-Mata – before joining near the confluence, where their combined flow continues southward into the Molopo River, and eventually to the Orange River. Over geological time, these drainage systems were transformed by tectonic shifts, sand accumulation and dune formation, leaving behind the fossilised riverbeds we see today.

The word **Nossob** comes from the **Khoekhoen language**, thought to mean '*soft and even flow*', perhaps referring to the gentle, intermittent movement of water. Other interpretations include '*black water*', '*black lung*', or '*black clay*', possibly describing the river's dark soils and winding course. The name **Auob** means '*bitter water*' in the Khoekhoen language and refers to the riverbed in the Kgalagadi Transfrontier Park, which is predominantly dry but is known for its salty or bitter water when it does flow.

Notice how much narrower the Auob valley is compared to the Nossob. For many visitors, the stretch along the Auob reveals the true magic of the Kgalagadi, a winding road that meanders across low dunes, often skirting calcrete ridges and looping into the riverbed towards the eastern bank. Every waterhole offers excellent visibility and attracts a wide variety of game. To the east and north of the Nossob's fossilised riverbed lies **wooded savanna**, sparsely traversed except by park rangers and authorised 4x4 routes. To the west, **rolling red dunes** stretch towards the Namibian border, largely untouched by human activity.

Both rivers are **ephemeral**, flowing only after exceptional rains. The upper Nossob, between **Union's End** and **Kaspersdraai**, once formed a wide floodplain now filled with sand and silt. It is, in essence, a **dead river**, its course marked by **trees growing where water once flowed**. Further south, the valley narrows and deepens, with steep, rocky banks. **The Auob River**, by contrast, floods roughly **once every 10 years**, while the Nossob might flow **twice in a century**.

The **calcrete cliffs** and **white ridges** that line these dry riverbeds tell of ancient groundwater processes. The Auob's cliffs are especially prominent, while the Nossob's are fewer and more subdued beneath thicker dune sand. Calcrete, also known as **hardpan**, is typical of the park's riverbed formations. It forms in calcareous soils through climatic fluctuations in arid regions, a process that began around three million years ago and continues today. As calcite dissolves in groundwater and re-precipitates during drying, it cements soil particles into an impermeable crust. Over time, this crust hardens into chalk-like rock, leaving the pale calcrete ridges that shape much of the Kalahari landscape. The two valleys also differ in their **mineral composition**; the Auob is rich in **sodium**, **calcium** and **magnesium**, while the Nossob contains more **phosphates**. As a result, **borehole water** from the Auob is generally **fresher and more drinkable**.

Though the rivers rarely flow on the surface, **subterranean water** persists below. The deep-rooted **camelthorn trees** thriving along their beds testify to this hidden resource. Seasonal pools form briefly after rain, notably at **Kwang Pan** along the Nossob, where sweet water collects and draws large herds of **blue wildebeest**, **springbok** and **gemsbok**.

The sweet water of the Nossob attracts an abundance of wildlife and large herds usually gather around its pans. For years, conservationists debated whether **boreholes** – being artificial water sources – should exist in the park at all. In severe droughts, however, they have proved essential for the survival of Kgalagadi's larger, wide-ranging animals.

The **dune roads** reveal a quieter, more intimate Kalahari than the riverbeds. Predators are here – lion, leopard and brown hyena – but seldom seen. Instead, life plays out in subtler ways. **Gemsbok** pick their way between tufts of grass, **eland** wander the valleys, and **steenbok** or **duiker** dart from shade to shade. The air belongs to **korhaans**, **larks**, **chats**, **sandgrouse** and the ever-watchful **ostrich**.

The dunes host a rich variety of plants. **Tsamma melons**, **tumbleweeds**, **devil's claw** and **devil's thorn** thrive after rain, while **shepherd's trees** and **grey camelthorns** anchor the sand and provide shelter, shade and food for countless creatures. **Agamas** bask on sun-warmed stones, **Cape cobras** hunt through the grass, and honey badgers dig for rodents and scorpions.

Rodents are among the most abundant and ecologically important animals in the Kgalagadi. During good rainy seasons, rodent populations explode across the dunes and riverbeds. Species such as the **gerbil**, **striped mouse** and **whistling rat** breed rapidly, feeding on grass seeds, roots and green shoots. Their digging and burrowing loosen the soil, improving aeration and allowing rainwater to penetrate more deeply.

Life without bulk grazers

Visitors often wonder why **elephants**, **buffalo** and **rhinos** are absent from the Kgalagadi. The answer lies in the lack of water and fodder to sustain such bulk grazers. These species require vast quantities of food and water daily, passing much of it undigested and wasting precious moisture.

Desert-adapted herbivores like **gemsbok**, **springbok**, **steenbok** and **duiker** have evolved remarkable efficiency. They extract nearly all available nutrients and water, producing small, dry pellets instead of wet dung. Even **blue wildebeest**, less specialised, produce drier dung here than their savanna counterparts. The presence of wildebeest is largely as a result of artificial water supplied by boreholes.

Similarly, **baboons** and **monkeys** are seldom seen. They rely on fruit, succulent plants and tall trees for roosting, none of which the arid Kalahari can provide.

Daniel Wipf
Gemsbok grazing on devil's thorns on a red dune after rains

ANIMALS NEVER DO NOTHING

Because of the open terrain along the riverbeds, visibility is mostly excellent. You can often approach animals closely, giving you the chance to observe them in detail, identify species and study their behaviour.

It's easy to name what you see but your experience deepens when you look beyond the obvious, noticing *where*, *when* and *how* they behave, and what their interactions might mean. The Kalahari reveals itself as a living puzzle; a web of patterns, relationships and unspoken rules waiting to be pieced together. It's not always simple to explain why animals behave as they do. Some actions are instinctive, others learnt and many are triggered by environmental cues.

Ask yourself: does this behaviour help the animal survive or reproduce? Could it be a remnant of ancestral habits that still shape modern species? Try watching the social structures within antelope herds. Many species are territorial, defending a home range from rivals of their own kind. Observe carefully. The dominant male is usually easy to spot, while others display subtle gestures of submission. Female herds, frequently accompanied by young males, move through territories on their way to food or water, signalling deference to avoid conflict.

You may also notice displacement behaviour. Those small, seemingly meaningless actions that ease tension, like a human scratching their head when uncertain. Animals do it, too: a springbok suddenly grooming itself after a standoff, or a wildebeest pawing the ground after retreating from a fight. Such moments may appear trivial, yet they speak volumes about instinct, emotion and the fine balance between fear and dominance.

All of this may sound complex but it is deeply rewarding to become a quiet observer ... a 'people scientist' of the wild. The more closely you watch, the more layers you will uncover, and your game drives will take on a whole new depth and meaning.

Scent marking by blue wildebeest

Red hartebeest bulls sparring for dominance

Road network and safety

The park's two principal tourist roads follow the **dry river-beds** of the **Nossob** and **Auob** rivers. Between them lies dune veld linked by two dune-crossing roads.

- A **4x4 vehicle is not essential for the main routes** between the traditional camps, but good ground clearance makes the journey far more comfortable. During the rainy season (December to April), the roads can become muddy and sandy sections more challenging, so a 4x4 is advisable.
- Roads to Gharagab and Bitterpan wilderness camps, driving the Nossob Eco-Trail and Leeudril Trail, Botswana roads (which do not fall under SANParks jurisdiction), **all require a 4x4 with high ground clearance and low-range capabilities**.
- Deflate tyres to around 1.6 bar before entering the park, and reinflate at Twee Rivieren before leaving the park (trailers 1.2 bar; caravan 2.0 bar).
- The **Twee Rivieren–Nossob** road is generally firm and passable by sedan.
- The **Nossob–Mata-Mata** route is far sandier and small sedans can easily get stuck.
- The **Mata-Mata–Twee Rivieren** stretch is again good.
- Caravans are allowed in the park, but the rough, sandy and corrugated roads can be hard on them. Standard caravans should stick to Twee Rivieren and, with care, Mata-Mata; the route to Nossob is better suited to off-road models.
- On the **Botswana side**, the wilderness deepens. Camps are simple – a wooden shelter, long-drop toilet, perhaps a tap or shower – with no shops or supplies. Travellers must be entirely self-sufficient and equipped with a proper 4x4. Fit a grass-net to protect your radiator from tall dry grass. It is advisable to travel in at least two vehicles.

The **Kgalagadi is vast and remote**, so vehicle trouble or getting stuck in sand can have serious consequences.

Getting stuck and mechanical breakdowns

- Should you get stuck on the road, ask passengers of a passer-by vehicle to notify the nearest reception.
- Send details of vehicle: **surname of owner**, **registration and make**, **colour**, **time** it was encountered, and the **approximate area** or GPS.
- The park will **transport passengers** to the nearest camp and can assist if you are stuck, but **cannot tow** a vehicle. Park staff will assist in calling a towing service. Charges may apply.
- The park has technical workshops and can help with minor repairs, but they do not stock tyres, batteries, etc.
- Emergency number for **Twee Rivieren: 054 561 2000 / 073 224 3484**.

Important: All visitors must **register and obtain a permit** before each drive and hand it in upon return. Each vehicle's intended route is logged daily; a vital safety measure should assistance be needed. Always carry **ample drinking water**, **emergency rations and fuel** as drives often last longer than expected and picnic sites are far apart.

Lioness on a road verge between Bedinkt and Langklaas

Nick Pawley

Cheetah at an important road sign

Don't underestimate the dangers of getting lost

Story: Fanus and Ruth Geldenhuys

On 17 July 2010, Ruth and I almost lost our lives because of an impulsive decision. It was our third night in the park, our first visit after retirement and a long-awaited trip to the Kgalagadi.

We rose early, packed a flask of coffee and a few snacks, and hurried to be first out of camp. The air was icy and Ruth kept her warm gown on as we collected our permit at the gate, noting our destination as 'going south'. Excited and full of expectation, we set off. The desert was still and empty, not an animal in sight.

After coffee and rusks at Marie's waterhole, we returned to camp, but it was still early, so we decided to drive north instead, without informing the office of our change in direction. That small oversight nearly cost us our lives.

Kilometre after kilometre, still no wildlife. At Langklaas waterhole we turned back, disheartened, then decided to explore the **Matopi** road, unaware that it was a restricted 4x4 track to Mabuasehube. There was no signpost to warn us. About eight kilometres in, the vehicle suddenly broke down. Something deep within the engine snapped, and we were stranded.

Panic set in. Ruth kept watch for predators while I worked under the bonnet but nothing helped. The vast silence pressed in on us. We took stock: no water, just a few mandarins, some droëwors and a little biltong. Eating would worsen dehydration, so we waited. Ruth suggested lighting a fire – surely someone would see the smoke – but it only drifted low, trapped between the dunes. We put it out and prayed.

Back at Nossob, park staff realised we had not returned and began a search. They drove south first, then north, but as night fell, the effort was called off until morning.

Meanwhile, we tried flashing the vehicle lights in SOS signals, but the dunes blocked the beam and soon the battery began to die. We had removed the back seat for packing space, so we spent the freezing night huddled in the front seats, using whatever we could find for warmth. It was a long, terrifying night ... one we will never forget.

Dawn brought hope, but also hunger and thirst. We shared our last mandarin and waited as the hours dragged by. Back at camp, staff and fellow campers were deeply concerned. Eventually someone had the idea to **follow our tyre tracks** from the campsite to see where we had gone off the main road. It worked. We were found on the second day; dehydrated, exhausted and profoundly grateful.

The experience changed us forever. Our advice to all visitors: **stay on official roads** and always **report your intended direction**. Carry **enough water and emergency rations** for unexpected delays. You do not want to experience what we did. Yet, despite everything, the Kgalagadi remains one of the most magnificent places on Earth: vast, humbling and unforgettable.

DRIVING ON SAND: ESSENTIAL TIPS FOR FIRST-TIMERS

You will be travelling on sand for most of your time in the Kgalagadi. If you have never driven in deep sand before, the following guidelines will help you stay safe, protect the environment and keep your vehicle moving.

Stay on established tracks wherever possible. The sand here is already compacted and keeping to the existing route minimises your vehicle's footprint and prevents damage to fragile dune vegetation.

Before you set off, **reduce tyre pressures**. This dramatically improves traction and reduces strain on your vehicle (most drivers drop to around **1.6 bar**, and in very soft sand, even lower may be necessary).

Drive slowly and steadily. Use **low-range** where appropriate, as it multiplies available torque and gives you a lower, more controlled gear for soft stretches. Keep gear changes smooth and at higher revs to avoid losing momentum.

On dunes, always travel **straight up** or **straight down**. Never attempt to turn on a slope. If a climb fails and you cannot reach the crest, reverse straight down in gear. Never coast and never try to turn sideways. Some dune crests are steep with very loose sand, and maintaining controlled momentum is vital.

Whenever possible, ease off the accelerator and **coast to a stop** rather than braking sharply. Heavy braking builds up sand mounds in front of the tyres, making it harder to pull away again. If you begin to bog down, avoid the instinct to 'gun' the accelerator as this just spins the wheels and digs you in deeper.

If stuck, first try **reversing gently** along your own tracks, which are already compacted. Back up far enough to gain a fresh run before moving forward again. With patience, repeating this manoeuvre often allows you to pass through a stubborn section.

If reversing fails, get out and assess the situation. Deflate your tyres further and clear sand away from behind and beneath the wheels. Check whether the chassis is touching the sand; if it is, dig it free before trying to move again. You may need several attempts ... and possibly a gentle push from passengers.

If you are still bogged down and tyre pressures are at their safe minimum, you will need recovery gear. A **snatch strap** is the simplest solution, provided another vehicle is available. If you are alone, you may have to resort to winching (if you have a winch and an appropriate anchor point) or **jacking**.

Above all, stay calm. Sand driving is as much about patience and finesse as it is about power. With the right techniques, you will ease your way through some of the most beautiful dune country on Earth.

Sandy tracks on a 4x4 route

David Elston

LOOK OUT FOR SCORPIONS

Scorpions are **nocturnal**, so always take care after dark. Do **not walk barefoot at night**, and avoid lifting rocks or stones. Never handle scorpions with your bare hands.

IF YOU ARE CAMPING:

- Avoid sleeping directly on the ground; use a **camp bed** or **inflatable mattress**.
- **Shake out bedding**, clothing, shoes and containers before use.
- Keep your campsite **tidy** and **free of clutter**, especially around sitting or sleeping areas, as scorpions hide wherever they can.

IF SOMEONE IS STUNG:

- The seriousness of a sting depends on the **species**, **size** and **location** of the sting.
- Those most at risk are **small children**, **elderly people** and anyone **allergic to insect stings** or with **respiratory problems**.
- Stay calm and, if possible, **identify the scorpion species**.
- Stings from **thick-tailed** (*Buthidae*) scorpions are **potentially dangerous** and require **immediate medical attention**. Get the victim to a **doctor or hospital** as quickly as possible.
- **Do not** try to suck out the venom, or apply a **tourniquet** or **ligature**, or give the victim **alcohol**.
- Apply **ice** or a **cold compress** to the sting site to reduce pain and swelling.
- **Paracetamol** or **aspirin** may help relieve pain.
- **Clean the wound** and cover it with a sterile dressing or bandage.
- An **anti-tetanus injection** may be required.
- **Anti-venom** is available but must be administered only by a **trained health professional**.

Scorpions glow under ultraviolet light owing to a substance in their exoskeleton that fluoresces. On warm nights, shining a small UV torch across the sandy ground will reveal them glowing an eerie blue-green, a thrilling and harmless way to observe these secretive nocturnal hunters.

Daniel Wipf

Scorpion glows under ultraviolet light

Daniel Wipf

Scorpionidae species or slender-tailed scorpion

Nico Smit

Buthidae species (extremely toxic) or thick-tailed scorpion

Scorpions are a favoured food source for insectivorous birds, such as lilac-breasted rollers

Elmar Venter

Skill, not immunity, allows insectivorous birds like fork-tailed drongos to use them safely

Daniel Wipf

Scorpions are a protein-rich food source even for a tree skink

Suricates or meerkats are notably resistant to scorpion venom

Kathy Kay

Autumn

Myburgh du Plessis

BEST TIME TO VISIT

Choosing your perfect season

The Kalahari is a semi-arid region with an average annual rainfall ranging from **150mm in the southwest** to about **350mm in the northeast**. Rainfall is unreliable and irregular, arriving mostly in dramatic summer thunderstorms between **November and April**, sometimes accompanied by gusting winds and dust storms.

The first rains transform the red dunes, carpeting them with the yellow flowers of the **devil's thorn**. Within two weeks, fresh green grasses appear, but if the rains fail to return, the vegetation quickly withers and the semi-desert harshness reclaims the land.

Temperatures vary widely; from **–11°C on icy winter nights** to **42°C in the shade during summer**, when the ground surface can reach a blistering **70°C**. In winter, frost is common, and the ground can be up to **25°C colder than the air**.

Broadly speaking, **winter (May–October)** is cool and dry, while **summer (November–April)** is hot and wet.

Autumn (March–April)

Early autumn, following good rains, is the Kalahari at its **most spectacular**. Sun-baked dunes and riverbeds erupt in a fleeting display of colour, a floral spectacle of rare beauty. Large herds of antelope gather along riverbeds and pans where sweet new grasses sprout. Termites emerge in huge numbers, drawing raptors from across the region.

Rainfall is patchy and unpredictable, but temperatures are pleasantly mild and the winds are calm. After particularly good seasons, a second springbok lambing may occur in March.

Winter (May–August)

In winter, temperatures in the riverbeds are often lower than in the dunes, prompting some herds and predators to move into the dunes for warmth and food. During prolonged dry cycles, when food becomes scarce elsewhere, impressive concentrations of wildlife can still be found in the riverbeds where limited grazing and water persist.

Nights are cold, frequently **below freezing**, yet the days are gloriously sunny and clear. **Honey badgers** are especially active during daylight hours. **August**, the windiest month, fills the air with dust that scatters sunset light into vivid colours. Bat-eared foxes tend to continue their foraging during the early morning hours.

Myburgh du Plessis

Winter

Spring (September–October)

Spring is typically dry, with many antelope retreating to the dunes unless the riverbeds still hold green grazing from good autumn rains. It is a prime season for **canids** such as jackals and bat-eared foxes, which den along the riverbeds.

Temperatures can fluctuate wildly. Chilly southerly winds may alternate with hot, dry **berg winds** from the north, veiling the horizon in fine dust. Despite the extremes, this is a beautiful time of transition before the first storms break the long dry spell.

Summer (November–April)

Summer in the Kalahari can be harsh for visitors unaccustomed to the heat. Daytime temperatures often exceed **40°C**, with warm nights offering little relief. Early starts and long midday rests are essential. The swimming pool or a shaded nap become welcome retreats.

Springbok lambing takes place now, filling the riverbeds with life and drama as predators lurk nearby. This is also the season of **spectacular thunderstorms**. Around **80 percent of the annual rainfall** arrives between **January and April**, another **18 percent between September and December**, and the rest during the cooler months.

After heavy showers, **termites erupt** in great swarms, creating feeding frenzies for birds, mammals and reptiles alike. Another reminder of the desert's cycle of renewal and survival.

Dominique de Beer

Summer

Lions are particularly active during early morning and dusk

Lions often use dune ridges as a lookout over the valleys

Hannes Lochner

Hannes Lochner

ONGOING RESEARCH

Lion Research Project at Kgalagadi Transfrontier Park

South African National Parks (SANParks), in partnership with the Endangered Wildlife Trust (EWT), is excited to announce a new lion research project in the Kgalagadi Transfrontier Park. This important study will help people better understand the lion population in the park, including how many lions live here, where, and how they move in the landscape.

Lions play a vital role in maintaining a healthy ecosystem. To manage them properly, scientists need accurate information. This is why their teams will be out in the field, using cameras, tracks, sightings and other safe, non-invasive methods to gather information. Each lion has unique features – like whisker spots and scars – which help scientists identify them individually.

Visitors to the park may notice research vehicles marked with SANParks or EWT logos. These teams occasionally locate the lions for research photographs. We ask all guests to kindly give them space and show support by driving respectfully and not crowding the area.

This partnership is a big step forward for lion conservation and we are proud to involve the public in protecting these iconic animals.

Routes and Recommendations

Dominique de Beer

Giraffes at dawn

Main rest camps recommended routes

FROM TWEE RIVIEREN

DESTINATION TR = TWEE RIVIEREN	DISTANCE & DRIVING TIME	BEST TIME OF DAY	RATINGS
TR to Confluence waterhole and back.	6 km + 6 km = 12 km. 20 min+.	Any time of the day.	One of the most rewarding waterholes. A pleasant drive when time is short. Don't miss the small waterhole just outside the camp gate.
TR to Melkvlei and over short dune road to Auchterlonie and back to TR.	51 km + 47 km + 42 km = 140 km. Six hours. Add time for a picnic.	Morning to noon. An excellent drive covering both dunes and two riverbeds.	For photographers this sequence is highly recommended. Morning light favourable for best viewing. 13 waterholes. Two places to alight from vehicle.
TR along Nossob River road to Nossob Camp via Melkvlei and Dikbaardskolk picnic sites.	114 km + 52 km = 166 km. Six to seven hours one way. Add time for a picnic.	Leave early morning, get there at noon.	15 waterholes. After Melkvlei, road gets sandy and often corrugated. Two picnic sites.
TR to Dikbaardskolk picnic site via Nossob riverbed, cross dunes along upper dune road to Kamqua picnic site and back along the Auob riverbed to TR.	144 km + 54 km + 70 km = 268 km. 9 to 10 hours on the road. Add time for a picnic.	Leave early in the morning, pack a picnic and take enough water. It will be an entire day's outing.	22 waterholes. A rewarding day trip but can also be exhausting if not prepared. Distances are deceptive. Do not speed as this will be a waste of time. Four picnic sites.
TR to Auchterlonie and back to TR.	21 km + 21 km = 42 km. Two hours.	Good afternoon route.	A pleasant short afternoon drive. This drive can easily be extended northwards depending on time available. Get out at Auchterlonie picnic site to stretch your legs.
TR to Mata-Mata and back to TR.	70 km + 56 km + 56 km + 70 km = 252 km. Nine to 10 hours.	Excellent day drive. Take breaks and pack a picnic basket.	Not necessary to go all the way to Mata-Mata when time is short. It is better to turn back at Dalkeith. 16 waterholes, two picnic sites.
TR to Leeudril, turn off onto 4x4 route to Auchterlonie, then back to TR.	15 km + 14 km + 18 km = 47 km. Two hours.	Permission and four-wheel drive a requirement.	Good as a 4x4 experience on dune driving. Not too demanding.

Western barn owl in a calcrete cave

Daniel Wipf

Controlled entry
No entry/exit
Entrance gate
Picnic site
Camp site
Camp site (A-frame)
Rest camp
Wilderness camp
Lodge
Borehole (sweet water)
Borehole (medium water)
Borehole (brackish water)
Pan
River
Main road
Main road (Five-star)
4x4 roads and trails
Direction
3 Distance
Bedinkt Picnic Site
Bedinkt
Kwang
Swartbas
Cubitje Quap
NOSSOB REST CAMP
Nossob camp waterhole
Ratel
Marie se gat
Rooikop
Marie's Loop
Bitterpan 4x4 Trail
Nossob 4x4 Ecotrail
Nossob
Klein Stofpan
Kaspersdraai
Cheleka
Nossob Road
BITTERPAN CAMP
Rosyntjiebos
Dikbaardskolk
Dikbaardskolk Picnic Site
MATA-MATA REST CAMP
MATA-MATA GATE
Nu-Quap
Eland
Upper Dune Road
KALAHARI TENTED CAMP
Sitsas
Strathmore
Moravet
Kameelsleep
CRAIG LOCKHART CAMP
Craig Lockhart
Dalkeith
Vaalpan
Jan se draai
14th borehole
Auob
13th borehole
Urikaruus
Kamqua
Kamqua Picnic Site
URIKARUUS CAMP
Rooibrak
Witgat
Kransbrak
Nossob 4x4 Ecotrail
Montrose
!Xaus Road
!XAUS LODGE
Batulama
Gunong
Kij Gamies
Lower Dune Road
Gemsbokplein
Melkvlei Picnic Site
Melkvlei
Auchterlonie Picnic Site
Auchterlonie
KIELIEKRANKIE CAMP
Tierkop
Kamfersboom
KijKij
Auob Road
Munro
Nossob Road
Rooiputs
TA SHEBUBE ROOIPUTS LODGE
Rooiputs Camp
Leeudril 4x4 Trail
Houmoed
Leeudril
DAWID KRUIPER CAMP
(under construction)
Samevloeiing (Confluence)
TWEE RIVIEREN REST CAMP
Tweerivieren
Two Rivers Camp
TWEE RIVIEREN GATE

FROM NOSSOB

DESTINATION	DISTANCE & DRIVING TIME	BEST TIME OF DAY	RATINGS
Nossob south along Marie-se-Draai and back.	4 km + 12 km + 4 km = 20 km. One hour.	Any time of the day.	Two waterholes. An extremely popular and rewarding route. Scenically pleasing. Usually good birding and game viewing.
Nossob south via Marie-se-Draai to Dikbaardskolk and back to Nossob.	4 km + 11 km + 48 km + 52 km = 115 km. Five hours plus picnic time.	Good morning drive.	Five waterholes. Scenically very different from the road to the north of Nossob. Picnic site at Dikbaardskolk.
Nossob to Kwang and back to Nossob.	23 km + 23 km = 46 km. Two hours.	Good short drive – either morning or afternoon.	Two of the best waterholes close to camp.
Nossob to Lijersdraai and back to Nossob.	85 km + 85 km = 170 km. Seven hours plus time for picnic meal.	Comfortable half-day drive with spot to hop out.	This is one of the most popular drives. Seven waterholes.
Nossob to Union's End and back to Nossob.	132 km + 132 km = 264 km. Ten hours.	All day drive. Two points to stretch your legs.	Plan well for this long drive. Union's End has an ambience of its own. Worthwhile to do this drive at least once.
Nossob to Polentswa Camp.	61 km. Two to three hours.	Sleepover at Polentswa.	Last section of the road into Botswana runs through the Nossob River. Very fine dust.
Nossob to Grootkolk.	112 km. Five hours.	Sleepover at Grootkolk.	Stop for a picnic at Lijersdraai. The silence there is breathtaking.
Nossob to Gharagab.	164 km. Six to seven hours.	Sleepover at Gharagab.	From Union's end to Gharagab is a 4x4 track. Be prepared for sand driving.
Nossob to Bitterpan.	53 km. Three hours.	Sleepover at Bitterpan.	4x4 track. Be prepared for sand driving.

Black-chested snake eagle

Edmund Aylmer

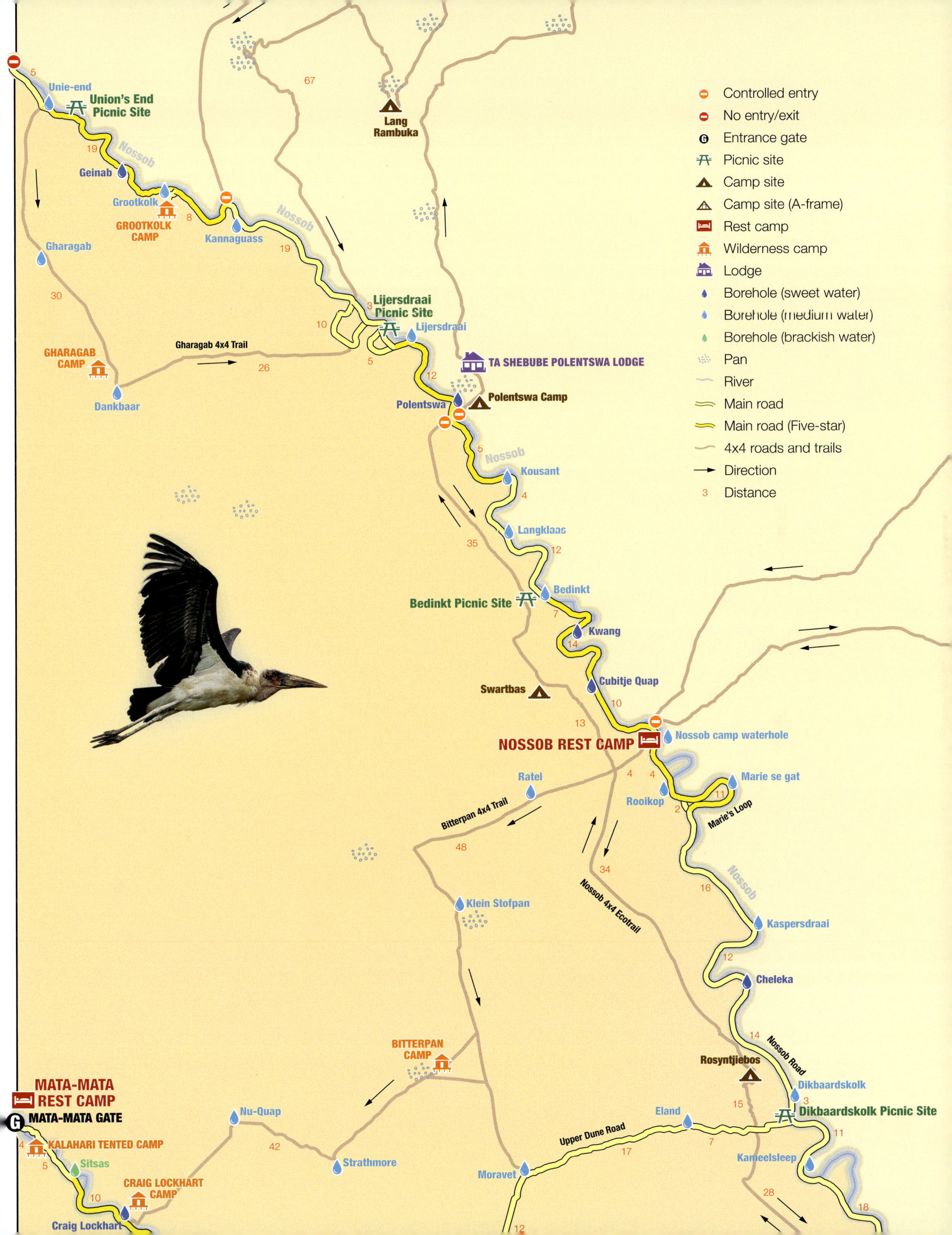

Controlled entry
No entry/exit
Entrance gate
Picnic site
Camp site
Camp site (A-frame)
Rest camp
Wilderness camp
Lodge
Borehole (sweet water)
Borehole (medium water)
Borehole (brackish water)
Pan
River
Main road
Main road (Five-star)
4x4 roads and trails
Direction
Distance
Unie-end
Union's End Picnic Site
Nossob
Geinab
Grootkolk
GROOTKOLK CAMP
Kannaguass
Gharagab
Lang Rambuka
Lijersdraai Picnic Site
Lijersdraai
GHARAGAB CAMP
Gharagab 4x4 Trail
Dankbaar
TA SHEBUBE POLENTSWA LODGE
Polentswa Camp
Polentswa
Kousant
Langklaas
Bedinkt
Bedinkt Picnic Site
Kwang
Cubitje Quap
Swartbas
NOSSOB REST CAMP
Nossob camp waterhole
Ratel
Rooikop
Marie se gat
Marie's Loop
Bitterpan 4x4 Trail
Klein Stofpan
Nossob 4x4 Ecotrail
Kaspersdraai
Cheleka
Nossob Road
BITTERPAN CAMP
Rosyntjiebos
Dikbaardskolk
Dikbaardskolk Picnic Site
MATA-MATA REST CAMP
MATA-MATA GATE
Nu-Quap
KALAHARI TENTED CAMP
Sitsas
CRAIG LOCKHART CAMP
Craig Lockhart
Strathmore
Moravet
Upper Dune Road
Eland
Kameelsleep

FROM MATA-MATA

DESTINATION MM = MATA-MATA	DISTANCE & DRIVING TIME	BEST TIME OF DAY	RATINGS
MM camp to Dalkeith and back to MM.	25 km + 25 km = 50 km. Two hours.	Ideal for a short afternoon drive	Three waterholes. The Dalkeith loop can be done more than once.
MM camp to 13th borehole and back to MM.	41 km + 41 km = 82 km. Four hours.	A good morning drive.	Game viewing is usually good and allow time at each of the five waterholes. This is a good route if you prefer coffee and rusks while game driving. Back by 11:00 at camp.
MM camp to Kamqua and back to MM.	57 km + 57 km = 114 km. Five hours.	The ideal destination for taking a picnic basket. Allow time for a rest.	A longish route but can comfortably be taken in the morning. It's a bit long for an afternoon drive unless you leave camp soon after lunch.
MM to Twee Rivieren.	57 km + 70 km = 127 km. Five hours one way.	Morning drives are always the best.	The distance can be deceptive since time may be lost at good sightings and at the picnic site.
MM to Nossob.	57 km + 54 km + 52 km = 163 km. Seven hours one way.	Morning drive and one way.	Two picnic sites and 14 waterholes. Takes the best part of the day. Pack a picnic basket.

A Gabar goshawk challenging a tawny eagle

Chris Speight

MATA-MATA REST CAMP
MATA-MATA GATE
KALAHARI TENTED CAMP
Sitsas
CRAIG LOCKHART CAMP
Craig Lockhart
Dalkeith
14th borehole
Auob
13th borehole
Urikaruus
Kamqua
URIKARUUS CAMP
Kamqua Picnic Site
Rooibrak
Montrose
Batulama
Gemsbokplein
Auchterlonie Picnic Site
Auchterlonie
KIELIEKRANKIE CAMP
Kamfersboom
Auob Road
Munro
Houmoed
DAWID KRUIPER CAMP
(under construction)
Samevloeiing (Confluence)
TWEE RIVIEREN REST CAMP
TWEE RIVIEREN GATE
Tweerivieren
Two Rivers Camp
Leeudril
Leeudril 4x4 Trail
Rooiputs
Nossob
Tierkop
Kij Gamies
Lower Dune Road
Witgat
!Xaus Road
!XAUS LODGE
Nu-Quap
Strathmore
BITTERPAN CAMP
Klein Stofpan
Moravet
Vaalpan
Upper Dune Road
Eland
Kameelsleep
Rosyntjiebos
Nossob Road
Nossob 4x4 Ecotrail
Kaspersdr
Cheleka
Controlled entry
No entry/exit
Entrance gate
Picnic site
Camp site
Camp site (A-frame)
Rest camp
Wilderness camp
Lodge
Borehole (sweet water)
Borehole (medium water)
Borehole (brackish water)
Pan
River
Main road
Main road (Five-star)
4x4 roads and trails
Direction
Distance

Wilderness camps recommended routes

GROOTKOLK

DESTINATION	DISTANCE & DRIVING TIME	BEST TIME OF DAY	RATINGS
Grootkolk to the north on Nossob River Road and back.	20 km + 20 km = 40 km. Two hours.	Short morning or afternoon drive.	Two waterholes and a picnic site.
Grootkolk south to Nossob Camp.	112 km. Five hours one way.	Leave early to allow time for game viewing.	Hop out for a picnic at Lijersdraai. The silence there is breathtaking.

GHARAGAB

DESTINATION	DISTANCE & DRIVING TIME	BEST TIME OF DAY	RATINGS
Gharagab to Lijersdraai to Union's End to Gharagab.	29 km + 41 km + 32 km = 102 km. Five hours.	Leave in the morning.	From Gharagab to Lijersdraai the road is a singletrack over undulating red sand landscape. Sandy.
Gharagab to nearby waterhole and back.	4 km + 4 km = 8 km. Short drive.	Late afternoon, early morning.	Short drive.
Gharagab to Lijersdraai to Nossob.	29 km + 85 km = 114 km. Four hours one way.	Leave in the morning.	From Dankbaar waterhole, the sand deepens and dunes become more pronounced. Extreme natural beauty.

BITTERPAN

DESTINATION	DISTANCE & DRIVING TIME	BEST TIME OF DAY	RATINGS
Bitterpan to Craig Lockhart and back to Bitterpan via Kamqua and Moravet.	61 km + 39 km + 42 km = 142 km. Six hours.	Leave early morning.	The drive up to Craig Lockhart is very scenic.
Bitterpan to Moravet to Kamqua and back to Bitterpan.	17 km +25 km = 42 km + 42 km = 84 km. Four hours.	Leave early morning.	A pleasant dune game-viewing drive. Take a picnic lunch.
Short circular route from Bitterpan and back.	15 km. One hour.	Late afternoon or early morning.	A pleasant short drive to see the surrounding dunes and pan.

URIKARUUS

DESTINATION	DISTANCE & DRIVING TIME	BEST TIME OF DAY	RATINGS
Urikaruus to Mata-Mata and back.	56 km + 56 km = 112 km. Four hours.	Morning or afternoon.	Several waterholes along this route are extremely worthwhile. Adjust the distance to time available.
Urikaruus to Twee Rivieren and back.	70 km + 70 km = 140 km. Six hours.	Morning or afternoon.	Several waterholes along this route are worth a visit. Adjust the distance to time available.
Urikaruus to Dikbaardskolk and back.	54 km + 54 km = 108 km. Four hours.	Morning or afternoon.	A route over the dunes may offer encounters at three pans along the way. Game often widely dispersed across the dunes.
Urikaruus to Nossob.	54 km + 52 km = 106 km. Four hours one way.	Any time.	A pleasant drive.

KIELIEKRANKIE

DESTINATION	DISTANCE & DRIVING TIME	BEST TIME OF DAY	RATINGS
Circular route from Kieliekrankie to Kij Kij, Rooiputs, Twee Rivieren and back along the Auob Road up to Auchterlonie to Kieliekrankie.	31 km + 39 km + 46 km = 116 km. Five hours.	Morning or afternoon.	Covers 11 waterholes and a picnic break at Twee Rivieren. Includes both river and dune roads. Close to best game-viewing locations for early morning starters.
Circular route from Kieliekrankie to Kij Kij, to Dikbaardskolk, Kamqua and back along the Auob Road up to Auchterlonie to Kieliekrankie.	31 km + 75 km +54 km +32 km = 192 km. Eight hours.	Day trip with three picnic sites.	Covers 18 waterholes and includes both river and dune roads. Close to best game-viewing locations for early morning starters.
Kieliekrankie to Auchterlonie and then to Kamqua and back.	4 km + 25 km = 29 km + 29 km = 58 km. Three hours.	A pleasant afternoon or morning drive.	Many excellent waterholes that can offer unexpected surprises.

KALAHARI TENTED CAMP

DESTINATION	DISTANCE & DRIVING TIME	BEST TIME OF DAY	RATINGS
KT Camp to Dalkeith and back.	20 km + 20 km = 40 km. Two hours.	Ideal for a short afternoon drive.	Three waterholes. The Dalkeith loop can be done more than once.
KT Camp to 13th borehole and back.	36 km + 36 km = 72 km. Three hours.	A good morning drive.	Game viewing is usually good. Allow time at each of the five waterholes. This is an ideal route if you prefer coffee and rusks while game driving. Back at camp by 11:00.
KT Camp to Kamqua and back.	52 km + 52 km = 104 km. Four hours.	The ideal destination for taking a picnic basket. Allow time for a rest.	A longish route but can comfortably be taken in the morning. It's a bit long for an afternoon drive unless you leave camp soon after lunch.
KT Camp to Twee Rivieren.	52 km + 70 km = 122 km. Five hours one way.	Morning drives are always the best.	The distance can be deceptive since time may be lost at good sightings and at the picnic site.
KT Camp to Nossob.	52 km + 54 km + 52 km = 158 km. Six hours one way.	Morning drive and one way.	Two picnic sites and 14 waterholes. Takes the best part of the day. Pack a picnic basket.

Bomber Kent

Gabar goshawk hunting Namaqua dove

Bomber Kent

Roads and Ratings

African wild cat

Dominique de Beer

The Nossob River Road

Twee Rivieren Camp is the main and **largest rest camp** in the park. Its name comes from the **confluence of the Nossob and Auob rivers**, just five kilometres upstream. This is where the South African park headquarters is located. Across the fossil riverbed, in Botswana territory, is the **Two Rivers Camp**. The reception area here is shared by both South African and Botswana staff, a symbol of the park's cross-border harmony.

Given its position and size, Twee Rivieren is usually busy and lacks the deep wilderness solitude found in the more remote northern camps. Yet, it remains the perfect introduction to the Kalahari. A place that gently reveals both its kindness and its harshness. If this is your first visit, give yourself time. The Kalahari does not rush to impress – it slowly seeps into you, grain by grain. But beware, once the red sand gets into your shoes, it rarely leaves your soul.

Twee Rivieren (Dutch for 'Two Rivers') has a story that reaches back to the early 20th century. **Before 1931**, the government purchased the farm of the same name, bringing the river confluence within the newly proclaimed Kalahari Gemsbok National Park. In **1938**, the first corrugated-iron warden's house was built for Joep le Riche at the confluence. Better accommodation followed further south, where the camp stands today. By **1950**, the first three tourist huts were added, and within a few years, the modest camp grew to **include a camping ground** and a handful of **additional rooms**. By **1957**, it could accommodate 12 guests, a far cry from today's modern chalets offering nearly a hundred beds, eight of them designed for visitors with physical disabilities. The campsite remains ever popular and often fully booked.

Take time to visit the **Twee Rivieren Interpretation Centre (TRIC)**. Here, the story of the park unfolds alongside the heritage of the **‡Khomani Cultural Landscape**, now recognised as a World Heritage Site.

The **Twee Rivieren Hide** and **waterhole** offer the perfect vantage point over the dune; a quiet place to reconnect with the wild. Beneath the spreading **Market Tree**, the ‡Khomani traders sometimes gather to sell their traditional crafts, offering a small, living thread that connects past and present, people and place.

The presence of a lioness disturbs a springbok herd

Hannes Lochner

Gnus Gnus
Polentswa
Mabua Kaa 4x4
Unie-end
Union's End Picnic Site
Lang Rambuka
BOTSWANA
Nossob
Geinab
Grootkolk
GROOTKOLK CAMP
Kannaguass
Gharagab
Lijersdraai Picnic Site
Lijersdraai
GHARAGAB CAMP
Gharagab 4x4 Trail
TA SHEBUBE POLENTSWA LODGE
Polentswa
Polentswa Camp
Dankbaar
Kousant
Mabuasehube Wilderness 4x4 Trail
Langklaas
Bedinkt
Bedinkt Picnic Site
Kwang
Matop
Nossob/Mabuasehube 4x4 Access Route
SOUTH AFRICA
Swartbas
Cubitje Quap
NOSSOB REST CAMP
Nossob camp waterhole
Ratel
Marie se gat
Bitterpan 4x4 Trail
Rooikop
Marie's Loop
Klein Stofpan
Nossob 4x4 Ecotrail
Kaspersdraai
Cheleka
Nossob Road
BITTERPAN CAMP
Rosyntjiebos
MATA-MATA REST CAMP
MATA-MATA GATE
KALAHARI TENTED CAMP
Nu-Quap
Eland
Dikbaardskolk
Dikbaardskolk Picnic Site
Upper Dune Road
Sitsas
CRAIG LOCKHART CAMP
Strathmore
Moravet
Kameelsleep
Craig Lockhart
Dalkeith
Vaalpan
Jan se draai
14th borehole
13th borehole
Urikaruus
Auob
Kamqua
Kamqua Picnic Site
URIKARUUS CAMP
Witgat
Kransbrak
Rooibrak
Montrose
!Xaus Road
Batulama
Gemsbokplein
Kij Gamies
Gunong
!XAUS LODGE
Lower Dune Road
Melkvlei Picnic Site
Melkvlei
Auchterlonie Picnic Site
KIELIEKRANKIE CAMP
Auchterlonie
Tierkop
Kamfersboom
KijKij
Auob Road
Munro
Rooiputs
TA SHEBUBE ROOIPUTS LODGE
Rooiputs Camp
Leeudril 4x4 Trail
Houmoed
DAWID KRUIPER CAMP
(under construction)
Leeudril
Samevloeiing (Confluence)
TWEE RIVIEREN REST CAMP
Tweerivieren
Two Rivers Camp
TWEE RIVIEREN GATE
Controlled entry
No entry/exit
Entrance gate
Picnic site
Camp site
Camp site (A-frame)
Rest camp
Wilderness camp
Lodge
Borehole (sweet water)
Borehole (medium water)
Borehole (brackish water)
Pan
River
Main road
Main road (Five-star)
4x4 roads and trails
Direction
Distance

Twee Rivieren to Union's End

★★★★

TWEE RIVIEREN RECEPTION

5 km to Confluence

From the camp gate into the park, the road follows the western bank of the wide Nossob riverbed to its confluence with the Auob. This short section carries most of the traffic in and out of the park. The surface can become rough and dusty, especially before gate closing time, so drive slowly; speed enforcement here can catch the unwary.

The majestic camelthorn is a dominant tree in the Kalahari and can grow to a height of 15 m. The closely related grey camelthorn is much smaller and can reach a height of 9 m. These are two of the important tree species in the park.

Sociable weaver

Hennie Blignaut

The access road offers a fine introduction to the iconic trees of the fossil riverbeds. Towering, **dark-green camelthorns** *(Vachellia erioloba)* line the route towards the wildlife access gate. Some stand within the rest camp perimeter, allowing a close look at these remarkable trees that shape the Kalahari's ecology. Camelthorns grow in deep sandy soils and withstand drought and saline groundwater thanks to taproots that can reach more than 40 m. The oldest trees may live for over three centuries. Dead trunks remain standing for decades, their hard heartwood impervious to termites.

The nests of white-browed sparrow-weavers are placed in the outer limbs or branches of the tree, usually between 2–8 m (about 6.5–26 feet) above the ground. Most nests are strategically located on the leeward side (the side sheltered from the prevailing wind) of the tree.

Along the riverbeds, the camelthorn thrives but as you climb the dune roads, they become scarcer. The **grey camelthorn** *(Vachellia haematoxylon)*, typical of the Auob valley, is even more drought-tolerant and its roots can reach depths of 60 m, allowing it to survive on dune slopes where little else grows. Young trees expend great energy on thorn production and take 15–20 years before bearing their first pods.

Watch for camelthorns filled with nests. Two communal nesting birds dominate this landscape: the **white-browed sparrow-weaver** and the **sociable weaver**. You will often see both sparrow-weavers and sociable weavers here, and it is worth learning to tell them apart.

A small waterhole lies just beyond the gate on the river side of the road. Don't rule out the chance of spotting game this close to camp. **Antelope**, and occasionally even **lion or other predators**, come to drink, and **raptors** are frequently seen overhead.

Sociable weavers choose camelthorns for communal nesting

White-browed sparrow-weaver

Nests of white-browed sparrow-weavers look very different

Look for leopard and spotted eagle-owls on the calcrete ridge to the western side of the road

Hannes Lochner

Hannes Lochner

African wild cat kittens in a calcrete cave

The fossil riverbed here is flat and wide, offering excellent visibility across the border into Botswana. There are no fences and animals move freely between the two countries. Small herds of **springbok** are common in the riverbed, while **gemsbok** and **red hartebeest** can sometimes be seen on the distant dunes beyond. Despite the proximity to Twee Rivieren Camp, **leopard** are occasionally sighted along this stretch. Look carefully where the western bank steepens and the first calcrete ridges appear.

Notice the low, dull-blue shrubs called **blue pea** (or *Lebeckia linearifolia*) edging the riverbed. These hardy, fleshy plants are perfectly adapted to semi-arid life: their greyish tone reflects sunlight, while their rounded stems and tiny leaves help conserve precious moisture.

★★★★★

CONFLUENCE OR SAMEVLOEIING

11 km to Leeudril

Pass the turn-off to the Auob River route and continue to the Confluence waterhole. *Samevloeiing* in Afrikaans means '*confluence*' and refers to the meeting place of the Auob and Nossob fossil rivers. It is a scenic and almost magical spot, with dunes on one side and an open pan on the other. Visibility is excellent and animals can be seen approaching the waterhole from far away. This is one of the five-star waterholes worth lingering at. It is accessible from three sides, with the western approach slightly elevated and the eastern side level with the waterhole. Even if your plan is to take the Auob route, it is always worth stopping here first.

Be the first to arrive at this waterhole in the morning. Predators may drink at any time, but they are most active at **dawn and dusk**. Use your binoculars to scan the riverbeds for movement.

The waterhole is **fed by three boreholes**, the first drilled in 1913, and two more in 1984 and 1987, ensuring a reliable supply for wildlife emerging from the dunes. Though the water is slightly brackish, it draws a steady procession of antelope and predators. Lion, leopard, hyena, wild cat, genet and caracal have all been seen here, especially in the early mornings or late evenings.

If this is your first time in the Kgalagadi, you may think this semi-desert is devoid of life, but you will soon be surprised by the multitude of small creatures not easily spotted from your vehicle. Reptiles of all shapes and sizes abound; insects such as termites, ants, beetles, butterflies, locusts, wasps and many others form the pantry for insectivorous birds and several small mammals. Scorpions, solifuges and spiders all have their place in the web of life. Many predators depend on the vast rodent populations, especially after good rains. It is little wonder the Kgalagadi is known as a raptor haven. Food is plentiful and the wilderness remains free of the killing pesticides that plague more cultivated lands.

As you leave the waterhole, continue on to the Nossob road and watch both sides of the road. On the left, a **rocky dune** with **scattered shrubs** provides cover for small predators such as **caracal** and **African wild cats**. This is their perfect habitat, where rodents, reptiles and insects abound. They are nocturnal hunters but if you are early, you might just witness a kill. It pays to drive this stretch as early as possible in the morning. You may even be lucky enough to witness a martial eagle preying on an African wild cat.

A lioness and her cubs on the way to the water

Hamman Prinsloo

Hannes Lochner

A black-maned lion coalition keeps together

Common ostriches are often seen dust-bathing along this road

Hamman Prinsloo

Look out for sparring springbok late afternoons

Pierre Labuschagne

Hamman Prinsloo

Secretarybirds favour the riverbeds for hunting

Secretarybirds are the iconic hunters of the open dune plains and the banks of the dry riverbeds of the Nossob and Auob. These elegant, long-legged raptors sometimes move on foot in the cooler parts of the day and may be perched on trees or dunes in the early morning. Here in the Kgalagadi, they have large territories, around 140 km² per pair. Sadly, these giants of the bird world – proudly featured on South Africa's coat of arms – are endangered. They nest on top of camelthorns but a recent study revealed they average only about 2.2 young per breeding attempt.

Along much of this stretch from Twee Rivieren to Leeudril, **bluebush** (*Calobota linearifolia*) forms a regular roadside band, its solitary yellow flowers brightening early spring. This blue-tinged shrub is extremely nutritious, and its high nutritional value remains unchanged with age. A particular beetle feeds mainly on this plant. However, it is not of much use as fodder for livestock.

Notice the **many camelthorns** lining the riverbed. Use your binoculars to scan each tree, even those far away, for raptor nests. Some of the trees near the road are occupied by sociable weavers or white-browed sparrow-weavers. It is quite entertaining to stop next to such trees and watch the comings and goings of the weavers. Camelthorns here and elsewhere are **favourite owl trees**. Owls are not easy to spot but stop and scan the branches for these nocturnal raptors. Once you find such a tree, chances are good that next time you drive past, you will see them again.

Ostriches are common in the Nossob riverbed, where they often gather for dust-bathing sessions to rid themselves of parasites. Perfectly adapted to arid life, they seldom drink and obtain most moisture from plants, insects and small vertebrates. They also swallow stones to help grind food in the gizzard.

By mid-morning, **blue wildebeest** arrive from their grazing grounds, trudging in long columns to drink. Wildebeest are gregarious – living in herds of 20 or more – though territorial bulls appear solitary as they defend their patches of ground. Females and non-territorial males form separate herds, while dominant bulls challenge any rival that ventures too close. Watch their posturing, head tossing, horn digging and tail swishing, each movement part of a complex ritual of dominance. During the short rutting season, which coincides with the end of the rains, these displays intensify into full battles, the **bulls clashing horn to horn before one finally yields**.

Before reaching Leeudril, scan the **calcrete ridge** on the Botswana side as these ridges always hide some form of life. Perhaps it is the haunt of a leopard or even a brown hyena. The small caves formed here are suitable hides for owls or porcupines.

Stephan Swanepoel

Porcupine finds shelter in a calcrete cavity

The ground squirrel is not fearless of the Cape cobra, but retreat is more dangerous than standing your ground. This is calculated, inherited survival behaviour on the part of the squirrel.

Bomber Kent

Hannes Lochner

Cape cobras are not a real threat to adult leopards

★★★★★

LEEUDRIL
11 km to Rooiputs

It is easy to guess where this waterhole got its name. In Afrikaans, *leeu* means **lion** and *dril* means to **tremble**. The story goes that a man named Matthys once walked over the dune and found himself face-to-face with a lion. Without his gun, he froze, his trousers shaking uncontrollably. The lion stared, turned and calmly walked away, hence the place was named **Leeudril**, 'where the lion made a man tremble'.

A large reservoir with **brackish water** supplies the nearby waterhole. The river course lies to the left, offering **wonderful morning game viewing** when antelope, ostrich and flocks of seed-eating birds come to drink. The red dunes and broad river valley make this an excellent spot for photography. Tawny eagles, bateleurs and other raptors perch in the surrounding camelthorns, while an unexpected visitor, the **grey heron**, is sometimes seen spearing small birds at the reservoir's edge.

Gemsbok gather here in the dry season, often to **lick mineral salts** deposited in sediments rather than to drink. These desert antelope spend their nights feeding in the dunes, taking advantage of plant moisture before returning to the riverbed.

The speedsters of the savanna favour the open riverbeds, hunting **springbok** that graze the nutritious grasses after rain. **Cheetah** rest flat in the shade, easily mistaken for branches or rocks. Watch for the faint flick of a tail or the lift of a head, signs that the hunt may soon begin. Most famously, the Kgalagadi riverbeds are some of the best places on Earth to watch cheetah, to follow their elegant hunting technique and, with luck, witness a kill. Researchers and photographers from across the world visit this area to study and record such remarkable events.

The **yellow bush** (*Galenia africana var. africana*) grows commonly along this stretch. Despite its bright green-to-orange leaves, it is toxic and avoided by grazers. Watch too for **kori bustards**, which may perform dramatic distraction displays if you approach their nests, fanning their tails and drooping their wings to lure intruders away from eggs or chicks (October–February).

If booked for the **Leeudril 4x4 loop,** do not miss the turn-off that follows.

Paul Nash

Cheetahs hunt mature male springbok, but they do so less often than females or young animals, and usually only under specific conditions

Paul Nash

A stand-off between an African wild cat and a black-backed jackal

Hannes Lochner

African wild cat

Hamman Prinsloo

Peace treaty

Hannes Lochner

About a kilometre further, you will find the **famous camelthorn** with its massive sociable weaver colony overhanging the road, a must-stop point for anyone in the park. The tree buzzes with activity and drama. **Cape cobras** raid nests for eggs and chicks, ignoring the furious dive-bombing of the weavers. These sleek snakes are expert climbers, scaling branches with ease. When raiding nests, they may consume up to a dozen chicks in a single tree. Over the years some nests become top heavy and crash down, together with the supporting branch.

Watch also for the **pygmy falcon**, Africa's smallest raptor and a close associate of sociable weavers. It commandeers two chambers within a weaver nest: one for roosting, one for breeding. Look for white droppings at the entrance to recognise its residence.

The turn-off to **Ta Shebube Rooiputs Lodge** and **Rooiputs Campsite** follows before you reach the Rooiputs waterhole.

A single sociable weaver nest may weigh over a tonne, housing more than 100 birds, providing shelter for snakes, lizards and owls alike.

Camelthorn heavy with sociable weaver nests

Hamman Prinsloo

The inquisitive stare, eyes wide open and ears turned forward indicates that this lion notices something in the distance

A caracal catches rodent prey with remarkable precision, using a single, lightning-fast forepaw strike

Caracals hunt rodents with a combination of acute hearing, patience, and explosive speed

Caracals

The **caracal** is one of the Kgalagadi's most elusive predators, more often sensed than seen. Sightings are most likely in the **early morning**, particularly along the **Nossob River road between Leeudril and Rooiputs**, when the light is soft and the cats are still active after a night of hunting. With their long legs, reddish coats and distinctive black ear tufts, caracals are superbly adapted to the open savanna and dune margins, where they hunt birds, rodents and small antelope with remarkable speed and agility. Their secretive habits and preference for low cover make encounters special and memorable.

Caracals are **solitary by nature**, coming together only briefly for mating. Males maintain large home ranges that **overlap those of several females**, patrolling their territories along riverbeds and dune edges. A male will associate with a female only when she is in **oestrous**, after which the pair separates again. This solitary lifestyle, combined with their nocturnal and crepuscular activity, explains why caracals are seldom seen despite being widely distributed across the park.

After action, satisfaction

★★★★★

ROOIPUTS
14 km to Kij Kij

The diggers who initially sank a well here had to cut through thick, fossilised sandstone, deep red in colour. In Afrikaans, *rooi* means 'red' and *puts* 'well'. The waterhole that resulted is now one of the most reliable drinking spots in the southern Nossob valley, attracting **springbok, gemsbok, wildebeest** and **ostrich**, serving as one of the park's most famous **lion hotspots**.

Scan the calcrete ridge on the eastern bank of the Nossob for lion. This is one of the favourite places for a mother to hide her cubs.

The view at Rooiputs is wide and uncluttered by trees, perfect for photography and long observation. Rooiputs is home to a large pride of **lions**, though it is rare to see them all together. The **black-maned Kalahari lion** is the undisputed monarch of all predators. The **females and cubs** form the pride's stable nucleus, closely related to one another. Males, meanwhile, form **coalitions** of brothers or cousins and defend territories that may overlap those of several female groups. These males are frequently displaced after several years by younger rivals, a natural process that ensures **genetic renewal**. When new males take over, they **kill the previous offspring** so females return to oestrus, a harsh but biologically effective means of preventing inbreeding. While dominant males rely on the hunting efforts of the females, their imposing size and heavy manes make them less agile hunters. Once ousted, displaced males rarely survive long as they are reduced to catching small prey. Within prides, hunting is largely the females' work; however, males dominate the feast after the kill.

A **lioness comes into oestrus** for only two to four days every two years, copulating repeatedly during this time. If ever you come across a mating pair, watch how she approaches the male, tail flicking provocatively, only to snarl and swat at him moments later. After mating, she rolls onto her back, paws in the air, behaviour that likely aids fertilisation. The cycle repeats endlessly for several days.

Males vigorously chase off competitors when a female is in heat

Hamman Prinsloo

When a lioness is in oestrus (in heat), mating is very frequent and intense

Lion cubs learn aggressive behaviour through a mix of learning, play, and instinct

Hamman Prinsloo

Lionesses do most of the hunting, while males defend territory and sometimes feed their cubs before allowing the females to eat. Hunting is largely nocturnal, as a lion's night vision is six times more sensitive than a human's. Their main prey are **gemsbok** and **wildebeest**, with **springbok** also taken. In the dunes, where stalking large antelope is difficult, lions may hunt smaller prey such as **springhare, fox, steenbok, aardvark** and, surprisingly, **porcupine**, prized for the thick fat layer beneath its skin. When tackling gemsbok, they leap onto the hindquarters, bite into the back, and wrench upward to break the spine before waiting out their prey's exhaustion.

Find the **meerkat (suricate) colony** that lives along this stretch of the Nossob. If you see them, watch for interaction between **fork-tailed drongos and meerkats**. Look out for the ever-alert sentinel on a mound, while **fork-tailed drongos** hover nearby, taking advantage of the insects stirred up by the foraging meerkats. These clever birds sometimes mimic meerkat alarm calls, tricking naïve youngsters into dropping their food before dashing for cover, only for the drongo to swoop in and steal the meal.

This area is a hotspot for **leopards** but also for **leopard tortoises**. If you come across one, drive slowly and give it right of way; these tortoises are most active during the rainy season, drawn by the scent of water from kilometres away. We once followed one such tortoise for about eight kilometres to the Kij Kij waterhole. It paused to drink, then turned around and patiently retraced its journey. During dry spells, they retreat into shaded shelters and aestivate, entering a state of summer dormancy to conserve moisture.

This is also **prime cheetah country**. The open riverbed and abundance of medium-sized prey make it an ideal hunting ground. When you come across cheetah, look around for springbok. Watch them for a while to see if they show interest in hunting. If so, linger a while to watch.

Lions can crack the shell of a leopard tortoise

Dominique de Beer

Caracal with black-backed jackal kill

Hannes Lochner

Hamman Prinsloo

Hannes Lochner

Honey badger attempts to crack the shell of a leopard tortoise

Leopard carrying cub by the nape of its neck on the calcrete outcrop close to Rooiputs

Grahame Murray

Playfulness is important in young cheetahs for developing skills

Grahame Murray

Hamman Prinsloo

Hamman Prinsloo

Bonding is enhanced by grooming each other

Cape fox antics – playfulness is essential training for life

Hannes Lochner

The Lost City of the Kalahari

A curious legend lingers in this area – the tale of the **'Lost City of the Kalahari'.** In the late 1800s, Canadian showman **Guillermo (William Leonard) Farini** claimed to have discovered stone ruins east of the Nossob River, near what he called the "Kij Kij mountains". His vivid account described paved causeways and cross-shaped walls, sparking decades of fascination and expeditions.

In the 1950s, South African author **Alan Paton** joined an expedition to search for these supposed ruins, but nothing was found. Later investigations by **Prof. AJ Clements** revealed that the 'city' was almost certainly a **natural formation** – weathered dolerite domes known as *Eierdopkopjies* near Rietfontein, just outside the park. The Kalahari dunes, stable for thousands of years, could never have buried such a structure.

Still, as you gaze across the endless red sand near Kij Kij, it's tempting to wonder what secrets lie beneath. Could shifting dunes one day reveal something more?

Elmar Venter

Tactile interactions are important for bonding in predators

★★★★

KIJ KIJ
12 km to Melkvlei

The name **Kij Kij** comes from the N|u or Nama languages and is said to mean 'looking around' or 'watching', a fitting name for this wide, open stretch of the **Nossob River valley**, where visibility is exceptional and game can be seen from kilometres away. The surrounding red dunes and calcrete ridges make this one of the most scenic areas in the park.

The **Kij Kij waterhole**, with its reliable water supply and broad open view attracts game throughout the day, particularly **springbok, wildebeest, gemsbok** and **ostrich.** The openness also suits **cheetah**, which rely on speed and clear terrain for hunting. Patience here is often rewarded. Visitors who wait quietly under the shade of a camelthorn have witnessed full hunts unfold from start to finish.

Lion are frequently seen moving through the Kij Kij–Melkvlei corridor, following migrating herds and occasionally resting in the dunes. This region forms part of several large **male coalitions'** territories, and the deep roars echoing through the valley at dusk are usually answered from far downriver.

Dune crests offer lions cooler conditions, better vision, safer resting sites and tactical control over an otherwise flat and exposed desert landscape – making them ideal lookout posts in the Kalahari

Ongoing research by SANParks and partners continues to gather data on lion movement, survival and population structure in the Kgalagadi. Results are preliminary and serve to inform management decisions. The recent studies in the Kgalagadi suggest a shift in the adult sex ratio of lions from roughly one male to two females (in the late 1970s) to about equal numbers of males and females by 2010. While adult female survival remains strong, sub-adult males now outnumber females in some cohorts, a pattern that raises concern about long-term population stability.

The tall **camelthorns** on the eastern side of the waterhole host a variety of raptors; **tawny eagles, bateleurs** and **black-chested snake eagles** are commonly seen perched high above the riverbed. Below, the dry channels are alive with smaller birds: **scaly-feathered finches, red-headed finches, yellow canaries, grey-backed sparrow-larks** and **sociable weavers.**

Scan the red dunes behind the waterhole for resting lions. This is a favourite lookout point over the valley, where predators can watch up and down the riverbed for approaching prey.

Daniel Wipf

No fear for giants

Hannes Lochner

Leopard tortoise shell and African monarch butterflies

Dominique de Beer

Hannes Lochner

The dance of butterflies

Gemsbok fighting for dominance

Paul Nash

Look for **pale chanting goshawks** and **lanner falcons** patrolling the airspace. Both are adept hunters of smaller birds arriving to drink. The **goshawk** appears composed, yet can attack swiftly and fiercely. Meanwhile, the lanner's stoop – its dramatic, rapid dive – offers one of the Kgalagadi sky's most impressive displays.

Keep an eye out for a honey badger on the move (often with a distinct gait and digging behaviour) and one or more pale chanting goshawks flying low behind or around it. **Goshawks** and **honey badgers** have a strange interactive relationship. The opportunistic goshawk, and sometimes a black-backed jackal, follow the badger and wait for it to find prey. Once it flushes prey, the goshawk goes for it. The badger loses out and the goshawk saves energy by playing the waiting game to steal a meal.

On the ground, **bat-eared foxes** are occasionally seen trotting through the riverbed in the late afternoon, listening for insects or rodents below the surface. Both bat-eared and Cape foxes den during November and December around the riverbed. If you come across a den, stay and watch the little foxes at play.

As you drive north towards **Melkvlei**, the vegetation becomes denser with occasional stands of **grey camelthorn** and **shepherd's tree** (*Boscia albitrunca*), both critical for providing shade and food in the harsh environment.

Bat-eared foxes are nocturnal, but often seen at dusk or dawn

The **Leeudril to Kij Kij** section of the Nossob valley records some of the **highest predator densities** in the Kgalagadi, particularly cheetah and lion, drawn by the constant herds of springbok and wildebeest.

Villiers Steyn

The gemsbok (oryx) is a striking, desert-adapted antelope with long, straight rapier-like horns and bold black-and-white facial markings, superbly adapted to survive the heat, aridity and open landscapes of the Kalahari.

Sightings of the red-necked falcon in the Kgalagadi are both notable and sought-after

Charl Weber

Scott Chalmers

This black-headed heron has become a resident at waterholes in the park

Cape turtle doves visit waterholes in huge flocks as there is safety in numbers

African wild cat sightings can be in unexpected places

Villiers Steyn

★★★

MELKVLEI
1 km to picnic site

It is easy to miss this waterhole, probably because, after a long morning of game viewing, you cannot wait to reach the picnic spot and stretch your legs. The waterhole, on the left of the road, is not a spectacular sight and blends well with the background and the white calcrete rocks that surround it. The name refers to the white chalk banks of the river: *melk* is the Afrikaans word for 'milk', and *vlei* means 'a place where water collects'.

Blackthorns are covered in blooms after spring rains

Corné Malan

Notice the blackthorns (*Vachellia mellifera*) next to the road. This plant plays a dual role in the Kgalagadi ecosystem, serving as a **crucial fodder and habitat resource for wildlife** while posing a significant challenge as an **aggressive invader** in overgrazed areas, leading to bush encroachment.

Blackthorn grows in relative abundance behind the waterhole along the dunes. Here they are merely shrubs, but further east on the Botswana side of the park, blackthorns can grow into sizeable trees. Notice their funnel-shaped to rounded crowns and multiple stems. Each stem bears small, blackish, hooked thorns carried in pairs. The modest, feather-shaped leaves are especially palatable, even after being shed in winter. The powder-puff flowers, with their honey-like scent, attract bees with nectar, and even the pods add to the blackthorn's value as a food plant.

As you drive toward Nossob Camp, you will pass many blackthorn bushes close to the road. The San people use twigs of this bush as toothbrushes, as it is said to contain fluoride. Blackthorns also attract **kori bustards**, since the plant secretes little balls of gum that they eat. In Afrikaans, the bird is called *gompou*, which literally means 'gum peacock'.

In essence, while *Vachellia mellifera* is an important native species that provides essential resources in the harsh Kgalagadi environment, its tendency to form dense, invasive stands under certain conditions presents a significant ecological challenge.

Lions do not appear to be discouraged by the occasional strong, dust-laden winds of the Kgalagadi

Hannes Lochner

The martial eagle's piercing eyes are cold and unwavering, scanning the landscape with lethal precision

Steph Vermeulen

Lion interactions are fascinating to watch

Hamman Prinsloo

Nadine Mather

Kittens playing in a camelthorn while waiting for their mother

★★★★

MELKVLEI PICNIC SITE
10 km to Gunong

You are allowed to leave your vehicle here, but always check carefully for predators resting in the shade of the tables or near the buildings before you step out.

The picnic site here is one of the most popular resting places along the Nossob road, offering shaded tables, toilets and a chance to stretch your legs. Melkvlei is an ideal place to pause before continuing your journey, either to turn back to Twee Rivieren, or to continue north towards Dikbaardskolk picnic site or Nossob Camp.

While you enjoy your picnic, look around and scan the environment for game. The area surrounding Melkvlei offers excellent game viewing. The **Nossob riverbed** here is wide and gently undulating, its golden grasses and dunes form a quintessential Kalahari scene.

Springbok herds move gracefully across the distant flats, and **gemsbok** regularly stand poised against the dunes – the perfect photographic subjects.

Scan the camelthorns for **lanner falcons, bateleur, Gabar goshawks** and **tawny eagles** that may perch on the nearby trees, while **martial eagles** are occasionally seen soaring overhead.

Kori bustards stride through the grasslands, and **northern black korhaans** may be heard giving their croaking calls from the dune slopes.

Hamman Prinsloo

Take care before disembarking from your vehicle at Melkvlei – lions may surprise you

The caracal is a taut bundle of muscle and focus, ears pricked and body coiled, always alert and ready to explode into a lightning-fast pounce

Hannes Lochner

Continue on the road northwards after the break at the picnic site. Leaving **Melkvlei**, the Nossob valley opens wide and level, with tall red dunes pressing close on the western side. The road follows the course of the fossil river, sometimes hugging the bank, sometimes crossing shallow calcrete pans where animals often congregate after rain. In the dry months, the landscape seems motionless and silent, yet, if you pause and listen, it hums softly with life.

Leopard sightings are occasionally reported along the low ridges north of Melkvlei. Their camouflage is superb; even when close, they vanish into the red-gold hues of sand and grass.

The **camelthorn and grey camelthorn** remain the dominant trees, interspersed with **shepherd's trees** *(Boscia albitrunca)*. Their pale trunks and evergreen leaves provide vital shade for birds and antelope. **Gemsbok, blue wildebeest** and **springbok** appear regularly, while **ostriches** move through the riverbed in loose family groups, feeding on the sparse grass and small succulents.

Raptors are ever-present. **Pale chanting goshawks** patrol from the treetops, **bateleurs** glide low over the dunes and **tawny eagles** perch near waterholes. Occasionally, a **lanner falcon** will flash past, scattering flocks of doves drinking below. On windless days, **white-backed** and **lappet-faced vultures** may be seen soaring on slow, steady wings, sentinels of the sky searching for carcasses far beyond the horizon.

Springbok herds often amble through the river valley, and **gemsbok lick mineral salts** on the crest of the ridge, but **lion** and **tawny eagle** are regular visitors, too. After drinking, lions might rest in the shade under picnic tables. Check your surroundings before leaving your vehicle.

Caracal, on the way to Gunong

Story and photos by Heiko Denker

Anja and I were on our way from **Twee Rivieren** towards **Nossob**, with our final destination being **Bitterpan**. **Leeudril**, **Rooiputs**, **Kij Kij** and **Melkvlei** were already behind us and not a single photo taken. On such quiet mornings, one of us would eventually say: *"Jetzt könnte mal langsam etwas passieren!"* ("It's about time something happens!")

The embankment along the road was quite high, so you could only just see over the edge. As I glanced to my left, I suddenly spotted a reddish shape – a cat! It was a **caracal**, sitting right on the embankment, almost within arm's reach. It was just before eight o'clock; the light was still soft and the caracal in no hurry, completely relaxed beside us. *Etwas war passiert!* (Something had finally happened!)

We spent the next hour and 10 minutes with the caracal, watching it hunt **Brants' whistling rats**. The first hunt was a success; the rat was caught and eaten within minutes. A few failed attempts followed, with long, patient pauses between them, until the cat eventually slipped away between the bushes about 80 m from the road.

The rest of the day was quiet again, with not another photo taken all the way to Bitterpan. But that caracal encounter … that is what the Kalahari is all about: long hours of stillness, rewarded by a moment of pure magic.

Heiko Denker

Caracals mostly hunt small, abundant prey

Heiko Denker

Caracals are among the more successful medium-sized predators, especially when targeting small prey

Gunong

★★★

GUNONG
8 km to Kransbrak

After heavy rain, the flats around Gunong shimmer yellow with **devil's thorn** blooms. Watch how ostriches move among them, delicately plucking the flowers one by one.

The borehole at **Gunong** was sunk as recently as 1963, though its water is still unfit for human consumption. It is usually a quiet waterhole, yet after good summer rain, the bare patches transform into a wonder-world of blazing yellow when the aptly named **devil's thorn** (*Tribulus zeyheri*) carpets the ground.

The **Khoekhoen** word *gunong* means 'place of many devil's thorns'. Anyone who has ever stepped barefoot outside a chalet or picnic site knows the pain of these sharp 'thorns'; actually small, spiny fruit capsules designed to cling to hooves, paws or shoes, dispersing their seeds far and wide. The plants survive the long dry spells through underground stalks and roots, sprouting fresh leaves and flowers within days of rain. The succulent runners are relished by many herbivores especially **ostriches**, which feed eagerly on the flowers. The devil's thorn provides valuable grazing after rain, but if the soil dries before follow-up showers, the wilted plants can become poisonous to livestock.

Do not confuse devil's thorn with devil's claw (*Harpagophytum procumbens*), which has large pink, trumpet-shaped flowers and occurs mainly in the dunes. This plant plays a dual and significant role in the Kgalagadi region: a **vital ecological role** in the local ecosystem and a crucial **socio-economic and medicinal role** for the indigenous communities. The plant is well adapted to the arid conditions of the Kalahari, with a deep main taproot and secondary **storage tubers** that allow it to survive droughts. Its deep root system helps to stabilise the sandy soils and prevent erosion, contributing to the overall health of its habitat. The secondary tubers are a **food source** for various animals, including porcupines and certain antelopes like duiker and steenbok.

From here northwards, the chance of encountering **eland** increases. When conditions on the Botswana side are harsh,

The beautiful auburn slender mongoose is usually seen among fallen branches of camelthorn trees

Daniel Wipf

huge herds migrate southwest in search of food and water. Although eland are among the park's eight most common antelope, they are largely confined to the Botswana dunes and are seldom seen along the Auob or southern Nossob roads.

Eland are the largest and most mobile antelope in the park. During drought they break into smaller groups, individuals moving up to 130 km in search of grazing. Primarily browsers, they are flexible feeders and can take in large quantities of grass when necessary. Adult bulls can weigh up to 900 kg, using their size to browse leaves from high branches. **Giraffe** can reach higher still but these introduced browsers have yet to spread far into Botswana's more remote dune systems.

As you approach **Kransbrak**, notice the rocky ridge on the right-hand side. **Leopard** regularly use the caves here as daytime shelters, their tracks often visible in the soft sand along the base.

The name *Gunong* is one of several in the park derived from **Khoekhoen** – the language of the region's earliest pastoral inhabitants – whose deep knowledge of the Kalahari landscape lives on in these evocative place names.

The devil's thorn in bloom after rains

The devil's claw is a vastly different plant

The opportunistic spotted hyena is always ready to steal prey

Daniel Wipf

★★★

KRANSBRAK
12 km to Jan-se-Draai

Scan the **rocky ridge** opposite the waterhole with binoculars. The caves often show traces of leopard activity: smooth entrance paths, scratch marks on calcrete or tell-tale paw prints in the sand below.

The name **Kransbrak** comes from the calcrete cliffs (*kranse*) across the riverbed and the natural salt lick (*brak*) that draws antelope to this spot. A few medium-sized trees offer scattered shade, and a short loop road towards the waterhole allows for closer viewing.

This stretch is renowned as a **leopard hotspot**. Though leopards are widespread in the park, sightings are less frequent than those of lion or cheetah. The calcrete cliffs here offer perfect cover, with ample prey and water nearby. Leopards thrive in the Kalahari because of their adaptable diet. Research has shown they prey on around **20 different species**, from small rodents to medium-sized antelope. These solitary cats are **highly territorial**; males and females occupy overlapping ranges but seldom share space except when mating or when a female is raising cubs.

Among the large predators, the leopard dominates only the cheetah. **Lion** and **hyena** can easily drive it off a kill, but cheetah generally yield rather than risk a fight. Cheetah hunt predominantly by day; leopard by night, though at Kransbrak, a leopard may sometimes steal a cheetah's kill and send it fleeing for safety.

Game viewing here depends on the time of day but never dismiss the element of surprise. In the soft morning light or the golden glow of late afternoon, these cliffs frequently reveal more than first meets the eye. Unfortunately, whether you approach from the south or the north, this area is usually reached by late morning or midday and seldom in the early hours when wildlife is most active.

As you drive north, **springbok** herds become scarcer, replaced by more **red hartebeest**, **gemsbok** and **ostriches** that favour the open plains farther from the road. Unlike some other parts of Africa where hartebeest have been eliminated from their historical ranges, the **Kgalagadi population is doing well**, with a generally increasing trend since the late 1990s. Red hartebeest in the Kgalagadi are **migratory**, moving seasonally within the park to find the best resources, especially congregating in the riverbeds during and after the rains when fresh vegetation appears. They are well adapted to the arid conditions of the Kalahari, able to live without freestanding water for extended periods as long as they can get enough moisture from their diet.

Black-backed jackal will devour birds feathers and all

Hannes Lochner

★★★

JAN-SE-DRAAI
18 km to Kameelsleep

Look for the elusive eland in this part of the Nossob. They are not often seen but sometimes single bulls wander on their own.

The waterholes along the **Nossob valley** tell a different story from those of the Auob. The name **Jan-se-Draai** recalls an early hunter, **Jan Matthys**, who, after journeying north up the Nossob, decided to turn back here, perhaps weary from the heat, or simply content with his load of meat and hides.

Eland are typically nomadic and appear in large numbers only from time to time, especially during droughts when they migrate into the South African side of the park in search of better grazing. They are generally shy and can be difficult to spot even when present. Those that inhabit the South African side keep to the dunes by day and wander into the riverbeds at night to visit waterholes. They disappear quickly when they sense danger, such as predators, and are most active at dawn and dusk.

Blackthorn shrubs and **young camelthorns** sometimes host loose, solitary nests a mere metre or two above ground, the handiwork of the tiny **scaly-feathered finch**. These restless seed-eaters, known in Afrikaans as *baardmannetjies* ('little bearded men') for the black malar stripes on their faces, are perfectly adapted to desert life. They can survive without drinking water, deriving moisture from seeds alone. At night, they roost communally in grass-ball nests or on open branches. If threatened, the flock bursts through the nest roof in a flurry of wings.

Bateleurs will readily take advantage of carrion of all sizes, from roadkill (birds, lizards, small mammals) to parts of large mammal carcasses left by predators. Scavenging provides a less energy-intensive food source than hunting, especially for younger birds still developing their hunting skills. They have strong beaks for tearing meat and a highly acidic digestive system, similar to other vultures, which helps them process decaying flesh and neutralise potential pathogens. They spend up to 8–9 hours a day in the air, flying low in a wide, zig-zag pattern across the dunes and riverbeds. This extensive, low-altitude searching allows them to quickly spot dead animals, often before other larger vultures or terrestrial scavengers.

Ann Gadd

Bateleur with Cape fox

Gemsbok are often seen along this stretch, sometimes forming nursery groups of calves guarded by one or two vigilant females, while the mothers graze nearby. Calving peaks around September but can occur year-round, depending on rainfall. Contrary to myth, gemsbok calves are not born with horns; these begin growing rapidly during the three-to-four-week hiding period before the young join the herd. Mothers return discreetly to nurse, calling softly until the calf emerges from concealment. All calves in a herd tend to suckle within a few minutes of each other, a remarkable synchrony in behaviour and survival. **Nursery herds** are frequently seen in the riverbed or among the dunes.

Louise Steenkamp

Thieves patiently awaiting their turn for a titbit

Kameelsleep

★★★

KAMEELSLEEP
13 km to Dikbaardskolk

The Kameelsleep waterhole is **unremarkable**, its water brackish and mineral-rich. The wide river valley stretches far from the road, and herds of gemsbok and springbok are often seen in the distance.

Uncontrolled hunting was rife in the 1800s. Among those who frequented the upper Nossob valley were the Sandersons, noted hunters of the time. On one expedition, they shot a giraffe and, fearing prosecution by the Cape authorities, dragged it with donkeys across the riverbed into Bechuanaland (now Botswana). Unbeknown to them, it was the last migrating giraffe in the Nossob valley. More than a century would pass before giraffes returned to this landscape.

Most of the park's place names predate its proclamation, and each reflects a fragment of the region's history. A few are Scottish in origin, but many are Khoekhoen, the language of the Nama and San who once lived here. Afrikaans, spoken widely by early settlers, shaped many others. The Afrikaans

Adult male leopards are notably larger than females

word for giraffe is *kameelperd* (shortened to *kameel*), and *sleep* means 'to drag'. The name **Kameelsleep**, meaning 'giraffe drag', thus commemorates the Sanderson incident.

A group of leopards is called a leap. It is also known as a prowl. However, leopards are typically solitary animals, so a leap or prowl is most commonly used to describe a mother with her cubs, as they are the only ones that form temporary groups.

Adult male leopards are noticeably larger than females, although the difference is less extreme than in lions.

Adult males are typically 30–50 percent heavier than females. In southern Africa, a male leopard usually weighs 55–75 kg, with large individuals exceeding this, while females commonly weigh 30–45 kg. Males are more powerfully built, with broader heads, thicker necks, heavier forequarters, and longer canines – adaptations linked to fighting rivals and defending territories.

Females are more lightly built and agile, an advantage for hunting smaller prey and raising cubs alone. While both sexes are superb climbers and hunters, the male's greater size reflects his role in territorial defence and competition, whereas the female's build favours efficiency and endurance.

Dave Miles

Lion chasing hyenas

Story and photos by Geo Jooste

A group of five lions was resting at the Kameelsleep waterhole. One male and three females were asleep under a tree about 60 m south of the water, while a single lioness lay apart, watching a brown hyena approaching the waterhole. It was mid-December and intensely hot.

As the hyena drew closer, clearly intent on drinking and bathing, the lioness made a mock charge and the startled hyena fled. The lioness returned to the shade of the tree but kept her eyes fixed on the retreating animal.

A short while later the hyena returned, advancing slowly and nervously, stopping often, alert to every sound and movement. The lioness had taken up a new position behind an old, dry tree log, watching intently.

The hyena entered the water, climbed out, circled the waterhole, and then stepped back in. At that moment the lioness launched herself from cover – this time it was no mock charge. She covered the 60 m in barely two seconds and caught the hyena on the far side of the waterhole.

Almost immediately the other lionesses joined the attack, overpowering the hyena. The male then arrived, pushing the females aside, gripping the hyena by the neck and delivering the final killing bite. He dragged the carcass to a nearby tree, where he fed alone.

Geo Jooste

Geo Jooste

Geo Jooste

Geo Jooste

Geo Jooste

★★★

DIKBAARDSKOLK PICNIC SITE
15 km to Cheleka

Before you alight from your vehicle, look around for predators. You may be surprised by the resident leopard that has discovered the roof of the ablution block is both cool and comfortable.

Dikbaardskolk picnic site lies to the left where the **long dune road joins the Nossob road**. Large **camelthorns** provide generous shade and the picnic tables are a welcome sight after a long drive through the dunes. Take your time here; stretch your legs, unpack your lunch and look up into the trees for movement or a flicker of feathers. This is a fine place for both birdwatching and quiet reflection.

Next to the camelthorn closest to the dune road stands a magnificent **shepherd's tree**. It's worth a closer look. This is one of the most remarkable trees of the Kalahari, a true survivor. The shepherd's tree is a **vital food source** in this arid landscape, easily recognised from afar by its rounded, evergreen crown and smooth white trunk. Peer at its tiny leaves and you may notice flowers after good rains or fruit ripening from autumn into winter. Though rarely seen near riverbeds, as here, it **thrives on the open dunes** where its deep roots tap into underground moisture.

The shepherd's tree in the Kgalagadi has the **deepest known roots of any plant**, with one specimen's root system found to extend an astonishing 68 m deep.

Locals call it the '**tree of life**' and for good reason. Throughout the year, it feeds and shelters an astonishing variety of creatures. Lions and leopards often **rest in its shade**; cheetahs use its sloping trunks as **play ramps**; and birds and mammals feed on its **sweet berries**. The hollows of older trees **collect rainwater**, a precious resource in this arid land. Even people have long relied on it. Nearly every part of the tree has a **use in traditional medicine** and, among the Tswana, it holds special reverence – **praise songs** to tribal leaders were once sung from the tops of shepherd's trees.

Look up into the fork of the camelthorns and you may spot the nest of a **black-tailed tree rat**. Unlike most rodents, this one builds its home high above the ground, using thorny twigs, **often freshly cut and green** to keep the nest cool and hidden from raptors. Over time, the constant damp from dew, urine and rain weakens the wood beneath. Eventually, the heavy branch splits and falls, evidence you might find near the picnic site, where one of these trees has lost a great limb in just this way.

The **black-tailed tree rat** (*Thallomys nigricauda*) is typical of the Kalahari, but do not confuse it with its close relative, *Thallomys paedulcus*, which lives further east in the wetter, broad-leaved and acacia savannas receiving over 500 mm of rain each year.

Flocks of lively birds eagerly await fallen crumbs at the picnic site. Identify **glossy starlings**, **tit-babblers**, **red-headed finch**, **sociable and sparrow-weavers**, **cape crows** and **familiar chats**. If you arrive early, study the sand for signs of the night's activity. The clear clawed tracks of a **honey badger** may cross the road or circle the tables, silent reminders of a restless forager's visit before dawn.

Janine Honiball

Janine Honiball

Beware of a sleeping leopard in the roof of the ablutions

Janine Honiball

Dikbaardskolk picnic site

Black-backed jackal

Edmund Aylmer

The road verges near Dikbaardskolk often show small holes and cleared patches of sand, evidence of **rodent burrows**. These tiny engineers are vital to the desert ecosystem as their excavations aerate the soil, disperse seeds and provide shelter for reptiles, insects and even small carnivores.

The name Dikbaardskolk dates back to the early hunting days of the 1800s. One of the farmers, Matthys, was known for his thick beard, *dik baard* in Afrikaans, said to resemble the black mane of a Kalahari lion. In local usage, *dikbaard* even became a nickname for lion. The word *kolk* refers to a whirlpool or eddy, and it was here that Matthys regularly camped during the hunting season.

A short loop road leads to an elevated viewpoint overlooking the waterhole, a busy gathering place for **gemsbok**, **springbok**, **blue wildebeest**, **red hartebeest**, **ostriches** and **kori bustards**. Raptors also visit to drink and bathe. This is one of the liveliest waterholes along the Nossob, where **cheetah** and **lion** are frequently sighted. Even when predators remain unseen, their **spoor** on the sandy road can reveal their presence.

Black-backed jackals are one of the **oldest surviving members of the *Canidae* (dog) family**, with their lineage stretching back over two million years, essentially making them living fossils among canids. Their resilience and adaptability have allowed them to persist in the African landscape for an extraordinary amount of time.

Look carefully for **black-backed jackals** scavenging near the water's edge. These canids are plentiful in the Kgalagadi owing to their **extreme adaptability, opportunistic omnivorous diet and unique co-operative social structure**. The harsh, arid environment of the Kgalagadi favours their resourcefulness in finding food and surviving in an ecosystem with large apex predators and highly variable conditions. They form monogamous pairs that mate for life, and their social structure allows older offspring to stay and help raise subsequent litters. This 'helper' system significantly increases pup survival rates, contributing to a stable population even amid environmental pressures.

Bat-eared foxes are regularly seen in the dry riverbeds. The association between bat-eared foxes and termites is a crucial predator-prey relationship; **termites, particularly harvester termites, are the primary food source** for the bat-eared fox, which in turn acts as a natural control for the termite population.

The surrounding dunes and ridges are prime hunting ground for **cheetah**, particularly during the cool morning hours when they use the slanting light and shadows to their advantage. The open terrain allows a full-speed chase, a breathtaking spectacle if you are fortunate enough to witness it.

Look out for raptor nests as you drive towards Kaspersdraai. Eagles sometimes maintain multiple nests within a territory, reusing and enlarging them year after year.

Brown snake eagles are regularly seen on this stretch of road. These raptors are not true eagles, since their **legs are not feathered**, but covered instead in thick **scales** that shield them from snake bites. These formidable hunters use their powerful talons to **grasp, hold and crush** slender-bodied snakes. When threatened, snakes strike and coil around the eagle's legs, but the tough scales are almost **impenetrable to fangs**. Feathers would only hinder their precision among grass and thornbush, which is why all **ground-hunting raptors** – from buzzards to harriers – have bare legs. Large snakes are crushed or torn apart; smaller ones are swallowed whole. When feeding chicks, adults carry big snakes in their talons, while smaller prey may be **partially swallowed**, the tail left dangling from the beak. At the nest, the chick tugs it free, a remarkable feeding ritual unique to these eagles. As you travel northward, keep scanning treetops and dead branches for them. **Brown snake eagles** are fairly common in the **upper reaches of the Nossob valley**, often seen perched motionless, eyes fixed on the sand below.

★★★★

CHELEKA
13 km to Kaspersdraai

At Cheleka, inspect the ground near shaded trees (from your vehicle). The fine, peppered texture of the sand can reveal delicate insect tracks, the marks of gerbils or the tiny drag trails of beetles moving between seeds and shade ... the minute signatures of desert life.

Cheleka waterhole lies a short distance from the main road, and it is easy to miss the small access track leading to a lovely big tree in the parking area. This is a rewarding stop and a good waterhole where you can relax in the shade while keeping an eye on the activity in the riverbed. It's a spiritual experience simply to sit there, listening to the natural sounds of this wild place. If you are lucky, a visiting predator may make an appearance, but it is almost certain gemsbok will provide your main entertainment.

The shade under camelthorns looks inviting, but do not be tempted to step out and rest beneath them. Not only do park regulations prohibit leaving your vehicle, but the **Kalahari sand** hides dangers few see until it is too late. Beneath the cool surface lurks the **sand tampan**, a soft-bodied tick that lies in wait where animals rest. Drawn by warmth and carbon dioxide, it surfaces to feed in swarms, attaching briefly to suck blood before dropping off again. The tampan transmits toxins and disease, a reminder that even the smallest desert dwellers have evolved formidable survival strategies.

Beyond Cheleka, the **Nossob River** meanders in wide **oxbows**, creating sweeping vistas of open grassland and red dunes. Though herds often graze far in the distance, **red hartebeest** are particularly common here, their russet coats vivid against the pale sand.

After good summer rains, this section can become challenging: the **road surface hardens** and acts like a channel, trapping runoff so vehicles seem to drive through rivers while the surrounding dunes appear dry. This is one reason why **high-clearance or 4x4 vehicles** are recommended for this stretch of road.

Pause at the huge camelthorn and observe how the bustling colony of sociable weavers attracts **reptiles**, **rodents**, **snakes** and even **raptors** searching for prey. The rustle of wings and chatter of the colony make this one of the liveliest roadside spectacles in the Nossob valley.

Crimson-breasted shrikes are striking in the bleak arid environment

Villiers Steyn

★★★★

KASPERSDRAAI
16 km to Rooikop

The name Kaspersdraai recalls the journeys of Kasper Sanderson, who travelled up the Nossob River in the late 1800s collecting tsamma melons for storage and later use. This was his turning-point, where he found no more melons and decided to head home. The well he dug here marked his seasonal camp, and the name lives on as a reminder of early desert life.

The **tsamma plant** (*Citrullus lanatus* var. *citroides*) is a sprawling creeper with small green melons streaked with pale mottling and is the **lifeblood of the Kalahari**. After summer rain, it flourishes across the dunes and, in dry years, the melons become a crucial **source of moisture and vitamin C** for countless animals, from **gemsbok** to **jackals, African wild cat**, and **brown hyenas**. Even the hyenas, mostly scavengers, will feed on tsamma to supplement their diet.

Brown hyenas are frequently seen here early mornings, solitary wanderers with shaggy manes, sloping backs and an unkempt, spectral look. They are **true desert survivors**, feeding on carcasses, ostrich eggs, insects and fruit. Unlike their insect-eating cousins the **aardwolves**, brown hyenas are opportunists, marking their territories with white pastes from their anal glands and using traditional **latrine sites**. They den in abandoned **aardvark burrows** and sometimes follow springbok ewes about to give birth, stealing the newborns. Spotting one in the open Kalahari light is a rare privilege.

Note the white eyebrow of the common fiscal

Daniel Wipf

A short loop leads to the **waterhole viewpoint**, shaded by scattered trees that attract flocks of small birds before they drop down to drink. After good summer rain, this area also bursts into colour as **Kalahari nerine lilies** (*Nerine laticoma*) bloom in profusion, their pinkish-lilac flowers glinting against the red sand. Related to the daffodil and crinum, they flower mainly from **December to February**, adding a delicate softness to the desert.

Sharp eyes may be rewarded with a glimpse of one of the Kalahari's most elusive residents, the **bushveld sengi** (also called elephant shrew). Neither elephant nor shrew, this little insect-eater is a truly African lineage, adapted perfectly to life in arid grasslands. With its long, mobile snout, large eyes and quick bounding gait, it darts between shrubs feeding on ants and termites, obtaining all the moisture it needs

The bushveld sengi (elephant shrew) of the Kgalagadi is a tiny, swift insect-eater, rarely seen as it darts between shrubs, using its elongated snout to probe the sand for ants and termites in the cool of early morning and late afternoon

Pierre Labuschagne

from its prey. Look for a network of tiny **runways radiating from a burrow** beneath a bush, signs of a sengi territory. Sit quietly and you may see it reappear, testing the air with its trunk-like nose before resuming its search for insects. Its long hind legs power its remarkable speed and are used for **foot-drumming communication**, a rhythm unique to each species. They also exchange high-pitched squeaks and purrs, and even scent-mark one another with secretions from glands in the mouth. Sengis are monogamous; breeding occurs mainly from **August to March**, when insect numbers peak. The bushveld species usually produces **twins**, which are independent within a few days.

Continue northwards until you reach the **second entrance to Marie's Loop**, which is recommended for a late-afternoon drive, a fine spot for game viewing and one of the most scenic stretches of the Nossob valley.

Despite their wild appearance, African wild cats are the **direct ancestors of the domestic cat** (*Felis silvestris lybica*), tamed by humans in the Nile valley more than **10000 years ago**.

Pierre Labuschagne

★★★★★

MARIE'S LOOP
Loop distance is 11 km

There are two entrances; best to begin the loop at the entrance closest to Nossob Camp.

The loop takes its name from Marie Brink, wife of borehole driller Henry Brink, who famously completed the drilling here herself after her husband became incapacitated. The borehole she finished became known as Marie-se-Gat ('Marie's Hole'). The water is of moderate quality but attracts abundant wildlife, making this one of the most rewarding loops in the Nossob valley.

Halfway around the loop lies the **waterhole**, an open area with wide views across the Nossob valley and a backdrop of red dunes. Large camelthorns and shrubs along the road offer perches for birds: **common fiscals**, **lilac-breasted rollers**, **shaft-tailed whydahs**, **Cape sparrows**, **scaly-feathered finches** and **yellow canaries** are regulars.

Afternoons are best for sitting quietly in the shade and waiting. **Ostriches** stroll the riverbed and **secretarybirds** may stride past with that measured regal gait. Predators are common. **Cheetah**, **lion**, **leopard**, **brown hyena**, **black-backed jackal**, **caracal**, **African wild cat** and the elusive **bat-eared fox** are all recorded here.

Occasionally, visitors are surprised by **kudu**, normally associated with more wooded parts of the park. They have adapted to the Nossob's tree-lined stretches, feeding on browse and supplementing their moisture needs with **tsamma melons**. Though not desert specialists, kudu are resilient browsers, able to thrive in semi-arid woodland where food and cover coincide.

Springbok are ever-present. During the **wet season (November–March)**, large herds graze the short green grass of the riverbed; in the **dry months (April–October)**, they split into smaller groups. Watch for their social structure:

- **Bachelor herds** of non-breeding males.
- **Female herds** with young, accompanied by one **territorial male**.
- **Mixed groups** outside the rutting season.

When the rut begins, males compete fiercely for dominance, locking horns in ritual combat. Only territorial rams mate, defending patches of prime grazing through posturing, pawing and a peculiar urination-defecation display used to mark their turf. Look for a ram stretching forward, tail erect and scraping the ground, the classic sign of territorial pride.

Along the loop's shaded stretches, notice the **paired paw prints and tiny dig mark**, which are signs of bat-eared foxes hunting. Their dens are marked by **multiple entrances** and often surrounded by well-trodden patches where pups play.

Bat-eared foxes can be seen foraging in the dry riverbed. In **winter**, these foxes become **diurnal**, foraging in daylight when freezing nights drive insects underground. **In November**, pups may play outside at dawn. Foxes feed mainly on **harvester termites** and **beetle larvae**. When termite colonies are active, family groups forage close together, but for beetle larvae they spread out, sweeping the ground with their oversized ears. By tilting their heads and

Daniel Wipf

Male black-backed jackals average 7.5 kg while females average 6.8 kg, but it's almost impossible to tell them apart in the field.

touching the sand with their ear fringes, they pinpoint prey movements and dig with astonishing speed and precision. Entirely **insectivorous**, bat-eared foxes are misunderstood and occasionally wrongly blamed for killing livestock. In truth, they play an essential role in controlling termite populations and maintaining ecological balance in the desert.

A single **bat-eared fox** can consume up to **1.2 million termites per year**, making it one of the Kalahari's most effective natural pest controllers.

Western barn owls take refuge in the safety of cavities in trees

Elsie Potgieter

Springbok

Annabé Marais

Bat-eared foxes are social animals, usually living in small family groups

Brown hyenas are regularly seen on their own, but they live in clans of several individuals that occupy a huge territory of about 350 km²

Daniel Wipf

★★★★★

ROOIKOP
7 km to Nossob Waterhole

At Rooikop waterhole, a dense thicket of young camelthorns marks where a great old tree once stood. Over time, these saplings will take its place. The site's name – Rooikop, meaning 'Red Hill' – refers to the striking red dune that rises beside the waterhole, a clear landmark in this open section of the valley. A short loop road circles the waterhole since the main route can flood after heavy rains.

Approach slowly in the **early morning**, when **brown hyena** or **lion** often visit to drink. Big cats, wary of disturbance, sometimes move off if startled, so stop at a respectful distance and wait quietly. Birds, however, soon resume their routines, hopping down to the water even with a vehicle nearby.

The surrounding dunes and ridges are prime hunting ground for **cheetah**, particularly during the cool morning hours when they use the slanting light and shadows to their advantage. The open terrain allows a full-speed chase, a breathtaking spectacle if you are fortunate enough to witness it.

Hares are also occasionally encountered here. Both the **Cape hare** and **scrub hare** occur in the Kalahari and are difficult to distinguish in the field. Mostly nocturnal, they feed on grasses and bark and can reach astonishing speeds when startled. The **scrub hare** favours bushy ground, while the **Cape hare** prefers open country. Unlike rabbits, hares do not burrow; they live in the open, and their young, called **leverets**, are born fully furred and with eyes open, ready to run within hours.

Include Marie's Loop or continue straight to Nossob Camp.

Cheetah cubs accompany their mother for six to eighteen months, learning hunting and survival skills

Hamman Prinsloo

Hamman Prinsloo

Daniel Wipf

Brown hyenas are **conflict-avoidant scavengers**, not aggressive brawlers. In the vast, open landscapes of the Kgalagadi, it is far more common to see them **yield and move away** than to fight. A true fight between two brown hyenas is therefore an **unusual and noteworthy** event, usually driven by food, territory or breeding pressure rather than constant rivalry.

Despite its dry riverbed, the **Nossob River** still channels **subsurface water** southwards. The camelthorn trees lining its course survive by sending roots **40 m deep**, tapping this invisible flow – the hidden lifeline of the valley.

Daniel Wipf

Daniel Wipf

Daniel Wipf

Brown hyena conflict between two males

Nossob waterhole

★★★★★

NOSSOB WATERHOLE
10 km to Cubitje Quap

The renowned viewing hide at the Nossob waterhole is located adjacent to the Nossob Rest Camp. From this hide, guests can watch the unfolding theatre of the wild not only during daylight hours but also throughout the night, should they wish. The hide is a significant attraction for many visitors.

Early mornings are prime time to spot the elusive **African wild cat**, often hunting along this section. Its **grizzled grey-brown coat**, **reddish ears** and **long, slender legs** distinguish it from domestic cats. When sitting upright, the cat's tall stance and vertical posture recall the feline forms seen in **ancient Egyptian art**. Wild cats are **solitary hunters**, preying mostly on **rodents**, but also on small mammals, birds, reptiles and insects. They detect prey by sound or sight, stalking low before pouncing with precision. A swift bite to the neck or skull ends the hunt … a highly efficient, silent kill.

The **Nossob lion pride** regularly patrols the road itself, using the soft sand for easy walking and the tall banks for concealment. These lions are powerful hunters, though only **one in six hunts is successful**. With many mouths to feed, they rely on regular kills but also drink when water is near. The **Nossob Camp waterhole** is a favourite gathering point, and night visitors to the hide may witness their moonlit silhouettes drinking in silence.

After good summer rains, the valley stirs with life. **Abdim's storks** arrive in large, chattering flocks, migrants from Ethiopia drawn south by the abundance of insects. Their appearance signals a brief period of plenty in this arid land. Other unusual visitors sometimes appear, too: **lesser kestrels**, **kites**, **steppe eagles** and **European bee-eaters**, all riding the seasons in search of food.

Wild cat spoor can sometimes be seen on the road near the camp; small, neat pawprints without claw marks. Lions' larger tracks show the rounded pad and clear toe lobes that tell of their passing during the night.

Abdim's stork

Steph Vermeulen

Lions do not usually hunt birds. However, if tempted, they may strike at them.

Continue north along the broad, sandy valley and keep your eyes open for raptors such as the **pale chanting goshawk**. The goshawk spends a large amount of time perched in visible locations like the tops of trees, making them easy to spot. They are sometimes called **Pirates of the Kgalagadi.** This informal name comes from their opportunistic and sometimes bold scavenging and hunting behaviours, including 'stealing' prey from other raptors and from honey badgers. Immature birds are brownish and streaked, quite unlike the smooth-grey adults.

Leaving **Nossob Camp**, you enter one of the most remote and unspoilt regions in South Africa. The wide, fossilised riverbed of the **Nossob** stretches northward, a pale ribbon between red dunes.

The **Mabuasehube turn-off** branches to your right. This route leads into Botswana and may be used only by **pre-booked four-wheel-drive travellers** heading for the wilderness camps of Mabuasehube.

Tawny eagles will also target Cape turtle doves at the water

Derryn Nash

Hennie Bignaut

Pale chanting goshawks catch a variety of prey items, including snakes

Hennie Bignaut

Rodents are favourite prey items of pale chanting goshawks

★★★★★

CUBITJE QUAP

14 km to Kwang

Cubitje Quap is one of the most active waterholes in the park and is a favourite drinking place for sandgrouse, jackals, bateleurs and others.

Cubitje Quap is pronounced with a click at the beginning and means 'the place of many aardvark holes on the pan', although some sources translate it as 'the place with many warthog holes'. The very sound of the name holds a strange fascination for many Kgalagadi regulars, for this is a favourite waterhole to spend time watching and photographing birds, especially sandgrouse in the mornings.

Hundreds of birds come and go throughout the day. You are likely to see **canaries**, **finches**, **whydahs**, **sparrows**, **weavers**, **starlings**, **doves** and, of course, flocks of **sandgrouse** by the dozen. Later in the day it becomes the turn of the **vultures** (especially in the hotter months) and other raptors, both large and small. It is fascinating to watch **lanner falcons** and **jackals** hunt doves and sandgrouse. In between these scenes of winged activity, **springbok**, **red hartebeest**, **blue wildebeest** and a variety of predators may appear.

Sandgrouse always arrive at the waterhole in large flocks. Presumably, the group grows as more birds join on their way to water. As they gather, the **Namaqua sandgrouse** gives its characteristic call – *kelkiewyn, kelkiewyn, kelkiewyn,* Afrikaans for 'glass of wine'. Hence the name *kelkiewyn sandpatrys*. The call may serve as an invitation for others to join the flock. Approaching the waterhole, the birds circle several times before darting in to drink. They spend only a few seconds drinking before lifting off again.

One of their most remarkable adaptations is the behaviour of **male Burchell's** and **Namaqua sandgrouse**, which soak their abdominal feathers to carry water back to their chicks, sometimes up to 80 km away. The chicks are raised in midsummer, when temperatures soar. While jackals may occasionally threaten sandgrouse, the main predators are lanner falcons. Drinking in flocks greatly improves survival chances. More eyes mean earlier warnings and sheer numbers dilute the risk for each bird. Gathering at waterholes en masse is therefore an elegant strategy to minimise predation.

Among the regular raptor visitors to Cubitje Quap are **secretarybirds**, those stately, long-legged hunters of the open dunes, and the ever-graceful **bateleurs**, which have a nesting site nearby.

Black-backed jackal hunting Cape turtle doves

Boshoff Steenekamp

Black-backed jackal hunting Burchell's sandgrouse

Kathy Kay

A successful hunt requires stealth, speed and planning

Peter Hall

Bateleur eagles fluff and shake themselves as part of feather maintenance and thermoregulation

Lanner falcon with Burchell's sandgrouse prey

Bateleurs engage in fighting, but it is infrequent and usually restrained

Burchell's sandgrouse chicks drinking water from male's feathers

Hennie Blignaut

The **Namaqua sandgrouse's 'kelkiewyn' call** is one of the most distinctive sounds of the Kalahari dawn, a name once used by early hunters and still fondly echoed by guides and travellers today.

Heading north from here, look out for low bushes lining both sides of the road, and on cool mornings you might see large numbers of **striped mice** sunning themselves at the edges of the bushes. This is a rodent pantry for raptors and many other animals, especially after good rains.

The striped mouse takes its name from the four reddish-brown stripes along its back. It inhabits a range of habitats that include some grass cover. At the base of a grass tuft, it excavates an angled burrow, about 50 cm long, ending in a chamber where two to nine young are born in summer. This rodent is active by day, moving quickly across open ground in search of grains, greens and insects. It also feeds on the fruits of buffalo thorn, raisin bush and blackthorn pods when available.

Rodents are the pantry for predators

The male Namaqua sandgrouse flies to a water source at dawn and soaks his specially modified belly and breast feathers which are uniquely structured with barbs and barbules to form a sponge-like network that can hold water. He then flies back to the nest, often many kilometres away, where the chicks drink directly from the wet feathers by sucking and nibbling at them.

A bit of important history

A few kilometres further, a no-entry road leads to Kwang Pan in the distance, which supplies part of the camp's water. The water here is less saline and in earlier years, it was the regular camping site of Piet de Villiers, Inspector of Lands, nicknamed 'Mof'. Piet de Villiers and Willie Rossouw, who married one of the Le Riche daughters, are regarded as the true founders of the Kalahari Gemsbok National Park.

By 1920, some farmers in the area had grown concerned: hunting had decimated much of the game between the Nossob and Auob rivers. Many farmers along the Nossob riverbank did little farming, relying instead on hunting and selling hides and biltong to survive. De Villiers and Rossouw decided to act and appealed to the Minister of Lands, Piet Grobler, one of the founders of the Kruger National Park and a visionary for conservation. After visiting the area, Grobler was convinced of its potential and initiated the process of proclaiming it a conservation area.

Despite financial constraints, he persuaded the government to declare 13 000 km^2 of desert a national park. The proclamation came in 1931 but there were no funds, no infrastructure and no one to manage this new park. Farmer Johannes le Riche, brother-in-law to Rossouw, had been badly affected by drought and the Great Depression. He was therefore easily persuaded to accept the National Parks Board's offer of seven pounds ten shillings per month to serve as park ranger. He was given an assistant, Constable Gert Januarie, along with horses, a cart and donkeys. Together, they patrolled the entire park.

The hunters were unimpressed and continued to poach illegally. It took years of perseverance to curb the slaughter. Other serious challenges followed: lack of water, immense distances and the bone-shaking road to the nearest town. Communication was minimal and effective patrolling was almost impossible. Le Riche's 650 km round trips took two weeks, and one 250 km stretch offered no water at all. The resilience of those early pioneers – and their families – was extraordinary. The contribution of the Le Riche family to Kalahari conservation was immense and, until quite recently, several of Johannes's descendants remained involved in the management of the park.

★★★★★

KWANG
7 km to Bedinkt

Patience pays off at Kwang. Lions usually rest in the dunes during the day, moving down to drink at dusk or dawn. The lions north of Nossob are notably wilder than those in the south.

The **Kwang waterhole** is a classic Kalahari stop: broad, open and framed by shade trees that make it an inviting place to pause and watch the comings and goings of wildlife. Visibility is excellent, the outlook over the wide, sandy riverbed beautifully scenic, but beware: the **lions** know this shade, too, and may wish to share it with you.

Lion sightings here are frequent, and the famous **Kwang lions** are among the most impressive in the park. One might imagine that such powerful predators live in constant abundance, regularly bringing down large prey, yet research has shown that in the **Kgalagadi's semi-arid environment**, lions depend surprisingly often on **smaller prey** such as **steenbok**, **aardvark**, **springhare** and even **porcupine**. When conditions improve and game is plentiful, they shift to larger antelope, their preferred prey.

Lions typically target **old or weakened animals**, or **solitary bulls and rams**, which are more vulnerable than those that live in herds. Because prey density is low in this vast ecosystem, lions must roam **extensive home ranges, sometimes over 400 km²**, in search of food.

In the Kgalagadi, **lion home ranges** are among the largest recorded in Africa.

After copulation, the lioness may appear aggressive and the male is swatted away

Kathy Kay

This image is a striking example of how strength and delicacy coexist in large predators such as lions.

Daniel Wipf

North of Nossob Camp, the road runs along the **outer edge of the broad riverbed**, so binoculars are needed to observe the activity on the far flats. High banks and scattered shrubs can limit visibility but after good rains, this whole area transforms. The valley fills with **springbok**, **blue wildebeest**, **red hartebeest** and **gemsbok** in impressive numbers.

Springbok are **highly nomadic**, following the rains and the flush of new grass. They are quick to exploit favourable conditions, their herds forming and dispersing according to the seasons of the desert.

Rutting season in the Kalahari is unpredictable, depending largely on rainfall and grazing conditions. When the rut begins, **territorial males** work furiously to herd females into their chosen areas. Springbok are exceptionally fecund; each ewe produces at least one lamb per year, but in years of abundant rainfall, she may rear **two lambs within 13 months**. Young females can even conceive at **six months old**, leading to occasional **population explosions**.

Lambing can occur anytime between **September and January**, depending on when the rut begins. In wet years, it happens early and most ewes drop their lambs within a few days of each other – a remarkable synchrony that helps overwhelm predators.

When birth is imminent, the ewe isolates herself from the herd. The **newborn lamb**, still damp and unsteady, must stand within minutes. The mother nudges it gently to encourage movement. Soon it can totter upright, splaying its legs for balance. Once steady, it begins to suckle, imprinting its mother's scent. For the first days, the lamb lies hidden in the grass, motionless and scentless, its **only defence** against predators. The ewe grazes some distance away and returns briefly to nurse it. Within a month, the lambs are strong enough to run with the adults, joining together in **nursery herds** that offer collective protection.

A single springbok lamb is vulnerable, but a **nursery group in motion – with dozens of small, darting bodies moving in unison across the pale grass** – **is one of the loveliest sights of the Kalahari plains.**

The beauty of a springbok herd moving in unison

Mystery of the trekbokken

Almost eight decades have passed since the last great **springbok migrations** – the legendary *trekbokke* – swept across the Kalahari. The final recorded movements occurred in **October 1946** and **November 1950**, and none have been seen since.

At the time, the park warden **Joep le Riche** was patrolling north of Kwang when he noticed a massive **dust cloud** rising on the horizon. As he drew closer, he realised it was a vast column of springbok, an unbroken procession of thousands moving steadily down the riverbed. He estimated the herd at **around 15 000 animals**, stretching for at least **11 km**.

Further north, he encountered even more groups, some numbering **over 500 individuals**, all travelling in the same southerly direction. Three days later, on his return to Twee Rivieren, he discovered most of these herds had left the park altogether, crossing into surrounding farmland. Tragically, the majority were **shot by farmers** for meat and skins before reaching the **Orange River** and only a few made it through.

Four years later, another great movement followed. This time flowing **from Botswana into the Northern Cape**, along a front estimated at **300 km wide**.

To this day, **scientists remain baffled**. No satisfactory explanation has been found for what triggered these mass migrations. Were they driven by **climatic fluctuations**, **food scarcity** or **overpopulation**? Perhaps a combination of all these factors ... or something else entirely.

Whatever the cause, the great *trekbok* migrations are now part of Kalahari legend; ghostly memories of a time when the plains themselves seemed to move, shimmering with the life of countless springbok.

Villiers Steyn

Caracal sightings have become more common in the past few years

★★★★

BEDINKT
13 km to Langklaas

If your visit coincides with midsummer after good rain, watch for the sudden flash of pink from the nerine lilies.

The name **Bedinkt** comes from the Dutch word meaning *'to reflect'*. According to old accounts, surveyor **Jackson** reached this point with his oxen during the dry season and, finding no tsamma melons left to feed them, paused here to consider whether to push on or turn back. Today, visitors do much the same, pausing beneath the shady trees at this peaceful waterhole to reflect on the stillness of the Kalahari.

Two small viewing loops offer good vantage points over a vast, open floodplain, which is ideal **cheetah country**. Spectacular hunts have been witnessed here, so scan the far edges of the riverbed for those low, elegant silhouettes. In early morning you might see **brown hyena, lion or other predators**. As the day warms, **doves** arrive first to drink, followed by **sandgrouse** and later, the **antelope**. Occasionally even **warthogs** appear, which is a rare sight as they struggle in such arid conditions.

This area is excellent for spotting **Gabar goshawks**, which resemble small pale chanting goshawks. Melanistic (black) individuals are occasionally seen. These fearless little raptors take prey larger than themselves and may raid other birds' nests for chicks. They also feed on small mammals, reptiles and insects. When building their nests, they may incorporate **colonial spider webs**, which enclose and disguise the structure.

Villiers Steyn

Caracal drinking

Bedinkt picnic site: At the time of writing, the new picnic site at Bedinkt was under construction.

Hannes Lochner

While cheetahs are superb hunters, they are subordinate predators when larger carnivores are present

For birds, the quickest way to cool down is to **stand in shallow water**, allowing heat to dissipate through the featherless legs and feet. The **pale chanting goshawk**, with its slate-grey body, long orange legs and bill, and haunting, fluting call, is one of the most recognisable raptors of the Kalahari. The colouring of immature birds is often confusing.

If your visit coincides with the **flowering of the nerine or vlei lily** (*Nerine laticoma*), you may find entire fields in bloom. This striking bulbous plant flowers after midsummer rain in clay depressions, painting the calcareous plains pink. Sometimes called the **snake lily**, its bulbs contain **calcium oxalate crystals** that can irritate skin or poison livestock.

Beyond Bedinkt, the wide plains attract vast **herds of blue wildebeest** after rain. These nomadic antelope depend on water and are picky about its quality. A herd may bypass one waterhole entirely if the taste is brackish. From a distance, their dark lines ripple across the pale sand like moving shadows.

Wildebeest are **territorial**, especially during the breeding season. The many solitary males you will see spaced evenly along the riverbeds are not outcasts, but **territorial bulls** guarding their ground, the strongest and fittest of them all. When herds of females wander through, they will try to hold them briefly and mate with any receptive cows before the herd moves on. Males that fail to win a territory live celibate lives in **bachelor groups**.

Calving peaks between **November and January**, when the grass is greenest and most nutritious. Drought years take a heavy toll on calves, as milk production drops sharply.

Warthog is a rare sighting

After good rains, the first flush of green includes the **Kalahari sour grass** (*Schmidtia kalahariensis*), a fast-growing annual with a sharp, acidic smell that can irritate the skin and even cause hay fever. Animals avoid mature stands, feeding only on the young shoots. This grass can also collect under vehicles and, when dry, **ignite easily**, so avoid parking over it.

Blue wildebeest are highly water-dependent, needing to drink **every two to three days**, unlike gemsbok, which can go **weeks without a drop**.

Sparring between wildebeest bulls is a low-intensity form of combat that builds strength, tests rivals and establishes relative dominance

★★★★

LANGKLAAS
4 km to Kousant

Notice the **Bushman grass tufts** forming pale 'roofs' over the sand, or the **snake eagles** scanning silently from their high perches.

The surname **Matthys** appears regularly in the history of Kgalagadi place names. One member of the family, known by the nickname **'Langklaas'** – meaning *'Tall Nicholas'* – made this area his temporary hunting camp. Perhaps he was drawn to its remoteness and the song of seed-eaters gathering at the water, or perhaps the hunting here was simply good. Whatever the reason, his name remains … though the **water** itself is still of poor quality.

Around the waterhole, **Bushman grass** (*Stipagrostis obtusa*) grows abundantly. This small, tufted species is one of the most important grazing grasses of the Kalahari. In drought years, the base dries to form a dense, pale mat known as the **'blue roof'.** Even then, it remains surprisingly palatable and nutritious but also highly **flammable**, and fire is often the only force that can destroy it. The plants grow up to about **60 cm** high, with short stalks that have earned it the nickname **short-legged Bushman grass**. The San people have long used its seeds to make a simple, nourishing porridge.

While large game are less frequent here, **honey badgers** and **suricates (meerkats)** are frequently seen near the waterhole. A **pair of black-chested snake eagles** also nests nearby and can regularly be spotted perched on dead branches or the bare crowns of camelthorns, watching intently for movement below.

Look for a wide grassy plain that opens on your left, dotted with **termite mounds**. These indicate a thriving population of subterranean workers. Where termites thrive, their predators are not far away. Though many termite-eating species, such as **aardvarks**, **aardwolves** and **pangolins**, are nocturnal and rarely seen by day, this area is a good place to look for their signs: diggings, droppings or fresh earth mounds.

Far across the floodplain, large herds of **red hartebeest** are often visible. In good years, when the grass grows tall after heavy rain, **over a thousand** may gather here before dispersing again into the dunes once the veld dries. Nomadic and resilient, these antelope depend on **tsamma melons** for moisture when surface water disappears.

The **red hartebeest** can easily outrun a lion. Yet speed is not always enough; solitary or territorial males are particularly vulnerable, while herds gain safety in numbers. Their social structure resembles that of the **blue wildebeest**, with **territorial males**, **bachelor herds** and **female herds** each fulfilling their role in the cycle.

During the **rutting season**, territorial males expend enormous energy defending their space: chasing intruders, herding females and repelling challengers. Feeding becomes secondary and many lose condition. Eventually, a younger or stronger bachelor may take over. Former territorial bulls either join bachelor groups or fall victim to predators; their strength spent in the fight for dominance.

Even when the females leave because of the drought, a territorial male may **stay behind**, guarding his ground in the hope that conditions improve and the herds return. Such dedication carries a cost of constant vigilance and isolation. So, next time you see a **solitary red hartebeest**, spare a thought for his struggle: a lone sentry in a vast, unpredictable land.

Most **calving** takes place between **September and November**, timed with the first green flush of spring grasses.

The **red hartebeest** (*Alcelaphus buselaphus caama*) can reach running speeds of **up to 65 km/h**, making it one of Africa's swiftest antelope and a master of endurance across the open plains.

A female herd of red hartebeest includes young calves

★★★★

KOUSANT
8 km to Polentswa waterhole

As you drive further north, it may seem as though game density declines. This is probably not the case, but the great distances between waterholes create that impression.

The name **Kousant**, from the **Khoekhoen** language, means *'coarse white sand'*. The waterhole lies to the **left of the road**, reached by a short circular access track with the trough to the south. Like many Kalahari pans, Kousant has its resident **pair of black-backed jackals**, ever alert for a dove, ground squirrel or mouse unwary enough to come too close.

In this arid land, grass is rarely green and lush. It is usually dry, fibrous and low in minerals such as **phosphates**. Yet, animals like the **gemsbok** thrive here thanks to remarkable physiological and behavioural adaptations. Their **broad muzzles** allow them to crop large quantities of grass quickly when grazing is good, while their **slow metabolic rate** reduces heat generation.

These antelope can lose water and cool off efficiently because they possess a **larger internal water reserve** relative to body size than most mammals. Their mobility also helps them survive; they roam far and wide in search of food, covering **vast distances** between grazing areas and waterholes.

Gemsbok are among the **great survivors of the desert**. Despite their size and high food requirements, they endure extreme conditions with summer temperatures soaring above **45 °C by day** and dropping below zero at night in winter. Their secret lies in a remarkable **thermoregulatory system**. They allow their **body temperature to fluctuate**, storing heat during the day and releasing it at night. This protects their brains from overheating, an extraordinary adaptation to life without reliable water. These magnificent antelope are regular visitors at **Kousant waterhole**, their stately silhouettes perfectly framed against the pale dunes.

As you continue north, watch for **lion** near the dunes. These lions are often referred to as the **Polentswa lions**: large, golden-maned cats that dominate this section of the valley. Soon after, the turn-off to **Polentswa waterhole** appears on your **right**. This site once bore the name **Grootbrak**, and the original waterhole lay on the **eastern riverbank**. When the **Polentswa Camp and Lodge** were established, the waterhole was relocated to the **western bank**, closer to the main Nossob road, making it more accessible to travellers and wildlife alike.

The gemsbok survives blistering Kalahari heat through a **counter-current heat-exchange system** in its nasal cavity. Warm blood flowing to the brain passes close to cooler blood returning from the nose, losing heat before it reaches the brain. By panting instead of sweating, the gemsbok cools this venous blood without wasting precious water, allowing its body temperature to rise safely above **40 °C** during the day and release stored heat later, standing side-on to the cool evening breeze.

Lions do prey on gemsbok, but they do so cautiously and selectively

Gemsbok are large, powerful antelope armed with long, sharp horns and are among the most dangerous prey species in the Kgalagadi

Water conservation in desert antelope

Masters of survival without drinking

Desert antelope such as the **gemsbok**, **steenbok** and **springbok** have evolved extraordinary physiological and behavioural strategies to survive for months without drinking free water. Their secret lies in **efficient water management**, both in how they obtain it and how little they lose.

They derive most of their moisture from the **plants** they eat, especially succulents, bulbs and fruits such as **tsamma melons**. Their digestive systems extract every possible drop, and their **kidneys concentrate urine** so effectively that almost no water is wasted. Even their **droppings are dry pellets**, conserving every trace of internal moisture.

By being **active mainly at night** or during the cooler hours of dawn and dusk, they avoid excessive water loss through panting or sweating. In extreme heat, their bodies tolerate mild **dehydration** and fluctuating temperatures rather than expending water to maintain strict thermal balance.

These remarkable adaptations make the gemsbok one of the **true desert specialists**, perfectly equipped to endure the harsh, waterless Kalahari plains where few large mammals can survive.

Desert air conditioning

Life in the Kalahari demands smart timing and energy use. Many mammals – from bat-eared foxes and porcupines to lions and brown hyenas – are **nocturnal**, avoiding the searing daytime heat. Others rest in the **shade of camelthorns** or retreat to burrows that stay cooler underground. Activity peaks in the soft light of dawn and dusk, when predators hunt and antelope graze on dew-damp grass. Every behaviour – when to move, feed or rest – is a finely tuned survival strategy in a land where water, shade and energy must be carefully balanced.

★★★★★

POLENTSWA

12 km to Lijersdraai picnic site

Watch a **bateleur eagle** after it bathes. It may stretch its wings fully, lie flat against the ground and tilt its head to the sun. This seemingly lazy pose is not rest; it's a vital maintenance ritual. The heat liquefies oils that the bird later spreads through preening, while the ants scurrying over its feathers help remove parasites.

Polentswa waterhole was known many years ago as *Grootbrak*. The name *Grootbrak* was derived from the limestone outcrops nearby, where animals regularly gathered to lick mineral salts. The name *Polentswa* refers to this part of the river as *'the rogue river'* or *'the river that lost its way'*. Here, the Nossob River and a huge pan intertwine. The latter, a remnant of the Polentswa fossil riverbed, once a tributary of the Nossob, now long vanished.

It is well worth spending time at Polentswa waterhole. Park in the shade of a large camelthorn or a scrubby shepherd's tree and simply wait; there is usually plenty of action here.

This area has one of the highest concentrations of **bateleurs** in the park. With their red faces, legs and feet, distinctive plumage and characteristic rocking flight, these masters of the skies are unmistakable. *Bateleur* is the French word for **juggler** or **buffoon** and, indeed, the bird's swaying, side-to-side motion in flight is one of the most striking sights in Africa. Bateleurs soar over immense distances in search of food. They scavenge more than most other eagles, often the first to arrive at a carcass, but they also hunt small mammals, birds and reptiles.

Arno van den Berg

Young lions often drink pressed closely together, bodies touching, for several practical and social reasons. This behaviour reflects both the inherent vulnerability of young lions and the strongly social nature of the species.

Pride sizes in the Kgalagadi typically vary, with average pride sizes around 11 individuals in the wider park. Specific sightings at Polentswa have reported groups of 5–10 lions, including lionesses, males and cubs.

In the Kgalagadi, bateleurs are sometimes seen lingering at waterholes during the heat of the day, **bathing** and then **spreading their wings wide** for anting and to sun themselves. Locally common in protected areas, they require vast territories and do not fare well elsewhere; thus, they are classified as **Regionally Endangered** in southern Africa.

The big trees around Polentswa waterhole also make perfect perches for **lanner falcons**, highly adaptable raptors that thrive in arid landscapes. They hunt both from perches and in flight. At almost every waterhole you can expect to see one – or a pair – perched in nearby trees, waiting to ambush drinking birds. Lanners sometimes hunt co-operatively, one bird flushing prey while the other strikes. Sandgrouse, doves and smaller seed-eaters are favourites, but they will also take mammals, reptiles, insects and even carrion. Lanners dive from high above at **speeds of up to 150 km/h**, striking their prey to the ground before feeding or carrying it off to a tree for safety.

As the morning progresses, **secretarybirds** may cautiously approach the waterhole to drink, a time when they are most vulnerable and must be certain all is safe. The same applies to the other great ground-dwelling bird, the kori bustard. Both species occasionally drink and, though mainly terrestrial, can take flight swiftly when disturbed.

Cape turtle doves congregate in large numbers at first light to drink. If a falcon suddenly stoops for the kill, the doves erupt in a flurry of wings, creating a blur of confusion that may save some from its talons. These doves feed mainly on seeds, particularly those of camelthorns. Their name derives from the sound of their call. In French they are known as **tourterelles**, from the Latin *turtur*, meaning both 'dove' and 'turtle'; hence the English term *turtle dove* and its echo in *sea turtle*.

Polentswa waterhole is also a favourite drinking spot for **mammalian predators** and, at times, there can be great excitement.

Danger looms at the waterhole as a lanner falcon strikes with breathtaking speed

The **lions** that frequent the Polentswa waterhole are known to be active and may be seen on the road itself or resting under small trees on the raised verges on either side. They often visit the unfenced Polentswa camping sites or cross the open floodplain. Their presence near this camp can lead to thrilling encounters but also requires awareness, as they are still wild and powerful animals.

A **leopard** is seen here regularly, and **black-backed jackals** patrol the area, hunting **sandgrouse**, **red-billed queleas** and **doves**. A nearby **hyena den** ensures frequent

Red-billed queleas gather in large flocks in nearby trees, chattering and jostling, before dropping down together to drink

Hennie Blignaut

Only a single claw is needed to secure the catch

early-morning visits from those restless scavengers.

Read the poignant story of the geologist Hans Schwabe, who perished here in search of riches. His grave, marked with a rough cross made of camelthorn wood, lies on the Botswana side of the riverbed, a lonely memorial to the Kalahari's unforgiving nature.

The road further north to the Lijersdraai picnic site can be extremely rough and corrugated. Take care, and close your windows when crossing the riverbed before you reach the picnic site as the fine, powdery dust seeps into everything.

Hidden predators such as black-backed jackals lie in wait, alert and patient, for birds to arrive at the water's edge for a drink

Hennie Blignaut

Polentswa

There is something haunting about the lonely beauty of Polentswa. The rust-red dunes, the whispering grass, the ghosts of windblown dust. It is a place where the present feels fragile and the past lingers near.

Here, under the vast blue dome of sky, you are reminded that life in the desert is both **tenacious and transient**. Lions still drink at the same waterholes where pioneers once stopped; bateleurs still soar over the same windswept plains that swallowed explorers like **Hans Schwabe**, whose simple camelthorn cross endures as a monument to human fragility.

In the Kalahari, **the dust never forgets**. It holds the footprints of those who came before, mingled with those of the wild creatures that still roam free.

The lone grave at Polentswa
Und meine Seele spannte
Weit ihre Flügel aus,
Flog durch die stillen Lande,
Als flöge sie nach Haus.
1906–1958
In Liebe, deine Familie

This haunting inscription marks a **lone grave** on the outskirts of the Polentswa plain, a silent monument to the **shattered dreams** of those who once sought riches in the windblown riverbeds of the Kalahari.

Hans Schwabe, a German geologist, passed through the Kalahari in **1958** en route to South West Africa (now Namibia). Convinced that **diamonds lay hidden in the Nossob River**, he ignored the warning of the park warden, **Joep le Riche**, who assured him there were none. Denied permission to prospect, Schwabe left Twee Rivieren as if bound for Mata-Mata, but instead turned north along the Nossob. He drove as far as **Kwang**, then continued on foot. On his windscreen he left a note:

"No water for car, no water for myself, no food, follow this road. Monday 8am"

The following day, **Botswana police** found his abandoned vehicle and alerted Twee Rivieren. A search party soon discovered the radiator still full of water, an ominous clue. They traced his **fading spoor northwards**, past signs of shallow prospecting pits, until vultures circling in the distance revealed the tragedy's end. His tracks had grown erratic; his body was found soon after, almost consumed by hyenas and vultures.

The rangers **buried him there**, near Polentswa, marking the grave with a **cross of camelthorn wood**, his **pick and tin canteen**, and a simple inscription.

Died 22 October 1958

Years later, his family placed the **bronze plaque** that bears the moving epitaph translated from Joseph von Eichendorff's verse:

"And my soul spread its wings wide, and flew through the silent land as though flying home."

Haunting beauty

★★★★

LIJERSDRAAI PICNIC SITE
24 km to Kannaguass

At **Lijersdraai**, the Nossob River makes a wide, sweeping bend. According to local lore, the loop resembles a **baby's nappy** (Afrikaans: *'luier'*) fastened with a pin, a whimsical name for this quiet stretch of riverbed. Whether true or not is hard to judge from the road, for the river's course is hidden by dunes and vegetation.

This is classic **leopard territory**, a recognised hotspot where sightings are regular though never guaranteed. The **leopard**, ultimate of cats, is stealthy, secretive, solitary and, to many, the most beautiful of all. Adaptable and arboreal, it moves with silent authority through the landscape. Daytime sightings are rare, but here, at Lijersdraai, a few individuals have grown accustomed enough to vehicles to be glimpsed even in daylight.

Leopards hunt mainly by sight, detecting prey at distances of up to **a kilometre**, and their **night vision is six times sharper than ours**. Their strength is extraordinary; they can drag prey **10 times their own weight** up into trees for safekeeping.

The picnic site is a welcome break for travellers driving north from Nossob. Even by Kgalagadi standards, it is a long, demanding journey, and many visitors turn back here to return to camp. For those continuing on to Grootkolk or Gharagab

Ground agama sunning on a termite mound

Wilderness Camps, Lijersdraai provides the perfect pause before tackling the final leg, a stretch that feels longer than it looks. Do not rush this last section; this is what you came for. Take time to absorb the solitude, the vastness and the profound stillness of the desert wilderness.

Unpack your picnic lunch and relax under the **shade of the camelthorns**. Look out over the plains and notice the clusters of termite mounds scattered across the landscape. After heavy summer rains, the shallow depression to the south of the picnic site often transforms into a temporary sheet of water, attracting wildlife and birds.

From here, **tracks** lead to a loop into the wooded dunes to the west. Both are scenic drives, but if pressed for time, it is usually best to continue northward. However, if you do venture out, keep your eyes open as visitors have occasionally reported sightings of **aardvark on overcast days**, as well as **honey badgers** and **hyenas**.

On these open plains, the silence is profound

Rudi Schulz

Territorial red hartebeest bull in prime condition

Spending time alone at Lijersdraai picnic site for the first time can be a deeply spiritual experience. The silence here is tangible ... almost haunting. You can feel the absence of people, the incredible solitude amplified by the wind sweeping across the open plains. It brings with it a humbling sense of smallness. A reminder of the insignificance of being. This is it: a true wilderness experience.

After good summer rains, the grassy plains from **Lijersdraai to Grootkolk** come alive with the persistent, rhythmic calls of **monotonous larks**. Males of most lark species proclaim their territories with long, fluting songs, delivered from a conspicuous perch or in a fluttering display flight. These seemingly endless songs echo across the landscape. The soundtrack of a green Kalahari. A long, quiet stretch of road follows before you reach **Kannaguass**.

Kannaguass

★★★★★

KANNAGUASS
8 km to Grootkolk turn-off

Scan the horizon for **raptors** such as lanner falcon, bateleur, black-chested snake eagle, tawny eagle, martial eagle and kestrel using the thermals that rise from the hot valley floor.

The name **Kannaguass** is said to mean *'camelthorn tree pothole'*. This marks the threshold to the **magical north** of the park – the realm of vast spaces, vivid colours and the so-called *'crowded desert'*, where life gathers around every drop of water. This waterhole is a hotspot for **jackal, brown hyena, lion, leopard, suricate (meerkat), bat-eared fox** and **bateleur**.

The **brown hyena** and **black-backed jackal,** frequently maligned, are in fact vital recyclers of life in the Kalahari. What lions abandon, they reclaim. What the heat would waste, they return to the earth. Every scrap of carrion, every fallen creature, is stripped clean by their patience and precision. They are the **final link in the desert's chain of renewal.**

The **black-backed jackal** is a regular visitor to Kannaguass. Despite its reputation as a scavenger, it is an adept hunter, capable of taking small mammals, birds and even young antelope. Jackals are usually seen in **pairs**, the bond between male and female lasting for life. Both parents raise the pups, usually assisted by older offspring from previous litters who stay on as **helpers**.

When several individuals meet at a waterhole, their social hierarchy becomes apparent. **Dominant** jackals raise their hackles and tails, asserting rank, while **submissive** ones flatten their ears and lower their bodies. Bickering is common but serious fights are rare. An injury could mean starvation in this harsh land.

Their behaviour mirrors that of domestic dogs, yet in the silence of the Kalahari their communication is far more subtle; a flick of the tail, a soft whine, a quiet deference as the higher-ranking animal steps forward to drink first.

The **brown hyena**, less often seen than its spotted cousin, is a remarkable and highly specialised scavenger. By day it lies in the **deep shade of a shepherd's tree**, resting in a shallow depression it scrapes into the sand. At dusk, it emerges, a shaggy silhouette moving ghost-like through the dunes. Its massive head and long mane give it an almost prehistoric look. Solitary by habit, it roams great distances under cover of darkness, following scent trails to carcasses, discarded kills or even ostrich eggs. Though powerful, it seldom hunts. Instead, it performs an essential ecological service cleaning the desert of decay, recycling nutrients into the soil.

The resident large clan of spotted hyenas that frequent the waterhole has a den on the plains (right side of the road travelling towards Grootkolk but not visible to the eye).

Kathy Kay

The lioness on heat initiates contact with the male by gently swatting or nuzzling him if he is inattentive. Low vocalisations and scent cues reinforce her receptivity.

Grootkolk

★★★★

GROOTKOLK
7.5 km to Geinab

To drive north of Grootkolk is to feel like an explorer in uncharted country. The track winds through **soft white sand**, bordered by magnificent **camelthorn trees**, and there is little traffic here … only silence, wildlife and endless horizons. This is one of the most rewarding stretches in the park for both **special sightings** and **photography**.

With the onset of summer rains **Abdim's storks** (*Ciconia abdimii*) migrate in their thousands from the **Sahel region** (Chad, Sudan, Ethiopia) to southern Africa, covering over **5000 km** in search of insects and locusts.

After good rains, the skies come alive with **Abdim's storks, white storks and steppe eagles**, non-breeding intra-African migrants that arrive in their hundreds to feast on the sudden abundance of insects. By day they feed in open veld or gather around waterholes; by night they roost together in the trees. When they move between feeding grounds, they wait for the air to warm, then spiral effortlessly upward on thermals, gliding great distances before descending over a new stretch of grassland.

Brown hyena

Hannes Lochner

Grootkolk waterhole

Anja Denker

The sandy road surface captures the **tracks of a multitude of living creatures**: the soft, padded, nail-less print of a lion; the twin row of tiny dots left by a giant millipede; the double line of small footprints with the occasional abdomen-thumping hollow between them, the trail of a tenebrionid beetle (*toktokkie*); the small triangular footprints of whistling rats with the faint drag mark of a short tail between them; the three-pointed tracks of hopping scaly-feathered finches; the cluster of padded footprints and fine lines drawn in the sand by the dragging quills of a porcupine; and the large front footprints with clear nail marks and the smaller, twisted hind prints, resembling a flower, left by the brown hyena. These are just some of the telltale signs of the road's recent travellers. Each track hints at the quiet abundance of life that passes unseen between dusk and dawn.

The Kalahari's sandy tracks are nature's open notebook. Learn to read them and you will never travel blind again: Each set of tracks tells who passed, when and even what mood they were in; cautious, curious or on the hunt.

Footprints in the dust

Hannes Lochner

A lion walks with a measured, deliberate gait, lifting each paw high and placing it down with silent precision, as if weighing every step before committing to it

★★★

GEINAB

11.2 km to Union's End picnic site

Take a quiet moment to scan the ground near the picnic site for the conical holes of ants and the larger, ragged openings of termite mounds. These clues tell stories of the nocturnal life that unfolds here long after visitors have left.

Geinab's waterhole has been restored and there is a large overflow a couple of metres away from the concrete waterhole. The area is incredibly active and teeming with life; huge herds of springbok, red hartebeest, wildebeest, prolific birdlife and the resident lion pride that moves between Grootkolk and Union's End is ever-present.

Geinab was once a functioning borehole, but has not been in use since 2017 after a cave-in. Despite the dry trough, the area remains lively. Herds of **springbok** and **gemsbok** visit regularly to take advantage of two natural **salt-lick sites**.

Across the road to the left lies an old **quarry**, its exposed **calcrete** forming a natural phosphate lick favoured by **red hartebeest**, **ostrich** and **gemsbok**. A little further north, to the right, another lick in **salty clay soil** attracts **springbok**, which gather daily to feed on the mineral-rich earth. This area is also superb for spotting **honey badgers** and may be seen digging for rodents or trotting briskly along the roadside, always purposeful, always fearless.

To travel north from Geinab is to enter the **final frontier of the Kgalagadi**, a realm of deep silence and immense space. The soft, pale sand road winds between scattered camelthorn trees, their shadows stretching long and thin across the white dunes. Few visitors venture this far – most turn back at Grootkolk – and those who continue often describe a powerful feeling of isolation and awe. The track feels untouched, ancient and timeless, as if you are tracing the very edge of the Earth.

Between Geinab and Union's End, the traveller may notice several **large mounds** scattered along the roadside. These are the work of **termites**, crucial engineers of the desert ecosystem. Their mounds aerate the soil and recycle nutrients, sustaining the sparse vegetation that, in turn, feeds insects, rodents and larger herbivores. At night, the area becomes alive with **aardvark**, their deep burrows and foraging pits evidence of nocturnal activity. If you are fortunate, you may even glimpse one; an unforgettable sight of this shy, ancient mammal, its pig-like snout probing the earth for termites and ants. Normally, aardvarks emerge to forage late at night and are rarely seen on daytime drives. Despite their pig-like snouts, they are unrelated to pigs. Using powerful forelegs tipped with spade-like claws, they dig the burrows in which they live and excavate nests of ants and termites, their primary food source. Aardvarks rely on an acute sense of smell and excellent hearing to locate their prey, while their large, movable ears detect even the faintest sounds of danger. They lick up termites with their long sticky tongue. Their eyesight, however, is poor. Count yourself extremely fortunate if you glimpse one during the day. Look around for the tell-tale signs of their presence: fresh spoor, torn-up ant nests or newly excavated termite mounds.

Geinab waterhole after the rains

Anja Denker

Daniel Wipf

The deep sandy road to Gharagab Wilderness Camp

Battle of Geinab (16 March 1908)

The **Nama uprising** in German South West Africa (Namibia) ended in March 1907. When one of its leaders, **Marengo**, was killed by the Cape Mounted Police after fleeing into the Cape Colony, only **Simon Koper** and his Fransman Nama clan continued the resistance, operating from deep within the Kalahari.

From his base near **Geinab**, Koper raided across the border into South West Africa, striking German patrols and retreating beyond reach. Determined to end this defiance, **Captain von Erckert**, commander of northern Namaqualand, based at Gochas on the Auob River, was ordered to drive Koper into British Bechuanaland. Realising horses could not cope with the desert, Von Erckert's troops used **camels** for mobility.

At the end of the rainy season, two detachments – **400 rifles on 700 camels**, supported by 160 auxiliaries – assembled at **Geinab or Grootkolk** and set off in pursuit of Koper's men. However, the Namas were forewarned. Simon Koper himself escaped, leaving his followers to prepare for battle.

Before dawn on **16 March 1908**, the Germans surrounded the rebel camp. A fierce two-hour firefight followed. **Captain von Erckert** was killed in the opening minutes, along with 14 of his men. By the end, **15 Germans and 59 Nama** lay dead, with **19 Germans wounded**. Lacking water, the survivors withdrew, unable to pursue Koper's men across the arid flats.

Local legend tells that the Germans dug in around waterholes, expecting Koper's band to surrender to thirst but Koper's fighters lived on **tsamma melons**, the desert's hidden water source. From the cover of **camelthorn trees**, his best marksmen fired down on the trenches at dawn, killing several Germans before their comrades tried to flee westward. Koper's mounted men intercepted them, stripped the survivors and sent them marching home, **only to be cut down one by one**.

The wind soon erased the tracks of battle, yet the memory of Geinab's stand endures ... a haunting echo of resistance in the vast silence of the Kalahari.

Who was Simon Koper?

Simon Koper (sometimes spelled *Cooper*) was one of the last leaders of the **Nama resistance** against German colonial rule in South West Africa during the early 1900s.

A cousin of the famous Nama leader **Hendrik Witbooi**, Koper led a band of **Fransman Namas** who refused to surrender after the main uprising collapsed in 1907. From his refuge deep in the **Kalahari Desert**, he waged a guerrilla campaign across the border, raiding outposts and disrupting German patrols along the **Nossob** and **Auob** river systems. Their intimate knowledge of the Kalahari's terrain and seasonal pans allowed them to outwit German forces for years.

After the **Battle of Geinab** in 1908, Koper retreated eastward into **Bechuanaland** (Botswana), where his trail fades into history.

Today, the desolate riverbeds between **Grootkolk**, **Geinab** and **Gochas** still bear silent witness to this forgotten frontier war where camels, rifles and melon-fed rebels clashed in the shimmering heat of the Kalahari.

Pause to read the **information boards** at the picnic site; they tell the story of this remote frontier. The faint **bleating of sheep** drifting across the border reminds you life here still balances between wildness and human endurance.

The **Union's End waterhole** is the last one on the tourist road and the northernmost in the South African section of the park. Beyond it lies the invisible boundary where three nations meet: **South Africa**, **Namibia** and **Botswana**, a remarkable geographical landmark known as **Union's End**. The Nossob fossil riverbed enters South Africa here from Namibia, its ancient channels twisting and fading into the desert sands. This is a place of silence, wind and the illusion of infinity; the kind of place that leaves you reflective, humbled and moved by the sheer scale of the Kalahari wilderness.

Although the **resident lion pride** of this area is seldom seen at the waterhole itself, their **tracks** are visible in the soft sand each morning, a reminder that this landscape belongs to them. They drink here mostly at night, their low roars carrying far across the open plains. Early risers may also encounter brown hyena or black-backed jackal, moving quietly in the dawn light.

During the heat of the day, the waterhole becomes alive with **bird activity**. This is one of the best sites in the far north to photograph small, brilliantly coloured species: **violet-eared waxbills**, **shaft-tailed whydahs**, **canaries**, **red-headed finches** and **scaly-feathered finches** all flock to the water, their vivid plumage a striking contrast to the ochre sands. Occasionally, a **lanner falcon** or **Gabar goshawk** swoops down in pursuit, sending the smaller birds scattering.

Near Union's End, the landscape flattens and opens dramatically. The riverbed here is wide and open, framed by low, undulating dunes along the edges. Here, among the bare gravel plains and sparse grasses, lives one of the most remarkable of the Kalahari's birds, the **double-banded courser**. Perfectly adapted to desert life, it needs no drinking water and can endure searing heat. It thrives in open, arid terrain where visibility is everything, avoiding areas that have recently received rain because vegetation growth would obscure its view of predators. Its **breeding behaviour** is extraordinary. The double-banded courser lays a **single egg** on bare ground, fully exposed to the blazing sun where surface temperatures can exceed **70 °C**. Both parents share incubation duties, alternating between shading the egg when the temperature rises too high and warming it when the air cools below 30 °C. This delicate balance – maintained hour after hour under extreme conditions – is one of nature's quiet marvels. Each parent takes a turn on duty in the blazing sun. One shades or incubates the egg, while the other cools off beneath the sparse shade of a nearby tree, losing excess heat before returning to relieve its partner after about an hour. The downy chick that eventually hatches is precocial, able to walk within hours, and perfectly camouflaged against the sand.

A pack of African wild dogs may occasionally visit the park, but are not resident

Heiko Denker

Bat-eared fox

Elsie Potgieter

The electrified fence marking the border between the park and Namibia prevents lions from crossing to prey on livestock on neighbouring farms. Yet, some creatures – monitor lizards, tortoises and even smaller mammals – can often be seen testing the fence, searching for a way through. Informative boards along the boundary recount the history of this remote frontier.

Reaching **Union's End picnic site** is more than just the end of a journey … it is a symbolic arrival at the top of South Africa, where three great deserts meet and where human presence fades into insignificance. Standing here, surrounded by silence, you can almost feel the pulse of the Kalahari; vast, ancient and eternal.

Reflection: Union's End – remote, silent, deeply evocative – a true wilderness frontier where three countries meet and time seems to stand still.

The egg on bare ground

Double-banded courser

The Auob River Road

The fossil riverbed of the Auob forms part of an ancient drainage system that once flowed southward. For many visitors, this stretch reveals the true magic of the Kgalagadi: a winding road that meanders across low dunes, skirting calcrete ridges and looping into the riverbed towards the eastern bank. Every waterhole offers excellent visibility and attracts a wide variety of game.

Mega-predators, such as the impressive **Kalahari black-maned lion**, are regularly seen, while at the other end of the scale, the tiny **bat-eared fox** makes frequent appearances. Most famously, this is one of the **best places on Earth to watch cheetah**, to follow their elegant hunting technique and, with luck, witness a kill. Researchers and photographers from across the world visit this area to study and record such remarkable events.

The **elusive leopard** is also encountered here. Keep an eye out in the early morning or late afternoon. Mainly nocturnal, leopards have been seen at the most unexpected times and places. The Auob riverbed is home to **African wild cats**, **caracal** and **honey badgers**, while smaller carnivores such as **suricates** and **slender mongooses** are common.

Blue wildebeest need to drink regularly and, during autumn, **gemsbok** move in from the surrounding dunes. **Red hartebeest** are less common than in the Nossob valley, while **eland** appear only occasionally. Surprisingly, **greater kudu** are sometimes seen near Urikaruus. **Springbok** are plentiful and move in several herds along the river valley in search of fodder and water.

Giraffes were reintroduced many years ago, initially habituated at Craig Lockhart before being released into the park. They have largely dispersed south along the riverbed where they find their preferred browse trees, though some were seen moving north in the Nossob valley in February 2017.

Birding along the Auob road is particularly good. Look out for kori bustard, black-chested snake eagle, bateleur, steppe buzzard (in summer), southern pale chanting goshawk, black-shouldered kite, pygmy falcon, spotted thick-knee, pearl-spotted owlet, crimson-breasted shrike, Marico flycatcher and swallow-tailed bee-eater, among many others.

Calcrete, also known as hardpan, is typical of the park's riverbed formations. It forms in calcareous soils through climatic fluctuations in arid regions; a process that began around three million years ago and continues today. As calcite dissolves in groundwater and re-precipitates during drying, it cements soil particles into an impermeable crust. Over time, this crust hardens into chalk-like rock, leaving the pale **calcrete ridges** that shape much of the Kalahari landscape.

Hannes Lochner

Even the king of the Kalahari cannot escape the smallest irritations

Klein Stofpan
Nossob 4x4 Ecotrail
Nossob
Chele
Rosyntjiebos
BITTERPAN CAMP
MATA-MATA REST CAMP
MATA-MATA GATE
Nu-Quap
KALAHARI TENTED CAMP
Sitsas
Strathmore
Moravet
Upper Dune Road
Eland
CRAIG LOCKHART CAMP
Craig Lockhart
Dalkeith
Vaalpan
14th borehole
Auob
13th borehole
Urikaruus
Kamqua
Kamqua Picnic Site
URIKARUUS CAMP
Rooibrak
Witgat
Montrose
!Xaus Road
Batulama
Gemsbokplein
Kij Gamies
Lower Dune Road
!XAUS LODGE
Auchterlonie Picnic Site
Auchterlonie
KIELIEKRANKIE CAMP
Kamfersboom
Auob Road
Munro
Leeudril 4x4 Trail
Houmoed
Leeudril
DAWID KRUIPER CAMP
(under construction)
Samevloeiing (Confl
TWEE RIVIEREN REST CAMP
TWEE RIVIEREN GATE
Tweerivieren
Two Rivers Ca
Controlled entry
No entry/exit
Entrance gate
Picnic site
Camp site
Camp site (A-frame)
Rest camp
Wilderness camp
Lodge
Borehole (sweet water)
Borehole (medium water)
Borehole (brackish water)
Pan
River
Main road
Main road (Five-star)
4x4 roads and trails
Direction
Distance

Male and female common ostrich cooling down

Confluence or Samevloeiing to Kamqua

★★★★

CONFLUENCE OR SAMEVLOEIING
18 km to Houmoed

Look for the pattern of long parallel dunes; dune crests and dune streets

The first stretch of the Auob Road runs across the dunes west of the riverbed, descending into the valley only near Houmoed waterhole. This drive reveals the true character of the Kalahari's red fossil dunes. When overgrazed, such dunes can become bare, but here they are patched with hardy vegetation, the living skin of the desert. Though not teeming with large game, the area is rich in smaller, fascinating components of the dune ecosystem.

These **fossil dunes** are ancient and static, shaped by fierce winds, thousands – even millions – of years ago. The sand settled into **long, parallel ridges**. See if you can trace their pattern. The **dune crests** here are low, with wide, shallow valleys or dune streets between them.

Vegetation is dominated by **three-thorn bushes** (*Rhigozum trichotomum*) and **dune grass**. These resilient shrubs, common throughout the park, are not particularly palatable but become vital during droughts. After the summer rains, their whitish, pink-tinged flowers appear almost overnight, soon followed by fresh leaves and seed pods that feed antelope such as springbok. By binding the sand, three-thorns help to stabilise the dunes against erosion. Their **stems typically divide in threes, ending in spine-like tips**; an adaptation to extreme aridity. In very dry periods, they shed their leaves and appear lifeless, only to revive with the next rain.

Two **lark species** are frequently seen here. The **fawn-coloured lark**, the most common in the dunes, forages on the ground and blends perfectly with its reddish-fawn surroundings, usually betraying itself when it sings or takes off in display flight. The **spike-heeled lark**, with its longer, curved bill, also occurs along this route.

Three-thorn bush in flower after rain

Game density in the dunes is naturally low because of the vast open spaces but predators and antelope often move through on their way to the riverbed to drink. Look out for **steenbok** and other small animals that rarely need to drink at all. Slowing down reveals the smaller wonders that are easily missed at speed.

Watch a while when you come across a **ground squirrel colony**. If they are active, their playful antics provide endless entertainment while others dig or dash between burrows. These engaging little rodents are among the park's most visible residents, both inside and outside the camps.

The ground agamas in the Kgalagadi (*Agama aculeata*) are especially known for their **adaptations, enabling survival in the arid desert environment** and their **distinctive social and territorial behaviours.** In early summer, after rain, **male ground agamas** become conspicuous with their vivid blue and orange heads. These are among the Kalahari's most characteristic reptiles. They climb onto low shrubs to bask or display, while females, less colourful but equally striking when gravid, dig deep burrows in the damp sand to lay their eggs. Once covered, she may linger nearby until the eggs are safely warmed by the sun. The **ground agama tolerates intense heat** but retreats to shade when temperatures rise above 38 °C.

Ground agamas are territorial. Dominant males fiercely defend their territory and have exclusive breeding rights with the females in their group. Fights between rival males can be aggressive, using powerful jaws and tail lashing.

Daniel Wipf

A sunning ground agama on a three-thorn bush

The gentle touch of a leopard mother

Daniel Wipf

★★★

HOUMOED
6 km to Monro

Notice how much narrower the Auob dry river valley is compared to the Nossob.

The road descends gently over the rounded western bank into the Auob riverbed. The name *Houmoed* is Afrikaans for 'be stout-hearted' or 'keep up your spirits' – a fitting name, as perseverance was required to drill this borehole. Sand repeatedly collapsed into it but in 1913, after much effort, sweet water was finally struck. The reward continues to this day. The water is sweet and the waterhole remains a magnet for wildlife, especially ground-dwelling birds.

The Auob riverbed is a known **hotspot for predators**. Scan both the far dunes and the one behind you as the open terrain makes it easy to spot approaching animals from a distance. Initially you may find the riverbed quiet, with just a lone **kori bustard** or **secretarybird** in the distance. There is usually some grass growth in the middle of the riverbed, where the water table lies close to the surface and fresh green shoots reveal the hidden flow of the subterranean river. These tender shoots attract many of the terrestrial predators that patrol the dry riverbeds.

The **kori bustard** is the **heaviest living animal capable of flight**, with males weighing up to 20 kg. Despite its ability to fly, it is primarily a **ground-dwelling bird** and usually takes flight only as a last resort, preferring to run from danger. Males engage in impressive and elaborate **mating displays** to attract females. This involves inflating their neck sacs, puffing up their feathers into a 'great white ball' appearance, holding their head backward with their bill open, and producing a deep, booming sound that can be heard over long distances.

The **kori bustard** is an opportunistic feeder; it takes insects, small reptiles and even fruit. Keep count of how many you see on your drives. It is always surprising how many appear once your eyes adjust to their stately, slow-moving shapes. There are well over 200 kori bustards in the park. Elsewhere within their range they are considered vulnerable, though not yet endangered. Their movements are closely linked to rainfall, following the shifting patterns of food and moisture across the Kalahari.

Keep your eyes open for **suricate** (or meerkat) **colonies** living in the sandy dunes of the western riverbank. Early morning is the best time to watch them. As the first rays of sunlight strike the sand, they emerge from their burrows to greet and groom one another, warming up before their day begins. It is a delight to watch their **tight-knit family behaviour**. Some stand upright on their hind legs, balancing on their tails and facing the sun, while others take up sentry duty. The **sentinels**, often perched on a shrub or mound, scan the landscape – and the sky – for predators. Once the colony has soaked up enough warmth, they disperse into the surrounding dunes to forage, their teamwork and constant communication a hallmark of life in the Kalahari.

Displaying kori bustard

A short track crosses the riverbed to a lookout point on the eastern bank, **marking the end of the Leeudril 4x4 trail**. From here, you gain an excellent sense of place and wide views over the dunes, ideal for spotting movement on the horizon.

The kori bustard applies a unique way of drinking while sitting on its haunches. Unlike most birds that scoop water with their bills, the kori bustard drinks water using a peculiar sucking motion.

Leopard cub observes how to hunt a suricate

Dominique de Beer

Houmoed

Eland herd

Hamman Prinsloo

Eland

Eland in the Kgalagadi are present but relatively uncommon at main waterholes like Houmoed. These large antelopes are nomadic, wary and relatively dispersed all over the park, often moving widely in search of forage rather than clustering at waterholes. In years when forage quality is poor, they may shift into new areas and even into dunes in search of browse and grass – a movement that is unpredictable and driven by food availability more than the presence of surface water. Eland can obtain considerable moisture from the vegetation they consume and can survive extended periods without drinking, making them less dependent on waterholes than other antelope. When they do drink, it is often at less-visited waterholes, or in low numbers that make sightings at popular waterholes uncommon. Eland may use waterholes, particularly in the cooler evenings after gates close, but these visits tend to be sporadic and not as predictable as those of gemsbok or springbok.

Bulls are much bigger than cows

Hamman Prinsloo

To come across a herd of eland at Houmoed is a special sighting

Hamman Prinsloo

★★★

MONRO
8 km to Kamfersboom

Watch for Brant's whistling rats in the dunes beside the road or in the sandy riverbed. Their presence is revealed by small mounds of disturbed sand.

Monro was named after a policeman who lost his life when raiders from German South West Africa (now Namibia) crossed into British Bechuanaland (now Botswana). It is one of several waterholes in the Auob valley with distinctly Scottish names: Monro, Auchterlonie, Dalkeith, Montrose and Craig Lockhart. Back in 1914, before the park was proclaimed, a Scotsman named Roger Jackson was tasked with surveying the area. Perhaps feeling 'a wee bit homesick', he named the boreholes after places from his homeland.

The Monro waterhole lies in an open area with no trees or shrubs obstructing the view. Though its **water is not as sweet** as that at Houmoed, it remains a vital source for wildlife, especially during the heat of summer. Most of the park's pumps now run on solar power as it is less obtrusive than the old windmills and far more efficient.

The camelthorns along the Auob riverbed are **hotspots for roosting owls**. Look out for the impressive **Verreaux's (giant) eagle-owl**. During the day, the nocturnal owls roost in large camelthorn trees. Scan the branches carefully; this powerful bird blends perfectly with the bark. The park's largest owl hunts springhares, korhaans, small carnivores and unsuspecting raptors at night. When resting, its grey plumage and drooping tufts make it almost invisible among the branches.

Brant's whistling rats (*Parotomys brantsii*) play a key ecological role primarily as a **major prey species** for various predators. These plump rodents sit at their burrow entrances and whistle sharply at any sign of danger before vanishing underground. Wait quietly; they will soon reappear, nose first and ears twitching, a charming sight and a reminder that even the smallest residents of the Kalahari have stories worth watching.

Brant's whistling rat pups have a unique suckling behaviour where they **cling firmly to their mother's nipples** and are physically dragged along by her whenever she moves outside the burrow during the first 12–14 days of life.

Brant's whistling rat with two pups attached to her nipples

A black-backed jackal is an opportunistic hunter

Rudi Schulz

The martial eagle's claws are massive, scimitar-curved weapons – designed not just to grip, but to kill

This magnificent martial eagle caught an African wild cat unawares

The dark rosettes on the leopard's pale coat provide perfect camouflage in the dappled shade beneath a camelthorn tree

Hamman Prinsloo

Hamman Prinsloo

Look for leopards on the calcrete ridges

★★★★

KAMFERSBOOM
5 km to Auchterlonie

Scan the shadow of all the camelthorns for predators resting in their shade.

This waterhole was named after its original borehole guard, Kamfer. Here the Auob riverbed broadens into a wide, sweeping valley, allowing clear views across the landscape, which is an excellent spot for lion and spotted hyena sightings. Hyenas often den on the ridge behind the waterhole and on the western dune side, while lions patrol the open valley below. The water is of moderate quality, but that does not deter the wildlife.

In the Kgalagadi, the **gemsbok** (*Oryx gazella*) is among the most formidable prey species lions face. Their long, straight horns can be lethal and many lions bear puncture scars as proof. **Lions** rely on patience and teamwork. They use dune shadows and low vegetation for cover, attacking at dawn or dusk when temperatures are cooler and visibility is low. When attacked, gemsbok – with their elegant but deadly horns – are formidable opponents. They defend themselves and their young by kicking powerfully and charging head-down with sharp horns. If a gemsbok shows signs of weakness or injury, lions will persistently stalk and challenge it for hours until exhaustion sets in and the kill becomes easier. **Hunts often fail** as the open terrain gives gemsbok an advantage in spotting danger early. Successful kills usually involve co-operative hunting by females.

Spotted hyenas, though not typical of arid regions, are adaptable and opportunistic. Mostly nocturnal, they thrive in the harsh Kalahari environment. During the hot summer months, they are often seen lying in the waterhole to cool down, with only their heads visible above the surface, an unforgettable sight in the shimmering heat.

Nearby dunes and ridges hold echoes of history. During the **First World War**, the South African Government **drilled a string of boreholes** along the Auob riverbed to supply troops defending the border with German South West Africa (now Namibia). Guards from nearby communities were hired to protect them and, with their families and livestock, settled near the wells. When the war ended, they remained, building small homes and kraals from local calcrete stone. **Ruins of these homesteads and livestock pens** can still be seen on the eastern bank and ridge.

The **caves on the calcrete ridges** along this stretch provide ideal den sites and if you are lucky enough to pass early in the morning, you might glimpse cubs waiting near the entrance for their mother's return. When a **leopard** takes possession of a cave or ridge, it dominates the area and other animals wisely keep their distance. Leopards are primarily nocturnal and lack any special physical adaptations for surviving the semi-desert. Instead, they **rely on behaviour**; hunting at night, seeking shade by day, and using their surroundings with remarkable intelligence. The **calcrete caves provide cool, safe refuges and excellent vantage points to watch the riverbed below**. Where caves are absent, leopards make use of rocky shelves, disused aardvark burrows or even long grass for cover. These cats are masters of concealment, often flattening themselves in the shade or disappearing entirely as vehicles pass by. Unlike many predators, leopards are largely **independent of standing water**, obtaining most of their moisture from prey. However, when water is available, they will drink regularly, which is a useful tip for those hoping to catch a rare daylight sighting at a waterhole.

Lion and gemsbok depend on each other: lions regulate herbivore numbers, while gemsbok sustain predators during dry seasons when smaller prey is scarce.

★★★★

AUCHTERLONIE

2 km to turn-off, short dune road

Auchterlonie and surrounds are a hotspot for predators, not only lion and cheetah, but also leopard. Be vigilant and expect any of these anytime and anywhere.

Auchterlonie is one of several boreholes named by Scotsman Roger Jackson, who surveyed farms in this region in the early 1900s. The view over the riverbed is wide and uncluttered, broken only by a single grey camelthorn beside the borehole and a derelict windmill in the distance. A borehole guard, J Human, once lived here. His house has since been rebuilt and restored as a small museum. The water quality is average but the location is excellent for both scenery and wildlife.

Scan the shade beneath the lone camelthorn with your binoculars as **cheetahs often rest there**. Like most predators, they spend much of their time lying low, conserving energy. When stretched out, their slender bodies blend perfectly with the sandy landscape, resembling a fallen branch or rock. Watch for subtle movements: the lift of a head, the flick of a tail, the twitch of an ear.

The cheetah is built for speed and precision

Daniel Wipf

The Auob riverbed is a hotspot for cheetah

Daniel Wipf

The open terrain of the Kgalagadi perfectly suits the cheetah's swift, daylight hunting style. The Auob riverbed, with its springbok herds, is one of the best places in Africa to observe these cats. Though **springbok are their preferred prey**, cheetahs also take smaller antelope, birds, hares and rodents. They rely on speed rather than stealth, seizing prey by the throat and suffocating it quickly.

Among predators, cheetahs sit at the bottom of the hierarchy. Their jaws are comparatively weak and they sometimes abandon kills when challenged by stronger rivals. **Hunting by day allows them to avoid nocturnal competitors**, but even then, scavengers like jackals linger nearby, waiting for an opportunity. **Competition limits their numbers**; even in this cheetah stronghold, sightings remain special.

Auchterlonie is also a **good place to see lions**. They regularly drink at the waterhole and rest in the deep shade beside the restored museum on the ridge, a perfect vantage point from which to survey the valley below. The Kgalagadi's lions are renowned for their imposing **black-maned males**, which share the landscape with tawny-maned individuals. The dark mane gives a majestic, almost regal appearance and may serve both as a signal to females and as protection in combat. The **tufted tail** conceals a **horny spur**.

Each lion has a unique pattern of black whisker spots on their muzzle. This arrangement allows researchers (and keen visitors) to identify individuals. If you visit often, it is worth keeping a record ... you might just recognise a familiar face on your next trip.

Cheetah – Master of the semi-desert

The Kgalagadi offers excellent set-up for cheetahs: sparse vegetation, low large-predator densities compared to some savannas, and abundant medium-sized prey like springbok. Huge ranges and reliability on open terrain give them an edge. Yet they face major constraints: competition with lions, predation by hyenas, low prey density compared to richer ecosystems, and the ever-present need to avoid human conflict at the margins.

Where to look and what to watch

Head for open riverbed roads early morning. The Auob in particular is ideal: wide valleys, good visibility and frequent springbok herds, the cheetah's preferred hunt terrain.

Scan the shade of camelthorn or grey shepherd's trees near waterholes. Cheetahs lie low until prey moves into view. Spotting them before the sprint really comes down to noticing a subtle head shape or flick of a tail.

Watch for their hunting rhythm: a slow stalk, the flash of speed (often up to 90–100 km/h), the hooking of the fore-paws, then jaw to throat. But remember, a kill is only half the story. Regaining it from scavengers is a major struggle.

When a female has cubs, she may hunt less and pick more accessible prey. Look for her near reliable waterholes and browse lines.

A cheetah relies on speed, timing and precision to catch a blue wildebeest calf

Hamman Prinsloo

The southern white-faced owl nests in natural tree hollows, and its young become independent after about 47 days

Elsie Potgieter

When asleep, the white-faced owl has a cryptic stance, making it difficult to detect

Elsie Potgieter

AUCHTERLONIE PICNIC SITE
2 km from turn-off, short dune road

Look for scaly-feathered finches around the parking area. These remarkable desert-adapted bird species live in flocks of about 20 individuals. This finch is the only seed-eater able to survive for at least 62 days without drinking.

Just beyond the Auchterlonie waterhole, a short road crosses the Auob riverbed and climbs the hill on the eastern bank. Here you will find the restored dwelling that now serves as the **Auchterlonie Museum**, with an open picnic site offering a welcome break and a magnificent view over the dunes and riverbed below. It is easy to see why cheetahs and lions use these ridges as regular vantage points to watch for prey.

You are **allowed to leave your vehicle here** but always check carefully for predators resting in the shade near the buildings before you step out. There are toilets, shaded picnic tables and the small museum, which provides an evocative glimpse into the hard lives of the area's early settlers. A **well** nearby attracts bees during the hot, dry season but they disperse quickly once the rains come.

Auchterlonie was **restored in 2004** through the **Poverty Relief Project**, a collaboration between the local community, the Department of Environmental Affairs and Tourism, and the Tshwane University of Technology. Only ruins remained of the original dwelling, but together they reconstructed it using traditional materials and techniques.

Originally, borehole guards built simple **wattle-and-daub** houses, while the farmers who followed after the First World War used **calcrete stone**. Roof rafters were made from **camelthorn poles**, and **dune reeds** were bound with gemsbok or wildebeest hide for thatching. The earthen floors were finished with a **paste of fresh cow dung**, which dried into a hard, antibacterial surface. Recent studies have shown cow dung contains *Mycobacterium vaccae*, **a bacterium that boosts serotonin production**, literally helping to lift one's mood!

Scaly-feathered finches

Livestock provided milk but required fodder, water and protection. Farmers built **kraals** (enclosures) with sloping floors for drainage. The dried dung was sometimes cut into blocks and used as fuel. A short footpath leads to the restored kraal, which is worth exploring to better imagine daily farm life here.

Leather was essential for saddles, bridles and clothing. **Hides were tanned** in pits dug into the ground, soaked in lime to loosen the hair, then treated with salt and bark to soften and colour them.

Obtaining water was the hardest task of all. Wells were dug entirely by hand, often with the help of dynamite. Former sheep herder **Karel Raats** described how workers used long fuses and pulley systems to haul out loosened stones and sand, a risky, exhausting process. The well next to the toilet block shows the great depth they had to reach before striking water.

The restored dwelling and its surrounding features offer a poignant **window into a bygone life**, one of endurance, isolation and resilience. It is hard to imagine raising children in this stark, unforgiving landscape, where even a single cup of mealie meal would have been precious.

Christoffel le Riche was one of the earliest traders and pioneers of the area. His son, Johannes, was to play an important role in the establishment of the Kalahari Gemsbok National Park.

Malcolm Hoal

Auchterlonie museum and picnic site

The distinctive black 'tear marks' running from the inner corners of the eyes to the mouth help cheetahs reduce glare and sharpen focus during high-speed hunting

★★★★

TURN-OFF, SHORT DUNE ROAD
2 km to Gemsbokplein

The road continues to follow the calcrete ridge on the western side, which forms an excellent vantage point for cheetahs scanning the riverbed below for prey. Look closely into crevices and shaded nooks along the ridge. They often conceal nesting eagle-owls, resting porcupines or families of rock hyrax.

A **memorial plaque** near **Gemsbokplein** marks the site where the park's first warden, **Johannes le Riche**, and his wife **Bettie** built their modest wattle-and-daub home, raising nine children in complete isolation. Their sole neighbour was a constable ranger and his family, who assisted Johannes in his duties. Water was always scarce. After years of drought, the pans had dried up, and when the borehole guards left following the park's proclamation in 1931, they dismantled their windmills and took them away. The newly formed Parks Board could afford to maintain only two boreholes and two wells in the entire park; one of them here at Gemsbokplein, where the water was mercifully sweet and drinkable.

Poaching was rife, and Johannes had to patrol vast areas on horseback, covering nearly **650 km** from Gemsbokplein to Samevloeiing (Confluence), north along the Nossob to Union's End, across to Mata-Mata, and back down the Auob. It took more than two weeks, and for over **250 km** of that route, there was no water for man or beast.

Life was relentless: heat, hunger, drought and the constant struggle to survive. When the rains came, the land briefly turned green again, but malaria ultimately claimed Johannes's life in 1934. His perseverance, however, laid the foundation for the park we know today.

Try to imagine life here in those early days: no telephone, no radio, no vehicles, just horses and a donkey cart.

Notice the rounded mounds of **candle thorn bushes** (*Vachellia hebeclada*) in the Auob riverbed. In Afrikaans it is known as *trassiebos*, meaning 'neither tree nor shrub', since it grows low and dense, branching near the ground. What appears to be a cluster of plants is in fact a single individual. This hardy species, unique to the Kalahari, forms rounded mounds up to 20 m wide and rarely more than 2 m high. Its sprawling, multi-stemmed growth stabilises loose sand and provides vital shelter for small creatures. The name candle thorn comes from its stiff, upright seed pods, which resemble candles on a candelabrum. The leaves and white, bulb-shaped flower heads are relished by browsers, though its vicious 20 mm paired thorns guard the heart of the plant. Watch carefully; an **African wild cat** is often seen vanishing into its protective tangle.

Roots of the candle thorn may reach 30 m deep to tap the underground water table, a true survivor of the desert.

Villiers Steyn

The gemsbok's most striking head feature is its long, straight, spear-like horns, which are present in both males and females and used for defence against predators

Leopards are beautiful and fascinating – a rare blend of power, grace, and mystery

Elmar Venter

Leopard research in the Kgalagadi

Uncovering the secret lives of the desert's stealthiest hunter

In the arid heart of Kgalagadi Transfrontier Park (KTP), the elusive leopard (*Panthera pardus*) inhabits one of the world's most extreme environments for big cats. Yet this solitary felid has adapted remarkably and researchers have begun to decode its behaviour, space use and conservation needs in the dunes and dry riverbeds of this semi-desert.

What the research shows

- A key study in the southwestern part of KTP found adult male leopards have mean home ranges of approximately 2 104 km^2, and adult females about 1 259 km^2 – among the largest home ranges ever recorded for the species.
- Overlap between same-sex individuals (e.g. males with other males) and between opposite sexes was considerable. This behavioural flexibility helps leopards survive in prey-scarce, large-territory landscapes.
- A visitor-driven ID-catalogue initiative continues to build photographic records of individual leopards in KTP: visitors submit flank shots to help track movement, age and survival across years.
- The 2024 park management plan for KTP highlights leopards as a priority species for monitoring, given their large ranges, low densities and dependence on wide undisturbed habitat.

Why it matters

Because their territories are so vast and prey is sparsely distributed, every leopard sighting in the Kgalagadi is significant. It is not only a moment of wonder, but also a data point in a larger ecological story of survival, adaptation and conservation. Observing leopards in KTP means witnessing a species shaped by scarcity, stamina and stealth.

Visitor contribution

You can become part of the research story. If you photograph a leopard, try to get a clear flank shot (showing rosette pattern and whisker spots); note the date, time and location (GPS if possible) and send it to the KTP leopard ID project. Every image helps build knowledge of lifespan, reproduction and change in one of the continent's least-studied leopard populations.

ktp.leopards@gmail.com

★★★★

GEMSBOKPLEIN
7 km to Batulama

Scan the shade of camelthorns carefully for resting predators; also the distant dune ridges and to the left.

At **Gemsbokplein**, the water is sweet and reliable, drawing a variety of animals throughout the year. Blue wildebeest, ostriches and springbok visit regularly, while predators such as lion, leopard and cheetah are frequently seen nearby. The waterhole lies about 50–60 m from the road, with generally good visibility; although in the rainy season, taller grass can obscure the view. A small reservoir shaded by camelthorns stands behind the waterhole.

This area is a **favourite breeding ground for lions**. The caves and ridges provide safe dens for mothers with cubs. A lioness will leave her pride to give birth, returning when her cubs are four to eight weeks old and only if there are no older cubs already present. In Kalahari conditions, raising cubs alone is difficult: food is scarce, and prey is often too large for one lioness to manage. **Many cubs do not survive** and when new males take over a pride, they kill all existing cubs to bring females back into breeding condition (infanticide) … a harsh but natural cycle of survival.

Lion cub mortality rates are high, with only about one in two surviving to adulthood. Major threats include infanticide, illness, starvation and predation. Lionesses frequently have to move their cubs and they may travel long distances to ensure their survival.

Springbok are commonly seen near this waterhole, moving in nomadic herds along the riverbed. Safety lies in numbers. The more eyes and ears, the quicker they can spot danger. Springbok graze on the short, tender shoots that appear after even the lightest rainfall and browse on the flowers of three-thorn bushes after summer showers. During droughts, they switch to high-quality browse to survive. Despite the arid conditions, Kgalagadi springbok are impressively robust: males can weigh up to **45 kg** and females up to **38 kg**, larger than most of their kind elsewhere.

Look for **owls** roosting on camelthorn branches or in the shade below. Two species are regularly seen: the large **Verreaux's eagle-owl**, and the smaller yet equally striking **spotted eagle-owl**. Both are dominant nocturnal hunters, as regal and commanding as the eagles themselves.

Southern yellow-billed hornbills prefer woody areas along riverbeds.

Secretarybirds are renowned snake hunters, using swift, downward kicks to kill venomous prey safely

Nadine Mather

Villiers Steyn

Yellow-billed hornbills are omnivorous, feeding on rodents, small vertebrates, insects, fruit and seeds

★★★★

BATULAMA
6 km to Montrose

Batulama

Keep using your binoculars to scan the calcrete ridges, caves and towering camelthorn trees for owls, leopards or porcupines.

The **Batulama** waterhole provides good-quality water and was well used by early settlers before the park was proclaimed. The drinking place is ringed by large camelthorn trees, yet remains fairly open, offering good visibility. Lions are often seen resting in the shade of the distant trees, while the resident leopard occasionally reveals itself along the edges of the riverbed.

The way animals use **camouflage for protection** is truly remarkable. Their colours and shapes blend seamlessly into the surroundings, and it is only the faint twitch of an ear or the flick of a tail that gives them away. Patience is rewarded here; pause for a while, let your eyes adjust, and what first appears lifeless may suddenly reveal a hidden shape, a movement or a pair of watchful eyes.

Keep an eye on the sandy road verges for the charming **Cape fox**, one of the Kalahari's most endearing small predators. This is the only true fox in southern Africa, a petite animal with a long, bushy tail, slender legs and oversized ears that help it radiate heat. Weighing barely 2–3 kg and standing just 30 cm high, it feeds mostly on mice and insects, foraging at dawn and dusk. By day, it shelters in burrows, caves or thickets of candle thorn and is rarely seen. The best time to spot them is during the breeding season in **early summer (October–November)**, when pairs or family groups emerge from their dens to play. Watch for pups tumbling about in the soft light of morning or late afternoon.

A short loop in the road passes a weathered tree trunk that once supported a massive **sociable weaver nest**, now **collapsed into a heap of grass and twigs**. Pause here as the site usually teems with life. **Ground squirrels** and **striped mice** forage busily, while small predators such as **mongooses, meerkats** and **foxes** patrol for prey. Watch how the ground squirrels use their tails as **parasols** against the sun or as makeshift shields when threatened. This is also an ideal hunting ground for snakes, such as the **Cape cobra**.

The colouration of **Cape cobra** individuals varies from a deep yellow to a dark brown. Although the cobra is relatively docile, it is extremely venomous. It produces neurotoxic venom that attacks the nervous system. The result is paralysis and death. The cobra displays its characteristic hood when threatened.

Cape cobras are known predators of ground squirrels, and if the snake is successful, it will eat the squirrel. Cobra even feed on other snakes, such as puff adders.

There are numerous suricate dens along the Auob. Be vigilant and watch for the **tell-tale sentry** standing guard.

Daniel Wipf

Suricates (meerkats) live in co-operative family groups, and the entire group helps raise the young

Barry Hugo

Ground squirrel and suricate

Barry Hugo

Suricate siblings

Keen eyes

Meerkats

Species that must forage by day – such as **meerkats**, **ground squirrels** and **mongooses** – have evolved strategies to cope in the desert. They keep close to burrow systems for safety and escape the worst of the heat by standing upright to scan from shaded vantage points or by digging cool hollows in the sand. The pale colour of their coats reflects sunlight, while their communal living provides additional protection against predators and the extremes of temperature.

Important predator

Grahame Murray

★★★

MONTROSE
5 km to Rooibrak

Across the road, a **calcrete ridge** rises from the western bank. Scan it carefully with binoculars for any sign of life. Look for suricates, mongooses and ground squirrels.

Montrose is another of the Scottish names given by surveyor Roger Jackson. Look out here for **African wild cat**, **slender mongoose** and **Gabar goshawk**. Next to the waterhole signpost stands a fine **grey camelthorn**. Note its silvery leaves, pods (if present) and rounded growth form; then see how many others you can spot along the way to the next waterhole.

Owls rely heavily on their cryptic plumage for concealment, closing their bright yellow eyes to narrow slits and raising their ear tufts to enhance camouflage. The fringed feathers of their wings make flight completely silent, allowing them to swoop unseen and unheard on rodents and shrews that thrive among the fallen branches and thick camelthorn shade.

Among smaller residents, look for the **striped mouse**, the Kalahari's only truly diurnal rodent, abundant after summer rains. One of its main predators is the **Cape cobra**, often yellow in colour and occasionally active by day. Despite the danger, **ground squirrels** show remarkable boldness when encountering snakes. They confront them head-on, tails flicking in rapid warning, signalling both awareness and readiness to defend themselves. This bluff usually deters the snake or alerts others to danger. If threatened, the cobra raises its head, spreads its hood and strikes with lightning speed – up to **4.5 m per second** – fast enough to reach nearby prey in less than a tenth of a second. Yet the squirrels' lightning reflexes and agile leaps, sometimes flipping mid-air, usually save them. Other small mammals, such as **mongooses**, use similar tactics and even possess **natural resistance to snake venom**, a remarkable adaptation for survival in this harsh but vibrant desert world.

Verreaux's eagle-owl with prey

Dominique de Beer

Christiaan Ehlers

A cheetah mother gradually introduces her cubs to feed on meat

Barry Hugo

Springbok usually give birth at the end of the rainy season, when grazing is best and food is abundant

★★★★

ROOIBRAK
To Kamqua

Scan the area for black-backed jackal and Cape foxes. Look for the beautiful crimson-breasted shrike foraging on the ground under one of the camelthorns.

The red sandstone cliffs at **Rooibrak** are rich in minerals and game often gathers here to lick the salts that replenish their bodies. Apart from the occasional giraffe or circling eagle, it is usually a peaceful waterhole. This is also where the track from **!Xaus Lodge** joins the **Auob riverbed road**.

Gemsbok are frequently seen here, their striking horns and bold facial markings unmistakable against the red dunes. Perfectly adapted to arid conditions, they absorb moisture from food and can survive without drinking. They dig for succulent roots, rhizomes and bulbs, and feed on the **tsamma melon** and **gemsbok cucumber**. After the rains, they graze on mature riverbed grasses but as the land dries, they move into the dunes to feed on short annual grasses.

Giraffes are regular visitors. Absent from the park for many years, they were reintroduced in 1990 when eight individuals from **Etosha National Park** were habituated behind the dunes at **Craig Lockhart**. Today, they thrive in the riverbeds and surrounding dune fields; a remarkable success story of adaptation to a harsh, waterless environment.

Listen for the ringing whistles and grating calls of the **crimson-breasted shrike**, often seen darting through the lower branches of camelthorn trees. Brilliant in colour but restless and elusive, these birds mate for life and defend their territories fiercely. Once you spot a pair, you will likely find them in the same spot again.

Even large herbivores such as **gemsbok** and **springbok** alter their routines according to the weather. They feed in the cool of dawn and late afternoon, spending the hottest hours motionless in the shade, minimising movement and conserving precious body water.

Cape fox pups

Hamman Prinsloo

Hamman Prinsloo

A mother Cape fox responds to the calls of her pups, and engages in gentle play and mock-chasing, which helps the cubs associate her presence with safety, nourishment, and learning

KAMQUA PICNIC SITE

Look out for predators before you alight from your vehicle. People have been surprised before by predators resting in the shade of the ablution blocks.

The **Kamqua picnic site** offers a welcome break from long hours in the vehicle. If you are the first to arrive, take care and look around before getting out as **lion and leopard** have occasionally sought shade near the toilets, surprising unwary visitors.

There are **braai fireplaces**, picnic tables and benches where you can unpack breakfast or enjoy a cup of coffee. While stretching your legs, take a slow walk along the perimeter of the unfenced area and look for **lizards** and **ground agamas** basking on the sand. Several large **camelthorn trees** once offered deep shade here, but most are now standing dead … a stark reminder of the damage caused by careless **weedkiller use**.

Cape crows are regular visitors, their harsh caws followed by bubbling, gargling calls echoing across the stillness. Though not everyone's favourite bird, they deserve admiration for their resilience and adaptability. Usually seen in pairs or small groups, they **mate for life** and are strongly **territorial**, nesting high in camelthorn trees. After bathing at the nearby **Kamqua waterhole**, they can often be seen **preening** in the open, glossy feathers gleaming in the desert light.

The first part of the Auob road ends at the turn-off where the long dune road splits from it. The next part of the Auob road from Mata-Mata to Kamqua will be discussed in the following section.

Cape cobra

Elsie Potgieter

Boshoff Steenekamp

Swallow-tailed bee-eaters

Cape crows are all over the park and often visit picnic sites for scraps of food dropped by visitors

Mata-Mata to Kamqua

★★★

MATA-MATA CAMP
8 km to Sitsas

Once you are on the road, surprises await; perhaps a **magnificent sunrise** or the first **springbok** and **blue wildebeest** herds moving through the **Auob riverbed** before the turn-off to **Kalahari Tented Camp**. Sunrise here is pure magic. A fiery sky merging with the first dunes. Drive slowly; it is easy to miss great photo opportunities, especially when an animal pauses on a dune crest against that radiant light.

When the camp gate opens, everyone is eager to be first out, but patience often rewards the wise. There is only one route into the game-viewing area and, in the dry season, the first few vehicles raise dust clouds that can linger for kilometres. Many visitors **prefer waiting** a little while, letting the dust settle as the desert awakens.

While waiting, take time to watch the morning rituals of the **suricates (meerkats)** within the camp. These lively creatures live in **tight-knit, co-operative groups** and follow a fascinating daily rhythm. Just after sunrise, they emerge sleepily from their burrows and bask in the first warmth of the sun, using their sparsely haired, dark-skinned bellies to **absorb heat** quickly after the cold night. Later in the day, they may lie on cool rocks to shed excess heat. Notice the **dark patches around their eyes**. These are natural 'sunglasses' that reduce glare and enhance their long-distance vision. Their front feet bear long, curved claws, perfectly adapted for digging extensive burrow systems and unearthing prey beneath the sand.

Once warmed, the group **disperses to forage**. While most search for food, one or more **stand guard on a high perch** – a termite mound or rock – scanning for danger. These sentries communicate using a remarkable range of calls, each signalling a different kind of threat, from eagles above to jackals on the ground. At the alarm, the group instantly responds: freezing, flattening or dashing for the nearest burrow.

The entire clan helps **raise the young**, not just the dominant breeding pair. Subordinate members act as babysitters, guard the pups from predators (including rival meerkats), and even teach them how to handle dangerous prey such as scorpions. When faced with a snake or other ground predator, the mob unites, arching their backs, raising their fur and hissing in chorus until they resemble one large, bristling creature.

Look for **large camelthorn trees** adorned with **sociable weaver nests**, a signature sight of the Kalahari. These industrious birds usually select the healthiest trees and continually expand their 'apartment blocks'. Being **seed-eaters**, they rely on nearby grasses and plants, making their nest sites good indicators of local productivity. If you visit in the **wet season**, you will notice the **kidney-shaped pods** on camelthorn trees, rich in protein and a vital dry-season food source for many animals. The seeds, encased in a tough shell, can germinate only after passing through an antelope's digestive system, nature's clever way of ensuring both **fertilisation and dispersal**. Many seedlings germinate in the shade of adult trees, though just a few will survive the Kalahari's harsh conditions.

Blue wildebeest herd on their way to water. They need to drink every day.

Michael Ochse

Giraffe are regularly seen from the Auob Road

As you near **Sitsas**, the road runs close to the riverbed, offering excellent visibility. Watch for **ostriches**, **gemsbok**, **blue wildebeest** and the occasional **black-backed jackal** moving across the open plain. Always scan the dunes on both sides – the next special sighting might just be watching you first.

Blue wildebeest, the most water-dependent of all Kalahari mammals, are regularly seen making their way to water. They drink at almost any hour of the day except the last before sunset. During droughts, their reliance on water confines them to the fossil riverbeds and pans rather than the better-grazed dunes. They prefer sweet, clear water and this spot is one of their strongholds.

Since wildebeest are obligate drinkers and prefer short grass, their movements and herd sizes are largely dictated by sparse and patchy forage availability and water sources.

Greater kudu are a special sighting in the Kgalagadi

★★★★★

SITSAS
8 km to Craig Lockhart

In the **Khoekhoen language**, *Sitsas* means 'water with a bad taste', but judging by the steady stream of animals visiting throughout the day, it does not appear to bother them. This is one of the few waterholes shaded by a **large camelthorn tree**, close to the road; perfect if you enjoy **quiet game watching from your vehicle**. Expect regular visits from **predators**, **antelope**, **ostrich** and **black-backed jackals**. Antelope usually drink in the late morning.

Scan the calcrete ridge for movement. You never know what might be watching you from the rocks.

Gemsbok are frequent visitors, though not always for water. They come seeking **mineral salts**, since the grasses on the dunes behind the waterhole are poor in nutrients. By licking mineral-rich soil or drinking saline water, they replenish what is missing in their diet. The **clay-rich riverbed grasses** here are more nutritious than those in the dunes, but once the dry season sets in and these plants wilt, the gemsbok move back into the dunes.

The open area around the waterhole provides ideal habitat for **crowned lapwings**, which prefer bare ground and short grass. They nest in shallow scrapes lined with grass and pebbles, and their lively calls and quick movements make them entertaining to watch.

As you descend the hill, watch for **swallow-tailed bee-eaters** perched on dead branches of camelthorn trees. These agile hunters flash bright green and blue as they chase insects in flight, often landing to beat their prey against a perch. In summer, they move in pairs; in winter, they gather in flocks of 10 or more. On cold mornings, you may see several lined up together, **sunning themselves** before the day's hunt.

Check all the camelthorns next to the riverbed for **African wild cats and their kittens**. They are **highly adaptable predators** that can thrive in the desert environment by hunting a variety of small prey. Their ability to survive on a flexible diet – which includes rodents, birds, reptiles and even larger prey like antelope fawns when available – makes them a **key species in the ecosystem**. By keeping populations of rodents and other small animals in check, African wild cats are a crucial part of their ecosystem. Compared to domestic cats, they are slightly taller with longer legs, have a more upright posture when sitting, and a walking gait like a serval. Their fur colour is typically sandy, grey or brown, with faint stripes, and they have a black tip on their tail and russet-coloured backs of their ears.

A black-maned lion stops the traffic

Nick Pawley

Since wild cats are strictly nocturnal, the chance of spotting one during the day is slim but, when they have kittens, these are regularly seen in the early morning, playing before their bedtime. They breed at any time of the year but mostly in the hot, wet summer months.

Springbok herds are common along this stretch, moving up and down the riverbed in search of food and water. Pause to watch them; **cheetahs**, their primary predators, are often not far behind. Perfectly camouflaged, a cheetah may lie flat in the grass, only the shape of its head betraying its presence. The **wide Auob riverbed** offers ideal conditions for cheetah hunts: open terrain, good visibility and room to reach full speed. They usually prey on **adult springbok** but during **lambing season**, many young fall victim. Research shows **rams are nearly twice as likely** to be caught as ewes, perhaps as a result of their tendency to stray further from the herd.

Showers and storms are typical in the Kgalagadi, but they are irregular, highly localised and strongly seasonal

In coalition males, scent marking is done frequently and cooperatively, strengthening their territorial claim

Stephan Swanepoel

Craig Lockhart

★★★

CRAIG LOCKHART
7 km to Dalkeith

This waterhole is always rewarding for birdwatchers. A giant camelthorn tree near the drinking place serves as a safe perch for visiting flocks, while the thick candlewood stand beside the reservoir and solar panels attracts smaller species and shelters a variety of small mammals.

Look for **Cape glossy starling, red-billed queleas, masked weavers, Cape turtle doves, shaft-tailed whydahs** and **yellow canaries**. Even raptors, such as **Gabar goshawk** come down to drink at Craig Lockhart.

Giraffes were reintroduced to the Kgalagadi from Etosha in 1990 and there were just eight individuals to begin with. Since their release from the holding area over the dunes, they have settled mainly in the **Auob River valley**, where the tall **camelthorns** and **grey camelthorns** provide their preferred browse. They tend to remain close to the riverbed, drifting between **browse-rich waterholes** such as Craig Lockhart, Dalkeith and Veertiende Boorgat. Sightings are often of small family groups feeding quietly along the tree line or silhouetted on the dunes at dusk. Recent studies show giraffes are **reshaping the vegetation**, reducing the canopy size and flowering of key camelthorn trees, especially at browsing height. Despite the harshness of the desert, they appear well adapted, drawing much of their moisture from leaves and pods rather than from surface water.

Both the **ostrich** – Africa's largest bird – and the **kori bustard**, its heaviest flying counterpart, are regularly seen nearby. Though the kori can fly, it **prefers to stride** across the ground like its giant neighbour. Both species are polygamous and forage in open areas, pecking for seeds, insects or fruit. Because neither has a hind toe, they cannot perch in trees … true creatures of the earth.

Gemsbok also frequent this waterhole, lingering to lick the rocks for mineral salts. In the Auob, they usually appear in small family or nursery herds, or as solitary males. Within a herd, dominance is clear: adult bulls outrank females, though a senior cow leads the group while the territorial male brings up the rear. The sexes look similar but males are heavier and carry thicker horns. Lone bulls are likely defending territory. See if you can identify the dominant male when watching a herd. His confident stance and alert behaviour will give him away.

Driving along, the road is lined with stately camelthorns that hum with life. **Rats** and **mice** dart across the sand, while **ant-eating chats** and **scaly-feathered finches** probe the ant heaps for seeds and insects. The restless **chestnut-vented tit-babbler** – with its sharp *cherrik-tiktik* call – flits low between bushes, often heard before seen.

The reintroduction of giraffe to a landscape it historically occupied was highly successful

Daniel Wipf

A dense **candlewood thicket** in the riverbed frequently shelters **black-backed jackals**. They are most active at dawn and dusk and mate for life, sharing duties of guarding, feeding and raising their pups in abandoned aardvark burrows. Pups are born between July and October, and the sight of them tumbling and playing near the den in early morning light is a delight. Young from previous litters may stay to help rear the new brood. A close-knit family in one of the harshest yet most nurturing landscapes on Earth.

The tallest and the fastest mammals roam the Kgalagadi dunes and riverbeds

Peter Morton

Craig Lockhart

Cheetah research

The Kgalagadi cheetah is a specialist of wide open sands and fossil riverbeds. With few places that better suit their style of hunting, this park remains one of the best spots on the continent to observe and study them in action.

- Past spoor-survey findings suggest that density is roughly **one individual per 100 km²** in dune-savanna habitat.
- Reproductive success is higher here than in some other areas: about **1.5 offspring per litter** survive to independence (~45 percent of an average litter) in the Auob/Nossob system.
- Their survival depends on daylight hunting and open terrain: cheetahs rely on speed, select prey like springbok and young antelope, and must avoid losing kills to lions or hyenas.
- Their range overlaps Namibia–Botswana–South Africa corridors; in the park, they act as part of a wider, transboundary population with movement across the Auob and Nossob valleys.
- Although cheetahs are still found here regularly, no recent definitive census (with full confidence intervals) has been published since the major studies. So, while sighting rates remain good, exact numbers remain uncertain.

Zack Rheeder

The cheetah is a sleek, long-legged predator built for explosive speed

A juvenile pale chanting goshawk scares a feisty slender mongoose

Peter Hall

★★★★

DALKEITH

7 km to 14th waterhole

Dalkeith waterhole is situated on the loop road to the left. An excellent spot for bird photography. Approach slowly so as not to disturb animals at the waterhole, which lies close to the road.

Dalkeith, another of the Scottish-named boreholes, was likely named after the town in Midlothian. The water here is sweet and favoured by game, making this and the nearby 14th and 13th boreholes excellent for predator sightings. These loops are prime spots for cheetah hunts and kills, while lion and leopard are regular visitors. Because the Dalkeith waterhole lies so close to the road, it is a favourite with photographers and birders alike. The open surroundings – framed by red dunes and scattered camelthorns – offer a perfect backdrop for wildlife watching.

The trees around the waterhole attract a wealth of birdlife. **Kalahari scrub-robin**, **Marico flycatchers**, **scaly-feathered finches**, **Namaqua** and **Burchell's sandgrouse**, **turtle doves** and **lanner falcons** are frequent visitors. While you wait for the next drama to unfold, spend a while watching the birds. They tell the quieter stories of this desert valley.

Good sightings here are not limited to waterholes. Animals move across the dunes towards water and leopards are frequently seen crossing the road. The sweet water attracts **lions** and occasionally **leopards**. Although mainly nocturnal, they do roam by day, patrolling their territories. Solitary by nature, leopards meet only to mate or when females raise cubs. They mark their ranges with scent and claw marks, and their harsh rasping call is a signal to rivals or mates. When content, they purr softly; when threatened, they snarl and spit. When they do appear, it is often just for a moment before they melt back into the dunes, leaving silence and the echo of wild perfection.

A fork-tailed drongo challenges a martial eagle

Lee Norman

The **slender mongoose** is another treat along this stretch; a **fiery auburn flash** darting across the road, its tail tipped in black. Agile and solitary, it hunts rodents, reptiles and birds around fallen trees and calcrete outcrops. Less common than its yellow or banded cousins, it is a special sighting in the semi-arid reaches of the Auob. These fallen trees also shelter its prey – rodents, insects and reptiles – and in turn, attract raptors such as the **pale chanting goshawk**, one of its main predators.

The Auob dune road is true **raptor country**. The graceful flight of a **bateleur** can signal the presence of food to other scavengers circling higher in the sky. **White-backed vultures** rise effortlessly on the morning thermals, scanning vast distances for carcasses far below. At a kill, an unwritten hierarchy governs the feast: the powerful **lappet-faced vulture** tears open the hide first, followed by the **white-backed vultures** that strip the flesh clean. Above them, **Martial eagles** – the undisputed royals of Kalahari raptors – also nest in this valley, building massive stick platforms up to two metres across in the upper forks of ancient camelthorn trees. These nests are used year after year and during the breeding season (March to November), a single chick may rely on its parents for as long as eight months after fledging. Scan the treetops for these magnificent hunters, perched motionless before soaring high on broad, powerful wings.

The Auob valley is also home to **Verreaux's (giant) eagle-owls** and the tiny **pearl-spotted owlets**. The owlets are easy to identify by their diminutive size and bright white spots. Listen for their soft, fluting calls at dusk, one of the most evocative sounds of the Kalahari evening.

A pale chanting goshawk dive-bombs a tawny eagle

Christiaan Ehlers

An opportunistic terrapin snaps at a passing butterfly

Nick Mathios

★★★★

14TH BOREHOLE
7 km to 13th borehole

You could easily spend hours at this favourite waterhole, just waiting and watching.

The water at 14th borehole is sweet and potable, drawing many species to drink, though the lack of tall trees makes it less appealing to small perching birds. Instead, the openness suits the non-perchers that swoop down, sip quickly and leave. Blue wildebeest are almost always present in the riverbed, and seed-eating birds come daily.

Nick Mathios

A special highlight occurs two to four hours after sunrise, when **sandgrouse** arrive in their hundreds. Two species, **Burchell's (or spotted) sandgrouse**, which nests in the red dunes, and the **Namaqua sandgrouse**, the familiar *kelkiewyn* of rocky plains, gather here to drink. Their calls echo across the still air before they drop swiftly to the water, drink and vanish again. They come only once a day, always wary of raptors that could strike as they crouch to drink. After good rains, when puddles form near their feeding grounds, they abandon the main waterholes, leaving a silence that regular visitors miss.

Lanner falcons, **red-necked falcons**, **pale chanting** and **Gabar goshawks**, and even **tawny eagles** are among the most feared raptors hunting birds that come to drink at the waterholes. They strike with astonishing speed, catching their prey in mid-air as the unsuspecting flocks rise from the water. The lanner, in particular, is renowned for its spectacular stoop – a high-speed dive used to snatch smaller birds in flight – while the agile Gabar goshawk relies on surprise attacks launched from nearby trees. These aerial hunters are a constant presence at busy waterholes, turning an ordinary birding stop into a scene of sudden drama and precision.

Suné Eloff

In the Kalahari, curiosity is often the prelude to action

Suné Eloff

Suné Eloff

Tawny eagle

Scott Chalmers

Lanner falcon

Hennie Blignaut

Louis Lotter

Lion following a honey badger

This open stretch of the Auob is also **classic cheetah country**. The wide, unobstructed plains and **abundant springbok** make it one of the best places to witness a hunt. Scan the shaded trees in the riverbed. A resting cheetah is easily mistaken for a fallen branch until it lifts its head or flicks its tail. Once the chase begins, it is over in seconds; a blur of speed and precision ending in the quiet grip of jaws on a throat. Yet the victory is fragile, scavengers like jackals or lions often drive the cheetah from its kill within minutes.

In the early morning or late afternoon, when shadows envelop the dry riverbeds, **bat-eared foxes** emerge from their dens in search of termites. In **November**, when pups are born, you might glimpse them at dawn, playing outside their burrow before retreating underground. Adults forage in the cool of evening, their huge ears tuned to the faint rustle of termites or beetle grubs beneath the surface. These endearing omnivores feed mostly on insects but will also take lizards, rodents or even fruit.

14th Borehole ablutions

At the time of writing the new ablutions were under construction.

Rudi Schulz

Black-backed jackals at play

The calcareous ridges are hiding places for all kinds of leopard prey

Villiers Steyn

A wild cat breaks cover in a flash of speed

Villiers Steyn

Villiers Steyn

Speed meets power – the leopard closes in

Villiers Steyn

The leopard rushes off with its prize

Cherie Schlebusch

★★★★

13TH BOREHOLE
16 km to Urikaruus waterhole

Look out for **African wild cat** and other small predators on the way to Urikaruus waterhole.

The short loop to the 13th borehole often delivers far more than expected. **Birding** here is always rewarding. The trees and shrubs around the waterhole offer safe perches for small flocks of **red-headed finches** and **waxbills**, which flit down to drink before vanishing into cover. **Lanner falcons** frequently patrol overhead, waiting to launch their lightning-fast stoops on unsuspecting birds.

When scanning the scene, remember to look beyond the riverbed as predators such as **lion**, **leopard** and **cheetah** have been known to use the dune crests as lookout points, their tawny forms blending perfectly with the red sands.

Lions, the largest carnivores of the Kgalagadi, remain the most sought-after sighting in the park. The **dark-maned Kalahari lion is not a separate subspecies** but a magnificent regional form, lean-limbed and long-striding to cope with the distances of the desert. With little shade and sparse prey, these lions occupy vast territories. They survive largely on the blood and moisture of their kills but drink when water is available. In the fierce heat, they pant to cool their blood and even sweat slightly through their paw pads.

Honey badgers are sometimes seen trotting briskly through the dunes, digging for rodents and insects. They are usually accompanied by **pale chanting goshawks** or **jackals**, which wait patiently for prey flushed from burrows by the badger's energetic digging. If you see a goshawk unusually low to the ground, chances are a honey badger is not too far away.

Spotted hyenas are the opportunists of the Kalahari. Though not strictly desert specialists, they cope well by being largely nocturnal, spending the hottest hours in caves or shaded dens. Waterholes hold a special appeal: hyenas have learnt to lie in the troughs to cool themselves, often to the irritation of other thirsty animals. Members of the **Kamqua clan** are known to frequent the 13th waterhole for this purpose.

Spotted hyenas live in **matriarchal clans** led by a dominant female, larger than any male and ranking above all others. Females stay within their birth clan, while males are usually immigrants from elsewhere. The social order is strict and even young females outrank adult males. Males contribute nothing to rearing the cubs and females compete fiercely for food and status. Though sexes appear similar, adult females are usually in milk and their bellies hang lower and fuller.

Booted eagle and juvenile lanner

Peter Hall

Acceleration is the cheetah's weapon: from standstill, it reaches 100 km/h in seconds

Spotted hyena and cubs

Corné Malan

★★★★

URIKARUUS WATERHOLE
16 km to Kamqua

The Urikaruus waterhole lies about two kilometres south of the turn-off to Urikaruus Wilderness Camp. It is not the camp's private waterhole but a natural gathering point where rainwater pools in season.

The name *Urikaruus* means 'place of white calcareous rock', and predators are often spotted resting on the pale ridge above the riverbed, surveying the plains for prey. From the road, the waterhole is difficult to see, but a short track climbs onto the ridge, offering a rewarding vantage point across the scene.

A wide range of wildlife visits the Urikaruus waterhole: **leopard**, **hyena**, **lion** and **cheetah** are frequently seen, while herds of springbok and gemsbok graze the valley floor. Look out for **African wild cat**, and **Cape fox** at dusk or dawn.

The **greater kestrel** may be found perched on a nearby camelthorn or on a low branch, scanning for prey. It feeds mainly on insects sheltering in the stony calcareous soil, as well as on small mammals, reptiles and birds. Their presence, like the honey-coloured stones they hunt over, is a familiar feature of the semi-desert sky.

Among the larger herbivores, **red hartebeest** are regular visitors: tall, tan antelope with long faces, bracket-shaped horns and high shoulders that give them a distinctive sloping profile. Once widespread across Africa, their range has greatly diminished, yet in the Kalahari they endure by feeding on melons and tubers when water is scarce, and by following the paths of thunderstorms to new grazing.

Eland and **kudu** are rarer. Both occasionally appear here but seldom remain. Eland are more common in the eastern (Botswana) section of the park, while kudu, creatures of bush and woodland, struggle to survive in this open, waterless terrain.

Further south, the open valley around Kamqua is classic **cheetah country**. **Springbok herds** move steadily between Kamqua and Urikaruus, and cheetahs shadow them closely. If you find one resting in the shade, remain quietly as the **unfolding hunt** can be one of the most exhilarating spectacles of the Kalahari. The cheetah's burst of speed, reaching up to 100 km/h, lasts mere seconds before it hooks its prey with the dew claws, tripping it to the ground before grasping the throat in a suffocating hold. After the chase, the exhausted cat rests before feeding, drawing deep, rapid breaths through nostril slits designed for maximum airflow. Feeding begins at the soft groin area and the carcass is dragged to a bush for concealment. Lightweight teeth and a delicate frame limit the cheetah's power but enhance its speed.

Giraffe have adapted remarkably well to the Auob valley. Feeding on camelthorn and shepherd's trees, they draw most of their moisture from leaves but still drink when they can. Over time, their range has expanded steadily southward, and some have crossed into the Nossob valley, a sign of natural recolonisation.

In the Kgalagadi, leopards are highly water-efficient and drink only opportunistically, making waterhole sightings relatively rare

Kathy Kay

Hannes Lochner

Mane colour of lions varies widely and is determined by genetics and age

Hannes Lochner

★★★★

KAMQUA WATERHOLE
1 km to Kamqua picnic site

Scan the horizon and the calcrete ridges for hyena, for this is one of their strongholds.

Set slightly back from the Auob road but visible from the first rise of the long dune track, the Kamqua waterhole lies in a broad, open sweep of riverbed that seems to glow with a green shimmer after rain. This is a fine spot to stop and scan the landscape as cheetah, leopard and hyena are all regular visitors, and a range of antelope graze across the plain.

After good rains, the transformation in this valley is remarkable. The entire area turns into a sea of green, seemingly lush and fertile. The main architect of this sudden change is **Kalahari sour grass** (*Schmidtia kalahariensis*), a plant both beautiful and deceptive. It germinates rapidly after rainfall, carpeting bare sand in what looks like rich pasture but its value is short-lived. Once mature, the grass produces a fine organic acid at its nodes that, when mixed with dew, becomes caustic. Animals avoid walking or feeding among it, allowing the grass to reseed freely. Even for humans, brushing against it in shorts can cause a painful burning rash that may blister. The Kalahari's greening illusion is fleeting.

The long-established **Kamqua spotted hyena clan** often occupies burrows on the western ridge, opposite the picnic site. Early mornings and cool days are the best times to watch their movements as the clan members emerge from their shelter. Hyena society is ruled by females; dominant, assertive and physically larger than the males. When a male approaches a higher-ranking female, his submissive crouch and gaping grin are gestures of respect and survival. Observing their complex hierarchy in action is one of the most fascinating experiences the Kamqua area offers.

Spotted hyenas use **multiple communal and satellite dens** spread across their territory. Females with young occupy these dens at different times, moving cubs as conditions change or danger threatens. Adults know every den's location and can visit others' cubs, reinforcing the clan's strong social bonds and intricate hierarchy.

Elsie Potgieter

Check all trees on the way to Kamqua for wild cat

Dune roads

Driving the **dune roads** is a vastly different experience from the riverbed routes. Predators, though present, are rarely seen; gemsbok appear regularly but seldom in large herds. The dunes, however, teem with subtler life. Look for **korhaans**, **goshawks**, **kestrels**, **sandgrouse**, **larks**, **ostrich**, **brown hyena** and the ever-inquisitive **honey badger**. Vegetation is dominated by **shepherd's trees** and **grey camelthorns**, both vital to the dune ecology. The Kalahari's **rodents** play an equally important role.

If driven without stopping, the dune roads may seem monotonous … one rise after another, dune upon dune. Yet for those who travel slowly and look closely, an entire world reveals itself. This sea of dunes is one of the world's most pristine **semi-arid wildernesses**. If you can avoid it, travel when it's cool. In high temperatures the sand seems to become liquid and if you veer off the hardened section of the road in the slightest, you get stuck in the sand. Pause regularly, and listen to the silence. In this stillness lies the true magic of the Kgalagadi.

Away from the riverbeds, the dune roads offer silence, space and a deeper sense of wilderness

Barry Hugo

BITTERPAN CAMP
Rosyntjiebos
Nossob Road
Dikbaardskolk
Dikbaardskolk Picnic Site
Eland
Upper Dune Road
17
7
Strathmore
Moravet
Kameelsleep
12
Vaalpan
Jan se draai
8th borehole
13
Urikaruus
Kamqua
Kamqua Picnic Site
URIKARUUS CAMP
Rooibrak
Witgat
Kransbrak
Nossob 4x4 Ecotrail
Montrose
Auob
!Xaus Road
Batulama
Gunong
DGE
Kij Gamies
Gemsbokplein
10
Lower Dune Road
Melkvlei Picnic Site
18
Melkvlei
Auchterlonie Picnic Site
3
Auchterlonie
KIELIEKRANKIE CAMP
Tierkop
8
KijKij
Kamfersboom
Auob Road
Auob
Nossob Road
Nossob
Munro
Rooiputs
TA SHEBUBE ROOIPUTS LODGE
Rooiputs Camp
Houmoed
Leeudril 4x4 Trail
Leeudril
DAWID KRUIPER CAMP
(under construction)
Samevloeiing (Confluence)
TWEE RIVIEREN REST CAMP
Tweerivieren
Two Rivers Camp
TWEE RIVIEREN GATE
Controlled entry
No entry/exit
Entrance gate
Picnic site
Camp site
Camp site (A-frame)
Rest camp
Wilderness camp
Lodge
Borehole (sweet water)
Borehole (medium water)
Borehole (brackish water)
Pan
River
Main road
Main road (Five-star)
4x4 roads and trails
Direction
3 Distance

Lower Dune Road – Kij Kij to Auchterlonie

★★★

KIJ KIJ
8 km to Tierkop

Leave the Kij Kij waterhole and proceed onto the short dune road. Once over the first red dune, the **scene changes completely**. Gone are the towering dark-green camelthorns and the open expanse of the riverbed. In their place stretch stands of dune reed and Bushman grasses, dotted with stunted grey camelthorns scattered across the dune-veld.

Keep an eye out for **predators** moving towards Kij Kij. Lions may rest on the first dune ridge, where they command a wide view of the valley below. Overhead, raptors may be circling, watching for movement near the waterhole. Antelope, too, are often on their way to drink, moving cautiously through the dunes.

The dune roads are relatively narrow; yet they possess a stable foundation. Take care not to slip off the shoulder as once in the soft sand, getting stuck is easy, especially if you have not deflated your tyres. As the summer sun climbs higher, the Kalahari dunes become scorching hot. The fine red sand absorbs heat rapidly, reaching **surface temperatures of 60–70 °C by midday**, hot enough to burn skin or soften the soles of your shoes. Beneath the surface, however, the sand remains cool, offering refuge to reptiles, insects and small mammals escaping the midday furnace.

Scan the sand near low shrubs for **termite mounds**; tiny holes or fresh soil often indicate aardwolf feeding sites.

The heat also changes the character of the drive. As the sand warms, it loosens, offering less traction. Tyres tend to sink and engines run hotter. Avoid sharp acceleration on dunes. Steady, smooth power keeps you moving without digging in.

If you happen to be early on any of the dune roads, watch for one of the Kalahari's quiet night wanderers; the **aardwolf** or 'earth-wolf'. Despite its fierce name, it is shy, gentle and entirely insectivorous, feeding almost exclusively on termites. The 'earth' part refers to its habit of resting in burrows during the day. After dark, the aardwolf emerges to forage for termites and ants, listening intently for their rustling and cutting sounds beneath the surface. When it locates a nest, it rushes in, lapping up the workers with a long, sticky tongue before the soldier termites can retaliate with their noxious sprays. In a single night, an aardwolf may consume as many as **250 000 termites**, nearly a kilogram of pure protein. Harvester termites are abundant in the dune-field, so where you find their mounds, you may find aardwolf spoor.

The aardwolf is the only hyena that feeds exclusively on insects. It plays a vital ecological role by controlling termite populations, consuming up to a **quarter million** per night without damaging their colonies, ensuring a renewable food source.

First light finds the aardwolf's home, tucked safely at its den entrance

Bruce Crossey

Stephan Swanepoel

Dune crests are cooler than the valleys on hot days

Chris Cronje

Ostrich chicks are extremely vulnerable in their harsh Kgalagadi home

Pale chanting goshawks are often seen near honey badger activity

Villiers Steyn

Honey badger

Villiers Steyn

Villiers Steyn

The goshawk waits patiently while the badger raids a bird's nest

Villiers Steyn

Even the black-backed jackal is a patient opportunist waiting for prey disturbed by the badger

Steenbok obtain sufficient moisture from their food and are well adapted to life in the dune fields

Notice the big ears and absence of horns in females

★★★

TIERKOP
18 km to Kij Gamies

Pause near colonies of **whistling rats** and wait quietly as you may hear their sharp calls before spotting the first sentinel.

The name Tierkop has Afrikaans roots, literally 'tiger hill'. Of course, there are no tigers in South Africa but early settlers referred to leopards as tiers or tygers, just as in Tygerberg near Cape Town.

Among the small mammals of the dunes, **Brant's whistling rat** is a delightful find. Its warrens are easy to spot. They are clusters of sandy mounds riddled with burrow openings. These sociable rodents live in colonies of 10 or more, and their sharp, whistled calls echo across the dunes when danger is near. Sentinels sit upright on their haunches, stamping their hind feet to alert the group below ground.

Whistling rats are active by day, mostly during the cooler hours of morning and late afternoon. They lack the bushy tails that ground squirrels use for shade, so they remain close to their burrows, feeding near the entrances where they can retreat instantly if threatened. You may see them perched on a mound, nibbling seeds or grasses in the open sunlight, always alert, always within reach of safety. Their young cling to the mother's teats and follow wherever she goes, a small, endearing detail.

Steenbok are independent of water and therefore often seen on the dunes. These tiny antelope have a varied diet, including creepers, flower-pods, shrubs and fruit such as tsamma melon. To conserve water, they feed predominantly at night, or restrict their activities to the cooler parts of the day. Being territorial, they mark their territories with secretions from glands in the eye region, between their hooves and under their chin. With large ears and good hearing, they are able to escape predators like lion and leopard. Their extremely short fur allows them to cool down rapidly after a chase.

Brant's whistling rats (*Parotomys brantsii*) in the Kgalagadi Transfrontier Park play a key ecological role primarily as a major prey species for various predators and, during population eruptions, as significant herbivores that can impact local vegetation.

The gemsbok is the ultimate antelope adapted to arid conditions

Hannes Lochner

Dominique de Beer

Dominique de Beer

Hannes Lochner

Hannes Lochner

Kij Games

★★★

KIJ GAMIES
12 km to Auob River

Fresh, dome-like mounds indicate **active mole-rat colonies**. Sometimes you may spot loose soil still shifting as they dig below.

Dune fields cover almost the entire Kgalagadi Transfrontier Park, and most of its lion roam this vast sea of sand. The name Kij Gamies comes from the Khoehoen word for 'big lioness', perhaps recalling an encounter with a formidable female that once ruled these dunes.

Kgalagadi lions are not a separate subspecies but their **adaptability and strength** are legendary. Constantly traversing the soft dunes builds endurance and lean muscle, giving them their tall, athletic build. In this semi-desert, a pride's territory can stretch over **1 000 km²**, five times the range of a Kruger lion. **Prey is scarce**, so they rely on smaller animals like hares, foxes and porcupines between larger kills. After such meagre meals, little remains for the cubs and therefore survival here is a constant test.

When pride members meet, they greet by **rubbing heads**, an intimate act that reinforces family bonds. At night, their roars roll over the dunes, serving as both warning and reassurance; a way to claim territory, locate one another and strengthen the ties that keep the pride together.

Look for the stunted **grey camelthorn trees** near this pan and waterhole. Though they appear small, their taproots plunge over **60 m** into the sand to reach groundwater. Endemic to the southern Kalahari, these hardy trees provide shade, seeds and refuge to countless creatures.

Look out for the dome-shaped mounds of **Damara mole-rats**. These subterranean engineers live in colonies beneath the dunes, digging elaborate tunnel systems with their teeth. Most digging happens after rain when the soil softens; in just two weeks, a colony can shift **three tonnes of sand**. They feed on underground tubers, corms and bulbs, never drinking, relying solely on plant moisture for survival.

Damara mole-rats have a fascinating **social hierarchy**, led by a breeding pair supported by non-breeding helpers, much like meerkats. Occasionally, individuals venture above ground after rains to establish new colonies. Their compact, cylindrical bodies, conical heads and short limbs make them perfectly adapted to their hidden world below the Kalahari sands.

Tunnel networks of mole-rats help aerate the ground and recycle nutrients, supporting plant growth in the Kalahari's fragile dune ecosystem.

Tunnel network of a mole-rat

Mole-rat

Heiko Denker

Goshawk challenging a snake eagle

Anja Denker

Upper Dune Road – Dikbaardskolk to Kamqua

★★★

DIKBAARDSKOLK PICNIC SITE
10 km to Eland Pan

Between Dikbaardskolk picnic site and Eland waterhole, the landscape gradually shifts from wooded savanna to true dune country. Camelthorn, raisin bush, blackthorn and three-thorn shrubs thin out, giving way to low, stunted trees scattered over orange-red sands.

Once you crest the first dune, the landscape changes. Up one slope, over the crest, down into the next shallow valley ... dune after dune, endlessly repeating. It may seem monotonous but stop and the desert reveals its marvels: intricate tracks, hardy plants and the quiet persistence of life.

These vegetated dunes support browsers and smaller mammals alike. **Eland** and **gemsbok** wander here, along with **steenbok**, **honey badger** and **ground squirrel**. **Brant's whistling rats**, **elephant shrews** and **gerbils** scurry among the shrubs, while predators – lion, brown hyena and aardwolf – patrol the same dunes, often visible only by their tracks. The air belongs to the birds: **korhaans**, **goshawks**, **kestrels**, **sandgrouse**, **larks** and the ever-present **ostrich**.

Life here is defined by water, or the lack of it. Most dune dwellers seldom drink, relying instead on clever **behavioural and physiological adaptations**. Many stay underground during the heat of the day, where the temperature can be 10 °C cooler. Others feed at dawn or dusk when plants hold maximum moisture. Even the **steenbok**, a small antelope, survives partly on moisture-rich foods like **tsamma melons**, **gemsbok cucumber** and **young shoots**.

The **tsamma melon** (*Citrullus lanatus*) is one of the Kalahari's true lifelines, a fibrous, tough-skinned cousin of the watermelon with a water content of up to **95 percent**. Its fruits remain edible for nearly two years, providing a dependable reservoir for animals and humans. Without tsammas, the early **San** and hunters could not have survived their long journeys with ox-wagons across the desert. Along this road, look for round, green melons scattered on the sands. A half-eaten one may tell a story; a rodent's neat hole, an antelope's uneven bites, or a brown hyena's smashed fragments.

Gemsbok cucumber

Ground squirrel and tsamma melon

Mandy Mitchell

Another member of the pumpkin family, the **wild cucumber** (*Cucumis africanus*), is a smaller spiny fruit carried by runners that can stretch up to 50 m. Animals dig for its moisture-rich roots, while the San once scraped and squeezed them to drink the clear liquid that dripped from their hands.

The **raisin bush** (*Grewia flava*), or *brandy bush*, is another keystone species of the dunes. Its sweet berries feed both humans and wildlife. Its straight, flexible shoots have long served the San for bows, arrows and walking sticks. Even its bark, rolled into tubes, was once used as a makeshift straw to sip from underground seeps.

On the *dune crests*, look for *Bushman grass* (*Stipagrostis amabilis*), the hardy **dune bush** (*Crotalaria spartioides*), **lucerne bush** (*Hermannia tormentosa*), **tsamma melons** and the **gemsbok cucumber**, all species specially adapted to shifting sands and intense heat. In the **dune valleys**, where the sand turns pale pink or white and is more compacted, burrowing animals thrive. Here you will find an array of grasses and herbs: **sour grass**, **wild sesame** or *thunderbolt* (*Sesamum triphyllum*), **katstert** (*Hermbstaedtia fleckii*) and the soft pink-flowered **springbokopslag** (*Indigofera alternans*). Each has its own subtle season of bloom and purpose, feeding insects, grazers and browsers.

Raisin bushes often host **skipper butterfly larvae** and provide shelter for **gerbils** at their base.

★★★

ELAND WATERHOLE
17 km to Moravet

Watch ostriches around midday as their subtle posture shifts reveal how perfectly adapted they are to managing heat.

Like most waterholes in the dune-sea, Eland waterhole lies on the edge of a natural pan. These shallow, circular basins have hard, compacted floors that sit slightly lower than the surrounding dunes. After rain, water collects in them, precious for both drinking and for the salt deposits left behind as it evaporates.

The Eland pan is grassy and shallow, so its salt content is lower than that of bare, open pans like **Moravet** further west. Despite its name, eland are not ordinarily seen here. These massive antelope, the largest in the Kalahari, are wanderers, constantly on the move across vast tracts of land stretching deep into Botswana.

Eland are **predominantly browsers** but their diet shifts with the seasons. When browsing material becomes scarce, they graze on young grasses, or use their impressive horns to twist down branches for fresh leaves. A bull can weigh nearly **900 kg** and reach high into the canopy for food inaccessible to smaller antelope. They are skittish and wary of vehicles, so any sighting is a privilege. Herds often break into smaller groups that scatter across the dunes, reassembling during droughts when they move south-westward towards the fossil riverbeds in search of water and shelter.

The **ostrich**, a true emblem of the Kalahari, is a frequent companion along this stretch. Its scientific name, *Struthio camelus*, links it to the camel, both desert dwellers capable of conserving water with remarkable efficiency. Ostriches exhale air that is **not fully saturated with moisture**, thanks to their long trachea and intricate nasal passages that cool outgoing air and reclaim water vapour. Their kidneys, too, are highly specialised, producing extremely concentrated urine, a vital adaptation for desert life.

Cape hare is common in the dunes

Eddie Coombes

Female ostrich

During the heat of the day, ostriches orient their bodies **parallel to the sun's rays**, reducing the surface area exposed to direct sunlight. They shade their thighs with outspread wings and raise their back feathers to release trapped heat. When temperatures soar above 40 °C, they perform **gular fluttering** – a rapid vibration of the thin throat membrane that cools the body through evaporation. In winter, when frost bites, they wrap their wings tightly around their bodies and sit low to conserve warmth. Dust baths, common at midday, serve a dual purpose – cleansing and parasite control – as fine clay dust clogs the joints of ticks and fleas, immobilising them.

Before reaching **Moravet**, the **Bitterpan access road** branches off to the right. It is a restricted route, reserved for Bitterpan Camp guests re-entering the main road.

Ostriches can tolerate air temperatures exceeding 50 °C thanks to physiological cooling, water-saving respiration and dust-bathing behaviour, making them among the most desert-adapted of all birds.

★★★

MORAVET
28 km to Vaalpan

Search the dunes after summer rain for purple-flowered devil's claw, its hooked seedpods lying half-buried in the sand.

The Moravet waterhole takes its name from Oom Sarel Burger's beloved black-speckled cow, which used to hide her calves in the long grass of the pan. In those days, this was lion country and every search must have been tense and anxious. Back then, lions were considered vermin and shot on sight. This is a striking contrast to today, where these same lions are the pride of the Kgalagadi.

The **Kalahari lions** of Moravet are among Africa's toughest – powerful, resilient, and remarkably healthy – yet their future is uncertain. Research shows more **male cubs** than females are surviving, a pattern likely linked to harsh drought conditions. This imbalance poses a long-term threat, as too few females mean too few cubs to sustain the population. Historically, Africa once held millions of lions; by 1950, their numbers had fallen to half a million, and by 2014, fewer than 35 000 remained. Today, perhaps **20 000 wild lions** survive, occupying a mere **eight percent of their former range**.

Even here, protection is not absolute. **Lions** sometimes stray beyond park boundaries, where livestock losses can lead to retaliatory killings. Across Africa, rising human populations, shrinking wildlands, illegal wildlife trade and unsustainable trophy hunting compound the crisis.

For now, though, the lions of Moravet remain magnificent. Their **black manes glowing** against the sand, their calls rolling

Monarch butterfly

Hennie Blignaut

Butterflies seeking moisture: African migrants and brown-veined whites

over the dunes at dawn. Drive the loop road slowly, scanning every patch of shade or camelthorn bush; patience may reward you with one of the park's most unforgettable sightings.

Along this route grows another of the desert's wonders, the **grapple plant** (*Harpagophytum procumbens*), also known as **devil's claw** or *veldkruipspinnekop*. The explorer **William Burchell**, who first collected it in 1811, named it for its claw-like seedpods, which grip the hooves of passing antelope and hitch a ride to new ground. Farmers once cursed it for injuring livestock, and it was declared a **noxious weed in 1938**, but today it is valued as one of southern Africa's most important **medicinal plants**. Its tubers, growing deep in the sand, are rich in healing compounds used to treat arthritis, diabetes, high blood pressure and digestive ailments. Harvested sustainably, devil's claw now brings millions in export revenue to Europe, **a desert weed turned economic asset**. Its trumpet-shaped purple flowers appear only after good rains, a fleeting burst of beauty in an austere landscape.

After summer rain, stop beside roadside puddles to watch brown-veined white butterflies fluttering in their hundreds.

Grapple plant or devil's claw seed pod

★★★

VAALPAN
13 km to Auob Road turn-off

The road from Vaalpan to Kamqua winds through classic Kalahari dune country; a softly undulating landscape of long red ridges, shallow valleys and sparse vegetation. There are no striking peaks, just a rhythmic rise and fall of dunes that seem to go on forever. Despite the monotony, every dune and hollow tells a story of adaptation and survival.

Vaalpan itself is not truly a pan but a **saline depression**. Its brackish water, curiously palatable, once drew Oom Sarel Burger's livestock – including his beloved cow, Moravet – to graze here. A **grey heron**, an unlikely resident of this arid landscape, was often seen perched on the rim of the cement dam beside the trough. It likely fed on small fish, crustaceans and even unwary birds that came to drink. Herons are opportunists; when conditions turn harsh, they simply spread their wings and move to wetter places.

During the dry season, the dunes can appear lifeless and desolate, but the first good **summer rains** transform them almost overnight. Dormant seeds burst into life: **three-thorn shrubs** sprout buds, **grasses** shimmer green across the valleys, and the hardy **devil's thorn** (*Tribulus terrestris*) carpets the sand in bright yellow within days. Its flowers bloom briefly before producing the notorious spiny fruits known as *duwweltjies*. Beautiful as they are, these plants become **toxic to livestock** once they wilt.

Ant-eating chat

Rainwater pools in small road depressions. Soon, **clouds of butterflies** – especially the **brown-veined whites** – gather to sip the mineral-rich moisture. These delicate pollinators are finely tuned to the rhythms of the desert, emerging exactly when flowers bloom. The Kalahari averages only **150 mm of rainfall a year**, with moisture increasing gradually northeastward, shaping subtle shifts in vegetation. On the dune crests, sand remains coarse but surprisingly moist beneath the surface. In the valleys, it is finer and more compacted, supporting **stunted camelthorns** and other hardy shrubs that anchor the dunes against the wind. The result is a landscape that appears barren, yet hums quietly with life.

Northern black korhaan – male

Northern black korhaan – female

Scan the open dunes for black korhaan males performing their aerial displays.

This stretch between **Vaalpan and the Auob valley** captures the essence of the Kalahari; a vast, softly sculpted landscape where dunes, vegetation and wildlife have adapted to this harsh environment. The phenomenon of life springing from near-barren sand after the briefest rain is **unique to this semi-arid desert**.

Birdlife adds movement and sound. The **northern black korhaan**, a true Kalahari endemic, is often seen strutting beside the road, foraging for seeds and insects. Terrestrial and solitary, males perform flamboyant display flights, ascending steeply with exaggerated wingbeats, crest raised, calling loudly before descending in a fluttering glide.

Its close relative, the **red-crested korhaan**, prefers slightly more wooded areas but is still encountered here. Its display is even more dramatic. The male shoots 30 m into the air, flips onto his back and plummets earthward before opening his wings at the last possible moment, a performance as daring as it is spectacular.

Watch for the **greater kestrel**, a common sight hovering above the dunes or perched on a tall shrub. It feeds mainly on invertebrates and small reptiles, scanning patiently before dropping to strike. Alongside it, the **southern pale chanting goshawk** reigns as one of the most familiar raptors of the park. With its long orange legs, grey plumage and striking white primaries, it is easily recognised. These goshawks regularly perch on camelthorn tops or follow **honey badgers**, waiting to snatch prey flushed from underground burrows, a fascinating display of opportunistic partnership.

As you approach the **Auob River valley**, the scene softens. Camelthorns become more frequent, the dunes lower and the valleys widen. Along the dry riverbed, the vegetation thickens, and the pale sand gives way to stands of grey-green trees. On either side of the riverbed, look for **wild pumpkins** (*Radyera urens*), large, leafy plants belonging to the hibiscus family. Their deep red flowers are rarely seen. **Porcupines and ground squirrels** eagerly devour them before they can open, making a glimpse of one a small triumph for any keen observer.

The red-crested korhaan's display flight – a steep ascent, a backward flip and a dramatic free-fall – is one of the most theatrical courtship rituals in the Kalahari sky.

Accommodation

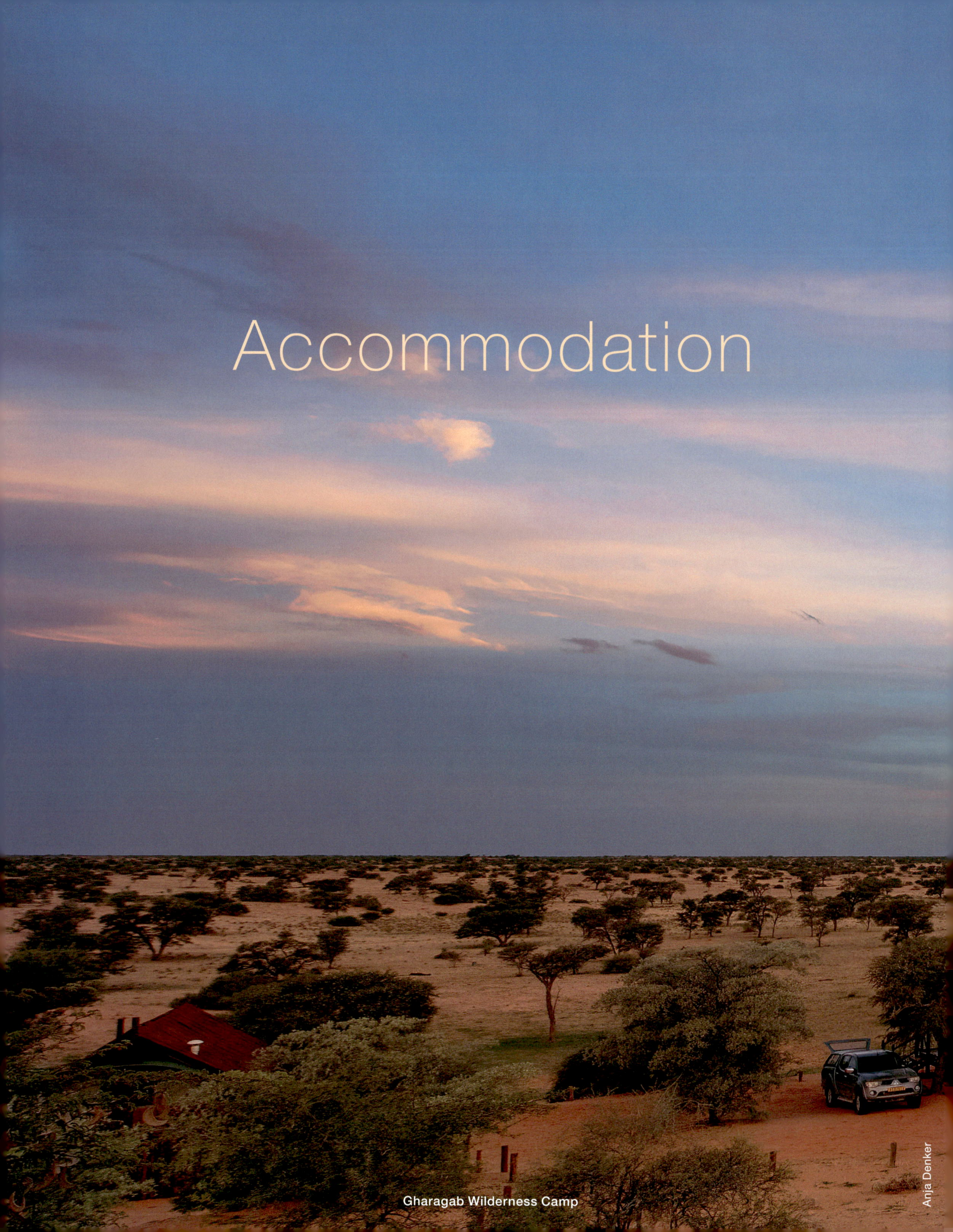

Gharagab Wilderness Camp

Anja Denker

Juvenile pale chanting goshawk

Bookings and border rules

The Kgalagadi Transfrontier Park (KTP) operates as one ecological system but is managed by two authorities:

- **South Africa:** SANParks (Twee Rivieren, Nossob, Mata-Mata, wilderness camps)
- **Botswana:** DWNP and concession holders (Mabuasehube, Polentswa, Rooiputs, Swartpan, Kaa area)

Although wildlife moves freely across the border, **visitors do not**. Cross-border movement inside the park is controlled and subject to immigration rules.

1. Enter and exit through the same gate

– No border formalities

If you enter and leave through the same country, you are treated as a normal domestic visitor.

Examples:

- Enter **Twee Rivieren (SA)** > visit Rooiputs/Polentswa (Botswana side) > exit **Twee Rivieren (SA)**
- Enter **Mabuasehube (Botswana)** > travel through the park > exit **Mabuasehube (Botswana)**

No passport control is required, even when driving on the opposite country's side of the park.

2. Enter one country, exit the other

– Immigration required

If you plan to cross an international border inside the park, you must complete immigration procedures **in advance** at the entry gate.

Examples:

- Enter **Twee Rivieren (SA)** > travel north to **Mata-Mata** > exit into **Namibia**
- Enter **Twee Rivieren (SA)** > drive Nossob > exit **Mabuasehube (Botswana)**
- Enter **Mabuasehube (Botswana)** > exit **Twee Rivieren (SA)**

In these cases you must:

- **Clear immigration at Twee Rivieren** (the only full border post inside KTP)
- Ensure **passports**, **visas** and **vehicle papers** are in order
- Declare goods and follow customs regulations

If you fail to clear immigration at Twee Rivieren, you may be forced to drive back to the gate for processing.

3. DWNP vs SANParks bookings are completely separate

Even though it is one park, accommodation must be booked with the authority responsible for that section.

SANPARKS (SOUTH AFRICA):

- Twee Rivieren, Nossob, Mata-Mata
- Wilderness camps: Urikaruus, Kieliekrankie, Gharagab, Bitterpan, Grootkolk, Kalahari Tented Camp, Dawid Kruiper and Craig Lockhart
- Book via www.sanparks.org

DWNP (BOTSWANA):

- Mabuasehube pans and campsites
- Botswana-side wilderness sites (Kaa, Swartpan, Thupapedi, etc.)
- Book via DWNP or authorised operators (e.g. Bigfoot Tours)

PRIVATE CONCESSIONS (BOTSWANA):

- **Ta Shebube Rooiputs** and **Polentswa**
- Book directly with the lodge or concession operator

4. Vehicle rules are country-specific

- South African rental vehicles **may require written permission** to enter Botswana or Namibia.
- Some Botswana tracks (e.g. Polentswa, Mabuasehube, Swartpan) require **high-clearance 4x4 only**, regardless of where you booked accommodation.

5. Cross-border movement between nodes

These routes count as international crossings:

- **Mata-Mata > Namibia** (official border post with limited hours)
- **Two Rivers (SA–Botswana)** at Twee Rivieren (official border post with limited hours)
- **Kaa > Namibia** (NOT an official border post – no immigration facilities)

You **cannot** legally cross into Namibia through Kaa or Polentswa.

6. Important note for lodge guests (Rooiputs and Polentswa)

Even though these lodges sit on **Botswana soil**, guests:

- **May enter via Twee Rivieren (SA)**
- **Do not clear immigration** unless they plan to exit via a different country
- Are treated as **domestic SANParks visitors staying in a Botswana concession**

Summary

- **As long as you exit the park through the same country you entered, no border procedures are required.**
- **If you enter and exit through different countries, immigration MUST be completed at Twee Rivieren.**
- **Bookings for SA and Botswana areas are made separately, even though it is one transfrontier park.**

Camps and lodges

The **main rest camps**, **wilderness camps**, **Botswana campsites** and **private lodges** are scattered across the Kgalagadi Transfrontier Park.

KGALAGADI CAMPS

- The **main** and w**ilderness camps** are managed by **SANParks**
- Three **privately operated lodges** occupy concession areas
- Mabuasehube campsites are managed by **Department of Wildlife and National Parks (DWNP)**

Main SANParks rest camps

- **Twee Rivieren** (the bustling gateway where journeys begin)
- **Nossob** (the heartbeat of predator country)
- **Mata-Mata** (the peaceful frontier along the Auob River)

Facilities in the SANParks self-catering chalets:

- **Kitchens** with fridge, stove, crockery and utensils, as well as bedding, towels, ceiling fans or air-conditioning, and a barbecue patio

Facilities at the SANParks campsites:

- Power points, ablutions with hot water and communal sculleries. A few premium sites at Nossob include private kitchenettes and bathrooms

Shops and payments:

- Basic goods available at Twee Rivieren, Nossob and Mata-Mata
- Credit and debit cards accepted at main camps and for fuel
- Only Twee Rivieren has a restaurant
- Cellphone reception at Twee Rivieren; limited/none at Nossob and Mata-Mata.

All three main camps:

- **Swimming pools** for overnight guests
- **Fenced and family-friendly**
- **Viewing hides** overlooking waterholes

Lighting and power:

- **Outdoor lighting** is limited; bring a torch or headlamp
- Main camps have **electricity**

Water:

- Purified but mineralised water; bottled water recommended

Wilderness camps

- Some wilderness camps are accessible only by a **4x4 vehicle**, offering a truly remote experience. Each wilderness camp has its own special atmosphere.
- Camps are unfenced and staffed by a single tourism assistant.
- Rustic, yet well-equipped cabins feature ceiling fans, gas-heated showers and outdoor decks with barbecue areas.
- For safety reasons, children under 12 are not permitted.
- Wilderness camps rely on solar power (no plug points).
- Water has a high salt content; bring your **own drinking water**.
- Bring your own firewood.
- No cellphone reception.

SANParks Eco-trail campsites

- Extremely basic and visitors must be self-sufficient.
- Some provide only a pit toilet and outdoor shower, others no facilities at all.

Private lodges

- The park's **three eco-lodges** offer fully serviced accommodation.
- Guided drives and walks, designed to blend seamlessly into the desert landscape.
- !Xaus is owned by the local Komani San and Mier communities and run by Transfrontier Parks Destinations (TFPD).
- **Rooiputs** and **Polentswa** by Ta Shebube, a small chain of camps in Botswana.

Mabuasehube

- All the camping sites are extremely basic and visitors must be completely self-sufficient.
- Some provide only a pit toilet and outdoor shower, others no facilities at all.

Mabuasehube

Corné Malan

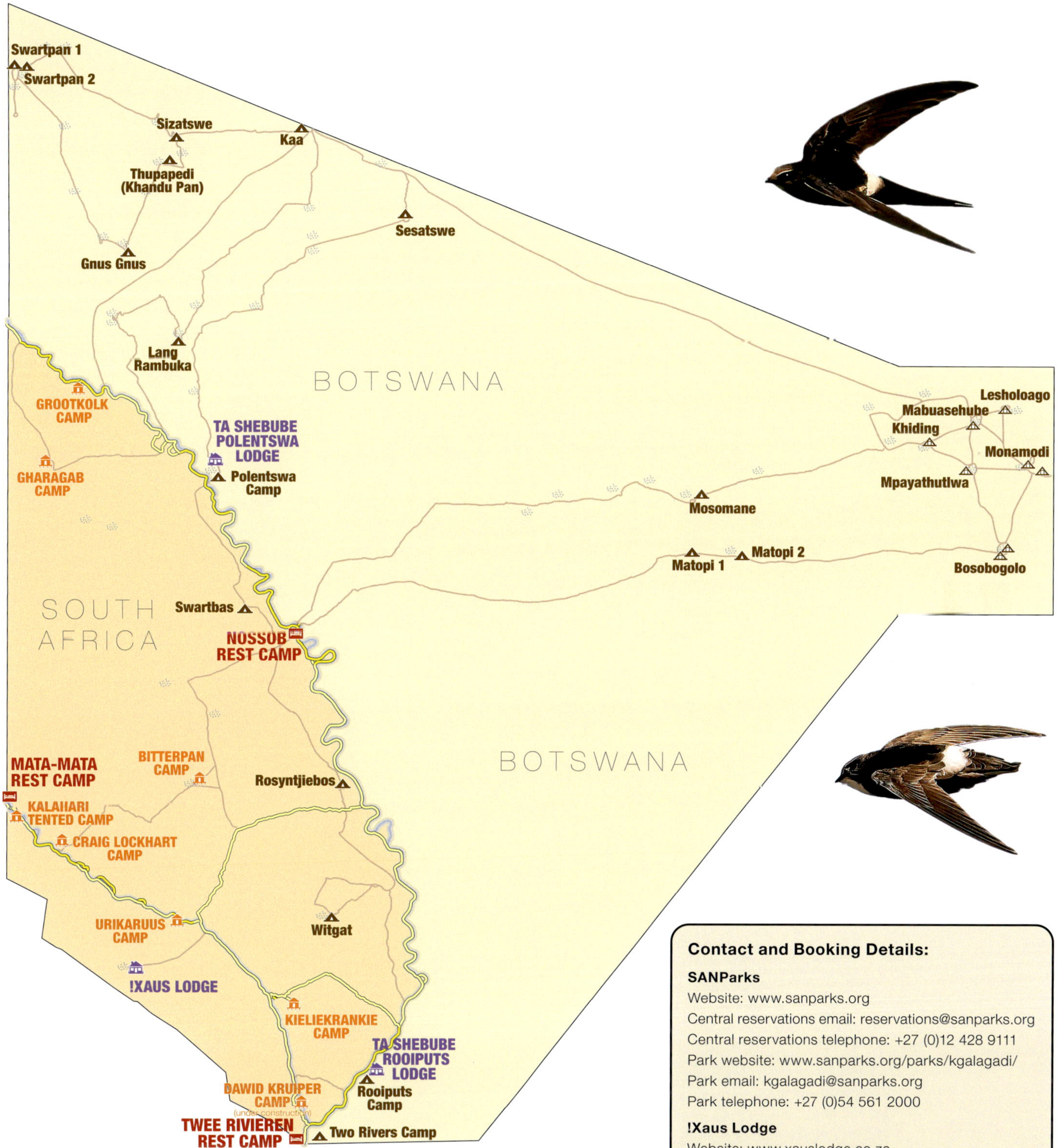

Contact and Booking Details:

SANParks
Website: www.sanparks.org
Central reservations email: reservations@sanparks.org
Central reservations telephone: +27 (0)12 428 9111
Park website: www.sanparks.org/parks/kgalagadi/
Park email: kgalagadi@sanparks.org
Park telephone: +27 (0)54 561 2000

!Xaus Lodge
Website: www.xauslodge.co.za
!Xaus telephone: +27 (0)21 701 7860
Email: info@xauslodge.co.za

Ta Shebube lodges
Website: www.tashebube.co.bw
Ta Shebube telephone: +267 316 1696
Mobile: +267 78 272 000 (whatsapp)
Email: info@tashebube.co.bw

Botswana Wildlife
Website: www.botswana.co.za/wildlife
Telephone: +267 686 or +267 318 0774
Gabarone telephone: +267 390 1999
Email reservations: dwnp@gov.bw

SANParks main camps

TWEE RIVIEREN CAMP

Twee Rivieren's surroundings teem with small desert life. Look for the huge harmless African giant millipede, known as shongololo or bongololo in the camp. **Huge millipedes** that grow to 33.5–67 mm size are common. Unlike centipedes, millipedes do not bite or sting. They are mainly harmless herbivores that feed on decaying plant material. They move slowly and curl up when in danger to protect their soft body parts. Their defence mechanisms consist mainly of the secretion of irritating but generally harmless secretions. Millipedes make a sudden appearance after rain.

From time to time you may encounter a **snake** in the camp. Snakes are most active during cooler parts of the day, specifically early morning and dusk, when they hunt, but their activity can also be influenced by other factors like temperature and several species are primarily active at night or during the day. Some snakes are most active in the midday sun to absorb warmth, especially during cooler periods. It is therefore a good idea to **wear shoes** and have a **torch** at hand when you go for a walk. Many snakes are harmless, but the **Cape cobra** and the **puff adder** are dangerous.

The **Cape cobra** is the most striking snake of the Kalahari. The colouration of individuals can vary from deep yellow to dark brown. Although this snake is relatively docile, it is extremely venomous. The neurotoxic venom attacks the nervous system. The cobra displays its characteristic hood when threatened. The **puff adder** is sluggish and emerges at dusk. When threatened, the puff adder will hiss and curl up ready to strike. The chevron patterning gives it away. The puff adder produces a cytotoxic venom that affects muscles and causes swelling and pain.

What to do in event of a snakebite: Keep victim calm, immobilised and transport them to the closest hospital without delay (Upington is the closest at 265 km from Twee Rivieren). Call the poison information centre at 0861 555 777. If victim stops breathing, resort to artificial respiration or make use of a bag valve mask. **Important:** Do not apply a tourniquet, do not cut and suck the wound, do not use ice or very hot water, do not give victim alcohol, nor apply an electric shock and do not inject antivenom randomly!

Puff adder

Edmund Aylmer

Ground squirrel and yellow mongoose with Cape cobra

Hannes Lochner

Yellow mongooses and **ground squirrels** are regularly seen near their burrows. Although fenced to exclude large predators, smaller creatures often find their way in. After dark, a **Cape fox** or **spotted genet** may wander past, and occasionally a **honey badger,** too.

Nights are peaceful, filled with the chirping of **barking geckos** and the soft call of **pearl-spotted owlets**, with faint sounds from across the border sometimes drifting in.

A distinctive shrub within the camp is the **three thorn (driedorings)**, a member of the pomegranate family with whitish trumpet-shaped flowers appearing after rain. Its branch tips end in three spikes rather than true thorns, and it is an important desert food plant. This shrub is widespread throughout the park and it is worth investigating it up close in the camp.

A thriving **bat population** roosts in the camp, supported by nesting boxes to keep them out of buildings. These bats play a crucial role in insect control.

Entrance to hide at Twee Rivieren

Campsite at Twee Rivieren

Nick Pawley

MATA-MATA CAMP

If you sit quietly near the ground-squirrel colonies, you may soon notice how these small mammals live in perfect cooperation.

Mata-Mata Camp itself is a delight, full of ground squirrels and meerkats digging and chattering among the chalets. The small waterhole, viewed from the hide, often attracts hyena, cheetah or even lion. After a long day's drive, take a seat there at sunset. It is one of the Kalahari's quiet pleasures.

Mata-Mata means 'give and you shall receive'. Give your heart to Mata, and you will leave with unforgettable memories. Perhaps the best gift the camp can offer is a sleepless night; lying awake while the deep roar of a lion echoes through the riverbed.

Suricates, and **ground squirrels** are permanent residents of the camp, providing endless entertainment with their constant foraging and playful antics. Suricates (meerkats) and ground squirrels may share burrows, taking turns as sentinels while others feed. The squirrels' warning chirps and the meerkats' barks form a shared language of safety, a remarkable example of interspecies teamwork in the Kalahari.

After dark, you may be visited by nocturnal wanderers such as the **Cape fox**, **black-backed jackal**, **spotted genet** or even the occasional **honey badger**.

Birding in the camp is rewarding. Regular visitors include the **crimson-breasted shrike**, **common scimitarbill**, **pearl-spotted owlet** and **white-faced owl**. Keep your binoculars ready as there is always something new to spot in the trees or around the chalets.

Geckos and **scorpions** are common, while the occasional **snake** may surprise an unwary guest. Be especially alert for scorpions on windy nights or after good rain. Campers should take care where they leave their shoes overnight. Always check inside your shoes or boots before slipping them on in the morning! The campgrounds are full of fascinating invertebrates if you take the time to look closely.

Suricate or meerkat at Mata-Mata

Gustav van den Berg

Spend time watching suricates. They live in colonies known as **mobs**, **gangs** or **clans**, sometimes numbering up to 50 individuals.

The **hide overlooking the waterhole** may not offer quite the same drama as Nossob's, but early mornings and evenings can bring special surprises. The semi-luxury chalets enjoy superb views over the waterhole, making it easy to enjoy the passing wildlife from the comfort of your veranda.

Meerkats are permanent residents at Mata-Mata

Suricates are alert and inquisitive creatures, constantly scanning their surroundings

Nossob Camp

NOSSOB CAMP

Spend time in the hide at dusk for unforgettable sightings, from geckos clicking nearby to lions passing in the dark. **Wildlife highlights include** lions, leopards, jackals, Cape foxes, owls, mongooses, ground squirrels, geckos and raptors.

Nossob Camp is a popular and frequently fully booked rest camp famous for its spectacular predator sightings, especially **black-maned lions**. Wildlife viewing is often centred on the camp's watering hole, which is accessible from a special hide and attracts animals like lions, leopards, hyenas and jackals. The camp itself is dry and dusty, but offers a swimming pool, a shop and a fuel station.

Nossob Camp retains much of its **natural vegetation**, offering superb opportunities to observe smaller creatures. A marked footpath follows the camp perimeter. This is perfect for short walks, though always wear closed shoes and carry a torch after dark. **Snakes** and **scorpions** can appear anywhere. Common snakes include the **puff adder** (sluggish and easy to overlook), the **small horned adder** and the **Cape cobra** with its yellow body and broad hood. Take care, especially around sandy play areas, and remember: the nearest hospital is far away.

Yellow mongooses and **ground squirrels** are common daytime companions. The mongooses are agile hunters of insects, the squirrel sociable foragers that share childcare duties and live in elaborate burrows.

The floodlit **Nossob waterhole and hide** provide hours of fascination. Visitors gather here in late afternoon, waiting for **lions** to appear, sometimes even from beneath the hide itself. **Jackals** and **Cape foxes** hunt insects under the lights, **barn owls** glide silently past, and bats flutter overhead. Occasionally a **leopard** visits, announced by the alarm calls of jackals.

By day, **springbok**, **gemsbok** and **raptors** dominate the scene, they are joined by **secretarybirds**, **storks and migratory kites**.

After dark, the desert comes alive with the **barking gecko**, its rhythmic clicks echoing like pebbles striking together. Harmless **Bibron's geckos** hunt insects near lights and can shed their tails to escape predators. **Barking geckos** are special in the Kgalagadi for their loud, barking mating calls that can be heard for hundreds of metres and form large choruses. These tiny desert lizards, **endemic** to southern Africa, are also unique for being **vociferous reptiles** that call from underground burrows to attract mates and defend territories. They spend most of their lives in these burrows, which are essential for mating, egg-laying and protection from predators.

Male barking geckos produce loud, specific barks to attract females and ward off rivals. At times, large choruses of thousands of males can be heard. Calling in chorus is unusual for reptiles.

Western barn owl

Myburgh du Plessis

Verreaux's eagle-owl

Leon Steenberg

Pearl-spotted owlet

Spotted eagle-owl

Peter Versfeld

Hamman Prinsloo

Southern white-faced owl

SANParks wilderness camps

At the time of writing, **SANParks** offers **self-catering accommodation** in **six wilderness camps**. Two additional camps are currently in the pipeline and already at an advanced stage of development: one planned as a **wilderness camping area at Craig Lockhart**, and the other the **Dawid Kruiper Rest Camp, self-catering cabin camp**, similar in style to the existing wilderness camps, on the bank overlooking the Auob between Confluence and Houmoed.

- Bitterpan Wilderness Camp
- Gharagab Wilderness Camp
- Grootkolk Wilderness Camp
- Kieliekrankie Wilderness Camp
- Urikaruus Wilderness Camp
- Kalahari Tented Camp

WHAT ALL WILDERNESS CAMPS SHARE

- Each is part of the **wilderness camp category** (not the larger 'rest camps') in the park.
- They are **unfenced**, meaning wildlife can move freely through the camp area; you are truly in the wilderness.
- Each has a **tourism assistant** on duty to maintain the camp, assist guests and monitor conditions.

Anja Denker

Lion in dune fields

- Access requirements: depending on the specific camp, you may need a **standard sedan** or a **4x4 vehicle**; all routes emphasise rough terrain and sand.
- **Facilities tend to be basic** compared to rest camps: often solar power lighting, no permanent grid electricity, and limited or no cellphone reception. Guests are required to bring their own water and firewood in many cases.
- Because of their remote nature and unfenced setup, campers must **exercise extra safety awareness**; children under a certain age may not be permitted, depending on camp rules.
- Visitors must be **fully self-sufficient** with fuel, water and supplies.

WILDERNESS CAMPS ARE SPECIAL

When darkness falls and the desert cools, the Kgalagadi transforms into a different world. Sit quietly on your veranda and let your eyes adjust. Movement will soon reveal itself. Watch for the **slender silhouette of a genet** slipping between the chalets, or the shape of a **black-backed jackal** trotting towards the waterhole. A **honey badger** may lumber past, nose to the ground, intent on beetles or scorpions. Listen for the soft, throaty call of the **white-faced owl** or the distant, yelping laugh of a **spotted hyena** carried across the dunes.

Even the smallest lives stir in the darkness: **black-tailed tree rats** rustling in the camelthorns, **geckos** stalking moths under the lights, and **barking geckos** trilling from the sand like tiny night watchmen.

GROOTKOLK WILDERNESS CAMP

Travel tips

From Nossob

- **Distance:** ±110 km
- **Travel time:** About **3½ to 4½ hours**, depending on corrugation and stops at waterholes along road
- **Route:** Nossob – Lijersdraai – Kannaguass – turn west to Grootkolk
- **Vehicle:** Accessible to **high-clearance vehicles and sedans**, corrugations can be severe

From Twee Rivieren

- **Distance:** ±330 km
- **Travel time: 8–10 hours**, best done over **two days**, with an overnight stop at **Nossob Camp** recommended
- Grootkolk is one of the most remote camps in the park, but **accessible by sedan** under normal dry conditions. The last stretch can be heavily corrugated. Always check road conditions with SANParks staff before departure.

The camp

Search the trees around camp for the **black-tailed tree rat** that nests in the forks of camelthorns.

Grootkolk Wilderness Camp offers one of the park's most remote and rewarding experiences. The four desert cabins, built from sandbags and canvas to blend with the environment, overlook a floodlit waterhole that draws an ever-changing procession of wildlife.

Wildlife moves freely between the units. Here, you are part of the wilderness, not apart from it. **Lions** are frequent visitors and their roars roll through the night. The waterhole attracts herds of **wildebeest**, **springbok**, **gemsbok**, **red hartebeest** and **kudu**, with occasional sightings of **leopard**, **cheetah**, **brown hyena**, **warthog** and **honey badger**.

In the drier months, **eland** are regular visitors, their approach often announced by the distinctive **clicking of their knees** before they appear like pale phantoms in the light. The **eland**, Africa's largest antelope, can weigh over a tonne, stand 1.7 m at the shoulder, and leap a two-metre fence from a standstill. The clicking sound, caused by tendons slipping over the knee joints, helps the herd stay together in the dark. Researchers have also shown that the frequency of these clicks reveals a bull's size and strength to rivals.

Leopard sightings are frequent in this region. Several females' territories overlap that of a dominant male. **Lions** visit regularly, usually heralding their arrival with deep roars that echo through the night. One of their routes passes directly between the chalets, offering thrillingly close encounters. At other times, they arrive silently, leaving only fresh tracks in the sand for early risers to discover.

There is even a faint chance of seeing the **elusive aardvark**, one of Africa's most unusual mammals. Feeding solely on ants and termites, it uses its tubular snout and long sticky tongue to probe the soil. This shy, solitary creature spends its days in burrows and emerges after dark to forage. Its powerful digging creates burrows later used by **porcupines**, **springhares**, **hyenas** and even **ant-eating chats**, making it an important **keystone species** in the Kalahari ecosystem.

In the trees around camp, the **black-tailed tree rat** (*Thallomys nigricauda*) is a familiar nocturnal resident. Curious but harmless, these agile rodents nest in hollows and forks of **camelthorn trees**, sealing the entrances with thorny twigs. At dusk, they emerge to feed on **seed pods**, **bark** and **tree gum**, which provides vital moisture in this arid landscape. Their main predator is the **pale chanting goshawk**, often seen perched nearby. These raptors will methodically raid rat nests, scratching at entrances until the occupant bolts, then pursuing it through the branches until caught. After feeding, the goshawk may return to raid again or take its prey to a nearby **sociable weaver nest** to feed or share with its young.

Female violet-eared waxbill

View from chalet at Grootkolk Wilderness Camp

Anja Denker

Adult male red-headed finch

Villiers Steyn

GHARAGAB WILDERNESS CAMP

Via Wilderness Trail from Union's End to Lijersdraai

Travel tips

From Nossob

- **Distance:** ±164 km
- **Travel time:** About **5–6 hours** (depending on road and sand conditions)
- **Route:** Via Union's End road (Nossob – Kannaguass – Union's End – Gharagab)
- **Vehicle:** Strictly 4x4.
- The track to Gharagab is strictly **4x4 only** owing to deep sand and remoteness. The route is scenic but extremely isolated, with no facilities between camps, so visitors must be **fully self-sufficient** with fuel, water and supplies.

From Twee Rivieren

- **Distance:** ±360 km from Twee Rivieren
- **Travel time: 10–12 hours or two days**, usually broken with an overnight stay at **Nossob Camp**
- **Route:** Twee Rivieren – Nossob (via Nossob River road) – Gharagab (via Union's End)
- **Access road:** 61 km deep sand and remote

Getting there and out via Gharagab 4x4 trail

The access road to Gharagab is a single sandy track winding through dune streets and over low to medium dunes. It is not technically difficult; steady, confident 4×4 skills are usually enough. The route reaches the **Gharagab waterhole** after 15 km, the **camp** after 32 km.

The trail beyond the camp begins as a two-way track to the first waterhole, **Dankbaar Pan**, then becomes **one-way only**, with deeper sand and more technical dune sections. This stretch requires careful driving, especially near the crests. If you are new to 4x4 sand driving, read the tips in the Wilderness Trails section.

The camp

Gharagab Wilderness Camp lies deep in the park's far north, near the Namibian border, a place where solitude and silence define the experience. Perched on a high dune, the four elevated log cabins overlook a floodlit waterhole and the vast, unbroken wilderness of the Kalahari stretching to the horizon.

This **isolated** camp is among the most remote in the park, reached via a one-way circular route through deep, rolling dunes between **Union's End** and **Lijersdraai**. The journey itself heightens the sense of remoteness, each dune crest revealing another sweep of red sand.

Lions are frequent visitors, often seen or heard near camp, while herds of **wildebeest**, **springbok**, **gemsbok** and **red hartebeest** gather at the waterhole. Occasionally, a **leopard**, **cheetah** or even the elusive **pangolin** may appear. A small **viewing platform** behind the cabins offers magnificent day-time vistas across the dunes.

As night falls, the desert transforms. The stillness deepens, broken only by the distant roar of lions and the rhythmic calls of **barking geckos**. Under the immense Kalahari sky, every star seems closer, every sound sharper. Dawn arrives softly, with the first light spilling over the dunes and the morning chorus beginning anew.

Perched high on a red dune, the elevated chalets at **Gharagab Wilderness Camp** offer sweeping views of the

Chalet at Gharagab Wilderness Camp

Heiko Denker

Sparring gemsbok

Daniel Wipf

arid landscape and its small, precious waterhole below. Day and night, the scene is never still, a living thread of life drawn to water in this dry wilderness.

Lions visit regularly, their roars echoing across the dunes as they rest in nearby shade during the heat of the day. **Cheetahs** and **brown hyenas** are also occasional visitors, their movements marked by fresh tracks at dawn. Small herds of **gemsbok**, **red hartebeest** and **springbok** come to drink, joined at times by **eland bulls** that appear like silent giants out of the dunes.

Perhaps the most special visitor here is the elusive **ground pangolin**, a shy, secretive creature seldom seen yet sometimes known to approach the waterhole at night. Covered in heavy yellow-brown scales, the pangolin moves awkwardly on its hind legs, tail raised for balance. It tears open termite nests with its strong foreclaws and laps up insects with a long sticky tongue. Lacking teeth, it grinds its food in a muscular stomach, aided by swallowed grit. When threatened, it simply curls into an armoured ball, almost impervious to attack. Tragically, these gentle insect-eaters are still hunted for traditional medicine and, outside protected areas, their survival hangs in the balance.

After dark, the Gharagab waterhole becomes a stage for the desert's secretive residents. Listen for the rasping call of a **gecko** or the bark of a **brown hyena** echoing through the still air. If luck is on your side, you might glimpse the glint of a **pangolin's scales** in the lamplight or the silent glide of an **owl** hunting over the dunes. Even in this harsh wilderness, the night teems with quiet life.

Landscape at Gharagab

Boshoff Steenekamp

BITTERPAN WILDERNESS CAMP

Via Wilderness Trail from Nossob to Craig Lockhart

Travel tips

From Nossob

- **Distance:** ±120 km
- **Travel time: 5–6 hours** (depending on sand conditions and stops)
- **Route:** Nossob – Upper Dune road – Bitterpan
- **Vehicle:** The last **53 km** from Nossob to Bitterpan is a **4x4-only one-way track** that crosses several red dunes – **no trailers allowed**.

From Twee Rivieren

- **Distance:** ±220 km
- **Travel time:** Around **6–7 hours**, best done as **Twee Rivieren – Mata-Mata – Bitterpan**, since the 4x4 access road links from the **Mata-Mata–Nossob dune road** about midway.
- **Route:** Twee Rivieren – Mata-Mata (120 km) – Bitterpan turn-off (±55 km south of Mata-Mata) – Bitterpan (via the 4×4 track)
- Bitterpan is **accessible only to 4x4 vehicles** and forms part of a **one-way 4x4 wilderness route** linking the **Auob and Nossob valleys**. The route is strictly for **overnight guests**, and drivers must be self-sufficient with water, recovery gear, and low tyre pressure (around 1.6 bar).

Getting there and out via Gharagab 4x4 trail

The sandy track from Nossob to Bitterpan is not known for abundant game, but it offers excellent birding and reptile sightings. The route is generally easy to drive, though the sand can become deceptively soft on hot days. Maintain steady momentum and avoid stopping in deep patches. Most visitors travel this section late morning to align with the 14:00 check-in at Bitterpan, an hour when animals rest but birds, snakes and agamas are still lively.

The track from Bitterpan down to the Auob riverbed is one of the most scenic 4x4 routes in the park. Broad red dunes, scattered shepherd's trees and pristine stretches of sand make for an unforgettable early-morning drive. Leaving camp at first light is essential. If you are the first vehicle of the day, the last tracks were laid almost 20 hours earlier. Countless small creatures – beetles, rodents, reptiles – have been active through the night, leaving intricate spoor that turn the road into a tapestry.

The camp

Game viewing is best enjoyed from the deck as wildlife moves silently across the pan. Early morning and late afternoon are the best times to stay quietly at camp, watching the waterhole, the pan and the surrounding dunes.

Bitterpan lies deep in the heart of the Kalahari dunes, midway between Nossob and Mata-Mata camps. Some see it as barren, others as enchanting; a silent landscape stretching endlessly beneath a blazing sky.

View of Bitterpan Wilderness Camp, pan and waterhole

Villiers Steyn

Barry Hugo

Brown hyena

The camp overlooks a vast, mostly dry **salt pan**, one of roughly a thousand scattered through the dune streets of the Kalahari. These pans form when wind and rain wash fine soil and minerals into shallow depressions. Over time, the accumulation of salts creates natural **licks** that draw herds of antelope – **springbok**, **gemsbok** and **red hartebeest** – along with their predators. When rains fall, the pans briefly transform into shimmering **waterholes**, sustaining a burst of life before drying again.

Some pans contain layers of mica in the fine soil, catching the sunlight and creating a **mirage-like gleam**, giving the illusion of water even when they are bone dry. The constant movement of hooves, dustbathing and wind erosion maintains the shallow basin, ready to hold rain again in the next wet season. Bitterpan Wilderness Camp rests at the edge of one such pan.

At night, the camp settles into silence broken only by the deep, chest-thrumming roars of **lions** that sometimes pass close to the chalets. Their voices roll across the dunes like thunder; a sound that is felt as much as it is heard.

After dark, **springhares** may bound into the lit areas in camp. These bushy-tailed, kangaroo-like rodents feed on roots, bulbs and grasses, moving in long, effortless leaps. By day, they rest in deep burrows where it is cool and safe, emerging after sunset to feed on moisture-rich plants that sustain them through the long dry months.

The **aardwolf** or 'earth wolf' is a shy, solitary insect-eater closely related to the hyena. Unlike its bone-crushing relatives, it feeds almost exclusively on harvester termites and other small insects, which it licks up with its long sticky tongue … up to 300 000 termites a night.

Although present throughout much of the park, sightings are most likely in the **northern dune areas** and along **quiet dune roads** away from the busier river routes. They favour **open grassy dune fields** where termite mounds are abundant.

Aardwolves are **strictly nocturnal**, emerging shortly after sunset to feed. In winter and on overcast days, they may appear earlier, occasionally just after dawn or before dusk. Look for them trotting slowly across the dunes, tails down, sniffing the sand. They often forage in patches of disturbed ground. Their distinctive black-and-cream stripes and bushy tails are unmistakable in early morning or late evening light.

A lion's roar can reach **114 decibels** and carry for **up to eight kilometres** across the open Kalahari night. It is not only a warning to rivals, but also a way to maintain contact between pride members spread out over vast distances.

Barry Hugo

Honey badger at Bitterpan

URIKARUUS WILDERNESS CAMP

Travel tips

From Twee Rivieren

- **Distance:** ±72 km from Twee Rivieren
- **Travel time:** Around **2–2½ hours** if driving leisurely with stops at waterholes
- **Route:** Twee Rivieren – Auob River road northwards – Urikaruus
- **Vehicle:** The road is **suitable for ordinary sedans**, though corrugations can be heavy at times.

From Nossob

- **Distance:** ±160 km
- **Travel time:** About **6–7 hours**, depending on road conditions and sightings
- **Route:** Nossob – via the Upper Dune road – Kamqua – Urikaruus
- This route crosses multiple dunes and is **accessible by high-clearance 4x2 or 4x4 vehicles** (not suitable for caravans or trailers).
- If you plan to travel between **Nossob and Urikaruus**, allow a full day and depart early as it is a long, scenic dune-crossing drive where animals are most active in the cooler hours.

The camp

Stay quietly on your deck after sunset and let the desert unfold. Listen for the soft rustle of **gemsbok** hooves, the low, throaty cough of a **leopard**, or the eerie yelp of a **brown hyena** echoing through the dunes. With patience, the lamplight may reveal the glint of eyes, each visitor a piece of the Kalahari's timeless rhythm.

Set along the dry Auob riverbed, Urikaruus Wilderness Camp is one of the park's most beloved destinations. The four raised two-bed cabins and a honeymoon suite overlook a floodlit waterhole, just 50 m away, where animals come and go throughout the day and night.

Lions, **leopards** and **wild cats** often pass through the camp, while herds of **giraffe**, **springbok**, **gemsbok** and **red hartebeest** drink nearby. **Spotted hyenas** from a local den are regular nocturnal visitors, padding silently between the cabins.

At night, the desert comes alive. A lion's roar reverberates through the valley, the rustle of movement below stirs the imagination, and the brilliance of the **starlit sky** makes sleep almost impossible.

Each stilted cabin is divided into two levels: an enclosed kitchen and sitting area below, and a bedroom and balcony above, a perfect vantage point for the unfolding drama at the waterhole.

Lions patrolling the riverbed in a dust storm

Springbok in the Auob riverbed during a sandstorm

Hannes Lochner

Many photographers sit up through the night here, waiting for the procession of nocturnal visitors; a leopard or male lion at dusk, a pair of lionesses later in the evening, a hyena or two after midnight, and sometimes eland or another leopard in the soft pre-dawn light.

The **eland**, Africa's largest antelope, move widely across the desert, following the rhythm of rain and vegetation. In times of drought, they drift southwestward towards the Auob River, where water lingers longer. To conserve moisture, they browse mainly at night or in the early morning when the vegetation holds the most dew. When threatened, they form a defensive circle – their powerful backward kicks can kill a predator in an instant – yet exhaustion or inexperience sometimes makes them easy prey for lions.

Even **kudu**, rare in this arid region, have adapted to the wooded dunes and riverbed near Urikaruus. At dusk, **Cape foxes** and **bat-eared foxes** sometimes venture close to the cabins in search of scraps.

The eland has a secret to surviving droughts. Eland seldom drink free water. Instead, they obtain nearly all their moisture from leaves and pods, especially at night when plants hold the most dew. Their ability to slow their metabolism and reduce body temperature helps them thrive in the Kalahari's extreme heat and scarcity.

KIELIEKRANKIE WILDERNESS CAMP

Travel tips

From Twee Rivieren

- **Distance:** ±55 km
- **Travel time:** Around **1½–2 hours** at a leisurely game-viewing pace
- **Route:** Twee Rivieren – via the **Auob River road northwards** – take the **Short Dune road** turn-off – ascend to **Kieliekrankie** on the dune crest
- **Vehicle:** Accessible by **ordinary passenger vehicle**, but **beware of soft sand and corrugations**, especially after rain or in summer heat.

From Nossob

- **Distance:** ±150 km
- **Travel time: 6–7 hours** depending on sightings and road condition
- **Route:** Nossob – south via the **Nossob River road** – at the junction, turn onto the **Short Dune road** linking the Nossob and Auob valleys – Kieliekrankie

The camp

In the rainy season Kieliekrankie sets the stage for spectacular thunderstorms with gusts of wind howling, rain lashing down and grandiose, terrifying bolts of lighting.

Before the park was proclaimed, a Scottish surveyor named Roger 'Malkop' Jackson was tasked with subdividing this arid land into farms. One of these, named after a small Scottish village, became the site of Kieliekrankie Wilderness Camp; today overlooking a vast red-sand landscape instead of the green glens of his homeland.

From the crest of the dune, the panorama is breathtaking. Below lies a pale pan fringed by undulating dunes stretching into infinity, each ridge aligned by the powerful northeasterly winds that shaped them. The dunes here average about **10 m in height**, some rising to 15, spaced roughly 200 m apart in graceful, parallel rows.

Kieliekrankie sits on a high dune ridge, open to constant breezes that help cool the midday heat. Look closely at the sand around your chalet. The grains at the crest are coarse, while the pan below holds finer silt. Interestingly, the coarse sand near the top retains moisture longer, allowing certain plants to persist even in dry times. Down near the pan, compacted sand provides ideal soil for burrowing creatures such as rodents and small carnivores.

The shifting vegetation mirrors the subtle differences in slope and soil. Hardy shrubs and grasses dominate the dune crests, while salt-loving plants and nutritious grasses flourish in the pans below, drawing **gemsbok**, **springbok** and **steenbok** to graze and lick the mineral-rich soil.

The camp's position makes it an ideal base for exploring both river valleys and several of the southern waterholes. From your deck, you might watch **black-backed jackals**, **gemsbok**, **ostriches** or even **brown hyenas** visiting the waterhole.

Lions appear occasionally, padding silently across the dunes at dusk. A gentle dune breeze cools the heat of the day and, as night falls, the sky ignites with stars, perfect for **stargazing** or long-exposure photography.

While wildlife may pass close by, large herds are uncommon on the dunes, giving Kieliekrankie its quiet charm.

The Kalahari dunes were shaped by strong northeasterly winds thousands of years ago. Their striking parallel pattern and gentle slopes make them among the largest continuous fossil dune systems in the world; stable, yet still subtly shifting underfoot with each passing breeze.

Thunderstorm in the distance as seen from Kieliekrankie Wilderness Camp

Anja Denker

Ian Morrison

Ian Morrison

Ian Morrison

Cheetah chasing a steenbok across the waterhole at Kieliekrankie Wilderness Camp

KALAHARI TENTED CAMP

Travel tips

From Mata-Mata

- **Distance:** ±**3 km**
- **Travel time: 5 minutes**
- **Route:** The Kalahari Tented Camp lies **just south of Mata-Mata** on a low dune overlooking the Auob River valley.
- **Vehicle: Ordinary passenger vehicles** are perfectly suitable.
- Most visitors use Kalahari Tented Camp as a quieter alternative to Mata-Mata, sharing the same entrance gate and fuel point. Because of its proximity to Mata-Mata, Kalahari Tented Camp is ideal for cross-border travellers heading to or from Namibia.

From Twee Rivieren

- **Distance:** ±**120 km**
- **Travel time: 4½–5 hours** at a relaxed game-viewing pace with stops
- **Route:** Twee Rivieren – follow the **Auob River road northwards**, passing waterholes such as Auchterlonie, Kamqua and Urikaruus – Kalahari Tented Camp
- **Vehicle:** Suitable for **ordinary sedans**, though roads can be **heavily corrugated**.

From Nossob

- **Distance:** ±165 km
- **Travel time:** 6–7 hours depending on dune conditions
- **Route:** Nossob – via the Upper Dune road – Kamqua junction – continue north along the Auob River road – Kalahari Tented Camp
- **Vehicle:** High-clearance recommended for the dune section; 4x4 preferred but not essential in dry weather.

The camp

At dusk, sit quietly on your deck and let your ears adjust. The Kalahari speaks in layers: the bark of a gecko, the whoop of a hyena, the owl's low screech and somewhere beyond, the echoing grunt of an ostrich. Each sound is a fragment of the desert's nocturnal symphony.

Perched above the Auob River valley, near Mata-Mata, the Kalahari Tented Camp offers an ideal mix of comfort and wilderness. Fifteen elevated wood-and-canvas tents blend harmoniously with the dunes, providing a peaceful retreat with views of the waterhole below. Slightly more luxurious than the remote wilderness camps, it even has a small splash pool tucked behind reception, a welcome relief in summer heat.

Lions are regular visitors and often roar through the night, though the deep booming call of an **ostrich** can sound deceptively similar. Herds of **springbok**, **wildebeest**, **gemsbok** and **red hartebeest** are frequent at the waterhole, joined at times by **cheetah**, **leopard** or **hyena**.

The nights here are unforgettable, filled with the sounds of the desert and skies so clear that stargazing becomes irresistible. However, **porch lights** left on can reduce the brilliance for photographers chasing perfect star trails.

Although the waterhole lies some distance from camp, the **chorus of night sounds** here more than compensates. In the still hours, you may hear what sounds like a lion's roar but listen carefully, it could be the deep, booming call of an **ostrich** echoing through the valley.

Springbok herds and **journeys of giraffe** frequent the waterhole, joined by other grazers and browsers that wander the Auob riverbed.

Giraffe head as seen from below

Hannes Lochner

After sunset, **spotted hyenas** sometimes move among the units, drawn by the lingering scent of evening braais. **Cape foxes** and **black-backed jackals** appear, too, snapping up moths and beetles drawn to the lights. The haunting cries of jackal's drift through the night, social calls that signal to mates or summon others to a carcass.

Even the elusive **leopard** is seen here. Its long whiskers help it navigate the dark, while its powerful jaws and canines are perfectly suited to the ambush … a swift pounce, a precise bite to the neck or throat and the hunt is over.

A leopard's night vision is about **seven times better than a human's,** thanks to a reflective layer behind the retina called the **tapetum lucidum**. This adaptation allows it to hunt effectively under starlight, moving almost invisibly through the dark.

African wild cat are regularly spotted at the Kalahari Tented Camp

Black-backed jackal frequent the riverbed

Tracey Slaven

CRAIG LOCKHART CAMP

A new SANParks wilderness camping area at Craig Lockhart camp is being developed.

SITUATION AT THE TIME OF WRITING

- SANParks has been building new Craig Lockhart campsites near the Craig Lockhart waterhole close to Mata-Mata Rest Camp, intended to expand accommodation options in the park.
- These sites will offer camping in a scenic dune area, expanding beyond the existing rest camps and wilderness camps.

WHAT IS PLANNED

About seven to 10 sites are being developed behind the dunes at Craig Lockhart. Exact opening dates, booking details and facility descriptions have not been formally published by SANParks at the time of writing.

Female Pygmy falcons have a chestnut-coloured back and a red eye ring

Kathy Kay

Giraffe drinking from Craig Lockhart waterhole against the setting sun

DAWID KRUIPER CAMP

A new SANParks rest camp is being developed in the Kgalagadi Transfrontier Park, named in honour of the late Khomani San leader Dawid Kruiper.

Dawid Kruiper (c. 1935–2012) was a highly respected **Khomani San elder**, storyteller, tracker and cultural custodian from the southern Kalahari. He became the public face of the Khomani San people during their long struggle to regain ancestral land inside what is now the **Kgalagadi Transfrontier Park**.

Kruiper was instrumental in the landmark **1999 land restitution settlement**, which restored land rights to the Khomani San and led to the establishment of community-owned conservation and tourism initiatives, including **!Xaus Lodge**. A gifted oral historian, he shared San knowledge of tracking, plants, animals and survival in the Kalahari, helping bridge indigenous wisdom and modern conservation.

Naming **Dawid Kruiper Camp** in his honour acknowledges not only his leadership and resilience, but also the deep cultural roots of the Kalahari landscape and the people who lived with it for millennia; an especially meaningful recognition in a park where wilderness and human history are inseparable.

The new camp was **announced by SANParks in 2017** as part of expanded tourism infrastructure in the park. It is being developed in the area between the **!Ae!Hai Kalahari Heritage Park** and the **Auob River**, within what is known as the park's V-Zone where the Khomani San and Mier communities hold preferential commercial development rights. Funding was allocated to build the camp, with SANParks operating it and a share of the benefits go to the local communities.

Plans envisaged the camp having about 10 accommodation units (a mix of two-bed and four-bed chalets), a reception building, swimming pool and internal roads. At the time of writing, the construction was still underway.

The secretarybird is a raptor hunting prey in the riverbed

The kori bustard is the heaviest flying bird and often seen in pairs

Ludwig's bustard is an uncommon nomad and a partial migrant to the Kgalagadi

Hamman Prinsloo

Botswana wilderness campsites

Camping areas in the Botswana section of the Kgalagadi

Camping on the Botswana side of the Kgalagadi Transfrontier Park is divided into **three very different types of experiences**, and visitors should understand the distinction before planning a trip.

Two Rivers Camp is situated at the international border opposite Twee Rivieren. It serves mainly as an **entry and administrative campsite** for visitors entering the park from Botswana. Facilities are basic but include ablutions. It is not a wilderness destination like the other Botswana camps and is generally used as a **stopover at the border gate** rather than a place, to spend several nights exploring the park. For more information contact tworiverscampsite2025@gmail.com.

Further north in the Nossob valley lie the **true wilderness campsites of Rooiputs and Polentswa**. These two camps are located directly along the Nossob riverbed, accessible from the main tourist road, yet offering a level of solitude and wildness that feels far removed from conventional rest camps.These small unfenced camps offer only the most basic facilities and provide an exceptional sense of solitude and immersion in the Kalahari. Wildlife sightings around these sites can be excellent, particularly predators along the Nossob riverbed.

A third and quite separate camping region is found in the **Mabuasehube area** on the eastern side of the park. Here camps are located around large fossil pans and are accessed by **4×4 dune routes** from Nossob or from outside the park in Botswana. Mabuasehube camping is more spread out and typically forms part of **longer overland or 4×4 trail itineraries** rather than a stay along the riverbed system.

Understanding these differences will help you choose the camping experience that best suits your interests.

TWO RIVERS CAMPSITE

The Two Rivers Campsite was previously operated by the Wildlife Department. Management of the campsite has since transitioned to the **Boravast Community Trust**, which now oversees its operations and maintenance. The campsite is unfenced, offering a natural experience in the Kgalagadi area. There are **four designated camping grounds**, each equipped with shelter structures. Visitors are required to bring their own tents, as the shelters are not enclosed. An ablution block is available for use by all tourists staying at the site. Bookings can be made via email or through phone or WhatsApp at +26773415687.

ROOIPUTS CAMPSITE

Rooiputs camping site is situated in the **Botswana side** of the Kgalagadi Transfrontier Park, approximately **25 km north of Twee Rivieren** along the Nossob riverbed road. This is a small, unfenced **camp among red dunes and camelthorn trees**, close to the Rooiputs waterhole. Being unfenced means wildlife, including predators, roams freely through the camp, so vigilance is important, especially at dusk and dawn.

You need a **4x4 vehicle** to reach the camp. The last stretch of road is soft sand, so a high-clearance 4x4 with lowered tyre pressures is strongly recommended for self-drive visitors.

Rooiputs does not have cottage or chalet accommodation. The campsite generally has **basic amenities**: shared A-frame sites, long-drop toilets, cold-water showers, fireplaces for cooking (bring your own firewood or gas) and wash-up areas. Water may be available for washing but should **not be relied on for drinking**; bring all drinking and cooking water with you.

Night driving is prohibited and campers should not wander outside tents after dark. Fires are permitted only in designated fireplaces; **collecting firewood in the park is illegal**, so bring your own or a gas stove. Keep food secured and least accessible to animals.

Campsites are managed by the **Botswana Department of Wildlife and National Parks (DWNP)** and must be booked in advance through DWNP reservations. The number of bookings and nights at each site is limited to preserve the wilderness experience. Permits are issued for specific sites and dates – you **may not change sites without prior permission**.

The closest shop and petrol station is at Twee Rivieren.

Rooiputs offers a **classic bush camping experience**: remote, quiet and rich in wildlife. The constant presence of animals and tracks around camp creates a vibrant, immersive wilderness feel.

Beware of predators in this wilderness camp

Anja Denker

The shade is meant for campers, but lions don't understand this

Anja Denker

When the opportunity presents itself, lions will pursue prey into the camp

Zack Rheeder

POLENTSWA CAMPSITE

Polentswa lies in the **far northern reaches of the Kgalagadi Transfrontier Park**, on the **Botswana side of the Nossob fossil riverbed**, close to the South African border. It is reached from **Nossob Camp (South Africa)** via a long, sandy 4x4 track and sits adjacent to the **Polentswa waterhole and pan**. Its remote position makes it one of the most isolated yet wildlife-rich camps in the park.

Polentswa is deliberately very basic, designed for experienced wilderness travellers rather than comfort-seekers. Polentswa campsite is unfenced with no water for drinking or washing, no electricity, no showers, no flush toilets (usually a simple long-drop or none at all, depending on site condition) and no rubbish disposal facilities.

Access is via deep sand and dune tracks. A **high-clearance 4x4 vehicle is essential** and tyre pressure management is critical. Bring your own drinking and washing water; all food and firewood (wood collection is prohibited); extra fuel (consumption is high in deep sand) and recovery gear (spade, compressor, tyre repair kit, snatch strap).

Lion, brown hyena, leopard and jackal regularly pass through camp, especially at night. Therefore, you should never walk away from camp after dark; never sleep outside your tent and keep food secured at all times.

Be prepared for weather extremes. Summers can become extremely hot with sand getting soft and difficult to negotiate in midday heat. Expect sudden storms and strong winds. Winter nights can get bitterly cold with minus temperatures and frost, but mild day temperatures.

Polentswa campsite is managed by the **Botswana Department of Wildlife and National Parks (DWNP)**. Booking must be done well in advance. Strict limits apply to vehicle numbers and length of stay. Check-in is normally done at Twee Rivieren for cross-border tracking and permits.

Polentswa is known for **excellent predator activity**, especially lion and brown hyena; large herbivores such as gemsbok and springbok; occasional eland moving through dune systems; and superb night sounds and spoor activity around the pan. Game densities vary but **the quality of sightings is usually exceptional**.

Polentswa is not convenient, comfortable or forgiving; no shops, fuel or help nearby and that is precisely why it is special. It offers solitude, true wilderness and the rare privilege of sleeping in a landscape where the Kalahari still feels vast, silent and untamed.

Barking gecko

Daniel Wipf

Kathy Kay

Kathy Kay

The Polentswa pan is the territory of the Polentswa clan and they regularly patrol the area

A stalking lion is pure stealth and restrained power, each step deliberate and purposeful

Private lodges and concession areas

PRIVATE LODGES OF THE KGALAGADI – AN OVERVIEW

Scattered across some of the most remote corners of the Kgalagadi Transfrontier Park lie three privately run lodges that offer a vastly different experience from the SANParks rest camps and wilderness camps. Though each lodge has its own character, setting and cultural story, they share several key features that define the unique style of lodge-based safaris in this vast semi-desert landscape.

All three lodges sit deep within the wilderness, far from any main camps. They offer **full-board accommodation**, including all meals and guided activities. Their locations were chosen for panoramic views, access to waterholes and a feeling of immersive solitude. **Cellphone coverage is limited or absent**, and accommodation is powered primarily by **solar energy**, with generators used sparingly. Night skies are among the finest in Africa, with no light pollution to dull the brilliant sweep of the Milky Way.

Because the lodges are unfenced and wildlife roams freely through and around them, guests must follow staff guidance at all times. A key element of their charm is the sense of unrestricted wilderness: lions may stroll past your cabin, jackals call through the night, and gemsbok appear silently in the dawn light.

All three lodges require **4x4 access**, either self-driven or via lodge transfer. Guests arriving in standard vehicles can leave their cars at designated points and continue with lodge staff through deep sand and dune fields. Each establishment employs and trains staff from nearby communities, providing vital employment in a region where opportunities are limited.

With these shared features in mind, the three lodges still offer diverse experiences; one deeply rooted in Bushman heritage, and two located on the Botswana side of the park overlooking classic Kalahari pans and waterholes.

Though they share similar remoteness and wilderness character, the three lodges offer distinctly different experiences:

- **!Xaus Lodge** – a cultural and landscape immersion on the ancestral land of the Khomani San and Mier communities.
- **Rooiputs Lodge** – accessible yet remarkably wild, overlooking the red dunes and a productive waterhole.
- **Polentswa Lodge** – the most remote of the three, set beside a sweeping northern pan known for exceptional predator sightings.

The king of the Kgalagadi against the rising moon

Hannes Lochner

Hannes Lochner

Leopards are often seen on night drives

!XAUS LODGE

- **Website:** www.xauslodge.co.za
- **Tel:** +27 (0)21 701 7860
- **Email:** info@xauslodge.co.za
- **Access:** Transfers depart from Kamqua picnic site, where guests meet a lodge vehicle. Self-drivers with a 4x4 may follow in convoy. Secure parking is provided behind the dunes for guest vehicles.

A remote heart of the Kalahari

!Xaus Lodge is a joint venture between the Khomani San and Mier communities and Transfrontier Parks Destinations. Reaching it is part of the experience. Guests meet lodge staff at Kamqua picnic site and then cross **91 dunes** over roughly 32 km of deep sand to arrive at the lodge, which lies tucked away in a vast, silent dune wilderness.

Water is scarce and electricity is limited to short generator periods. Days unfold at a gentle pace: guided drives, Bushman cultural experiences, dune walks, stargazing and the quiet wonder of watching animals gather at the distant water trough.

!Xaus is more than a lodge … it is a cultural homecoming. The crafts, stories and skills of the Khomani San are shared with pride, offering guests a rare opportunity to engage with one of the world's oldest living cultures in an authentic setting.

Perched high on a dune, the lodge overlooks the large, heart-shaped !Xaus Pan (meaning 'heart' in the Nama language). The pan may briefly hold water after exceptional rains,

The huge heart-shaped pan is usually dry, but a waterhole attracts a variety of wildlife

The !Xaus lodge is situated on a sand dune overlooking a heart-shaped pan

but it is usually dry, a pale, shimmering basin framed by red-ochre dunes. From your deck, you may watch lion, cheetah or gemsbok visiting the drinking trough below. In the dry months, the muted tones of sand and thornbush dominate; after rain, the desert transforms into a sea of fresh greens and waving grasses.

Land, heritage and renewal

!Xaus Lodge stands on the ancestral land of the Mier and Khomani San peoples. Under the !Ae!Hai Kalahari Heritage Park Agreement (2002), this land was returned to its original custodians, South Africa's first successful land claim of its kind. The lodge now provides vital employment and skills development in a region where opportunities are scarce. Today, an estimated 3.4 percent of the Mier Municipality's population directly depends on the lodge.

Local staff are trained as guides, trackers, cooks and hosts, interpreting both the natural and cultural heritage of this extraordinary landscape. Employment decisions are shared between the community and lodge managers, ensuring both ownership and pride remain local.

Visitors are welcomed into the living traditions of the San. At the nearby cultural village, modern San men and women demonstrate traditional crafts, tracking techniques and the use of medicinal plants. Elders who grew up here before the park was proclaimed share vivid memories of hunting, healing and life on the dunes.

Despite the pressures of modernity – poverty, illness and disconnection from ancestral lands – these communities maintain a deep respect for nature and a quiet resilience. Through tourism, their stories and knowledge continue to find new life.

The spirit of the dunes

Activities at !Xaus Lodge are immersive and sensory. Guided walks reveal the desert's hidden life: healing plants, water-bearing roots and the intricate architecture of shepherd's and camelthorn trees. Night drives unveil springhares, Cape foxes, aardwolves and occasionally aardvark or pangolin.

Yet the greatest treasure is the silence; vast, peaceful and almost tangible. Sitting on a dune as the sun sinks and the stars ignite, you feel the immensity of the desert and your own smallness within it. The experience is humbling, renewing and deeply personal. A journey not only into the Kalahari, but into yourself.

Members of the San community

TA SHEBUBE ROOIPUTS LODGE

- **Website:** www.tashebube.co.bw
- **Tel:** +267 316 1696
- **Mobile:** +267 715 78568
- **Email:** info@tashebube.co.bw
- **Turn-off:** S26°19'25" E20°44'14"
- **Access:** ±25 km north of Twee Rivieren on the Nossob River road. A 4x4 is essential for the final deep-sand section.
- **Closest SANParks camp:** Twee Rivieren (25 km)

A red dune refuge

Rooiputs takes its name from the *rooi* ('red') sands of the Nossob riverbed, but staff enjoy pointing out that red has other meanings too: love and danger. Both apply here. It is easy to fall in love with this peaceful, dune-fringed lodge. Yet, without fences, predators sometimes wander through camp, a reminder that this is true wilderness.

The chalets at Rooiputs lodge

Set along a mature red sand dune on the Botswana side of the park, Rooiputs overlooks a waterhole that draws wildlife throughout the day. While close to the park's main gate, it feels remote and uncrowded, a quiet frontier of the Kalahari where the rhythms of nature shape daily life.

The Rooiputs lion family

Lion are part of the lodge's identity. Staff know individuals by sight, understand the pride structure, and follow births, disappearances and the fortunes of young males pushed out to make their own way. The full pride of around 14 is seldom together, but when a kill happens, the news spreads by roaring and lions gather from across the dunes to feed.

During droughts, predators thrive. Prey animals must visit the scarce waterholes and lions simply wait. When rains return and grazing improves, herbivores disperse into the dunes, forcing lions to walk great distances and cubs are the first to feel the strain.

The pride regularly relaxes around the lodge buildings, sometimes lying in the shade beneath the raised decks for hours on end. Guests are accompanied to their chalets after dark, and staff keep a close watch during the day; exhilarating moments, but always a reminder of the wildness of this place.

Leopards, cheetahs and night creatures

For years, Warona – a well-known leopard from the Kgalagadi Leopard Project – frequently visited the lodge. She was often seen resting on the patio couch or drinking at the swimming pool, untroubled by observers. Once, she even arrived with two young cubs in tow. When absent from camp, she was usually spotted on the nearby calcrete ridge where caves offer perfect leopard shelter.

Cheetahs avoid the lodge when lions are present but may be seen in the surrounding dunes and Nossob riverbed, typically near springbok herds. Older and weaker springbok are their preferred prey.

Rooms overlook a waterhole

The rustic dining room matches the mood of the Kgalagadi

Barn owls nest in cavities nearby and sometimes glide past the chalets in a flash of white, hunting rodents attracted to the grasslands. Cape foxes have a den close to camp and occasionally slip into the circle of light at night. Genets are bolder and may investigate the dining area after dark.

An eco-friendly desert retreat

Rooiputs is an upmarket yet environmentally sensitive lodge, built to "experience the desert without having to rough it". Eleven elegant units – nine chalets, a family unit, and a desert suite with an outdoor bath – are spaced along the dune, each with its own deck facing the waterhole. Rooms feature canvas-and-wood construction, open-air showers, quality linen and warm ethnic décor.

The central lodge area is open-fronted, raised on timber decking and cooled by natural airflow. Solar power provides electricity, with generator backup on cloudy days. Winter nights can be icy, and the lodge supplies hot water bottles and thick blankets.

Activities and atmosphere

Guided morning, afternoon, sunset and full-day game drives explore both riverbeds and surrounding dunes. Educational nature walks close to camp reveal desert tracks, plants and small creatures. Evenings are ideal for stargazing through the lodge telescope, with the Milky Way arching brilliantly across the dark Kalahari sky.

Children over eight are welcome but a private vehicle is compulsory for families. Predators are regularly present within the camp and supervision is essential.

The lounge area

TA SHEBUBE POLENTSWA LODGE

- **Website:** www.tashebube.co.bw
- **Tel:** +267 316 1696
- **Mobile:** +267 715 78568
- **Email:** info@tashebube.co.bw
- **Turn-off:** S25°05'37" E20°24'33" from the Nossob road
- **Access:** ±59–60 km north of Nossob Camp on the Nossob riverbed road. 4x4 essential.
- **Closest SANParks camp:** Nossob (59 km)

The far northern pan country

Polentswa Lodge is the most remote of the Ta Shebube camps, a quiet frontier in the far northern dune veld, where a vast, dry pan stretches to the horizon. From your balcony, the view feels almost timeless, inviting you to imagine what this sweeping basin looked like millions of years ago when the Nossob still flowed.

The lodge stands on the edge of Polentswa Pan, a place shaped by ancient rivers, shifting dunes and geological change. The Nossob once joined the Molopo and flowed westward into the prehistoric Kalahari River. Over millions of years, the continent warped and tilted; river systems were captured, rerouted and finally choked by sand. Today, the Nossob flows only after exceptional rains, perhaps once or twice in a century.

The pan remains dry, etched with spoor in every direction, while a waterhole at the base of the dune draws a steady procession of wildlife.

Hans Schwabe, the geologist who searched these dunes for answers, is buried at the start of the Polentswa Pan track, a quiet tribute to the mysteries still held in this landscape.

A remote desert refuge

Polentswa's isolation is part of its appeal. Solar power, generator backup and purified (but naturally salty) borehole water keep the lodge running comfortably in a region with no cell signal. Emergency satellite communication is available at the office.

Only 4x4 vehicles can reach the lodge. Guests in 4x2 vehicles may leave their cars at Nossob and enjoy a scenic transfer. Because of the distance, travellers arriving in Upington should consider an overnight stop at Rooiputs before continuing north to Polentswa.

The tented camp overlooks the vast Polentswa Pan

The smart tented rooms of Polentswa camp

Life on the pan edge

Perched on the dune crest, the lodge looks out across the wide curve of Polentswa Pan; a classic Kalahari scene of space, silence and endlessly shifting light. Game viewing can be superb. Lions frequently patrol the pan's edge. Cheetahs favour the open flats, brown hyenas melt in and out at dusk, and leopard occasionally appear at the waterhole. The sheer solitude amplifies every sighting. Night skies are immense and unpolluted, and the silence is as profound as any in the park.

The Polentswa experience

Polentswa invites slow, quiet immersion. Watch the waterhole from your deck at dawn. Trace the spoor stretching across the pan. Listen for the distant call of a lion or the soft rustle of wind through dune grass. Like Rooiputs, the lodge offers guided game drives and self-drive guests may explore both the Nossob riverbed and surrounding dune country.

In every sense, Polentswa captures the essence of the northern Kalahari: remote, austere, beautiful … a place where past and present feel woven together by sand, wind and time.

Viewing deck

Choosing the best camp for your needs

Main rest camps

Choosing the right camp can shape your entire Kgalagadi experience. Each rest camp, wilderness camp and lodge offers a different balance of comfort, access, solitude and wildlife viewing. Some are ideal for first-time visitors and families, others suit photographers, birders or travellers seeking deep wilderness and silence. This section highlights the strengths and limitations of each camp to help you match your expectations, interests and available time with the place that will suit you best.

TWEE RIVIEREN CAMP

If you want service and convenience, Twee Rivieren is the best choice.

- Twee Rivieren serves as the primary entry point for most travellers visiting the Kgalagadi.
- The camp operates as the central hub for essential services, including bookings, permits and visitor information.
- It is family friendly and offers the full range of services, i.e. shop, fuel station, restaurant, best cellphone reception and accommodation options.
- From here you have easy access to the major self-drive routes and roads.
- Twee Rivieren tends to be noticeably busier compared to other camps within the park, particularly during peak season.
- Be prepared for an active atmosphere in comparison to Mata-Mata and Nossob, with higher foot traffic and more frequent interactions with fellow visitors.
- Animals are present, but not as frequently at waterholes around the camp compared to Nossob.

MATA-MATA REST CAMP

If you prefer quieter roads and dunes, solitude and good photography opportunities, Mata-Mata will suit you well.

- This is an excellent starting point for dune roads and the remote eastern side of the park.
- Fewer visitors add to the wilderness atmosphere.
- It offers good wildlife viewing along the dry Auob riverbed (a cheetah hotspot), especially early morning and late afternoon.
- The scenic riverbed setting offers delightful views, good for photography.
- The shop is smaller and offers fewer facilities than at Twee Rivieren.
- Limited cellphone reception and fuel not always available.
- Close to farming activities beyond the Namibian border.
- Long drives to and from other camps, especially Nossob.

NOSSOB REST CAMP

If your focus is predator density and remoteness, choose Nossob. Best for dedicated wildlife watchers, photographers and birders.

- Waterholes at and near the camp attract lion, hyena, predators and large antelope.
- The feeling of remote wilderness and striking quiet and openness is appealing.
- The waterhole at the camp is great for raptors and nocturnal sightings.
- The panoramas across the classic red sands and scrub is great for photography.
- There are fewer services, the shop is small and fuel not always guaranteed.
- Cellphone reception is patchy or absent.
- Fewer accommodation options; therefore, it is difficult to get a booking.
- It is furthest from the park entry points and central booking offices.
- A balanced itinerary would be to stay at Twee Rivieren to begin with, then explore Mata-Mata and end your trip at Nossob.

Wilderness camps

The wilderness camps of the Kgalagadi Transfrontier Park offer a rare opportunity to experience the desert at its most intimate and unfiltered. Facilities are deliberately simple, access is often challenging, and self-reliance is essential, but the reward is a deep sense of solitude and connection with one of Africa's last great arid wildernesses. For visitors seeking quiet, space and authenticity rather than convenience, these camps represent the very essence of the Kgalagadi experience.

All these camps are unfenced wilderness camps; predators roam freely and children under 12 are not allowed at most. None has shops or fuel; bring all supplies and drinking water.

GROOTKOLK WILDERNESS CAMP

If you are seeking true wilderness and solitude and prepared for long self-drive logistics, you will love this camp.

- Situated in the northwestern Kgalagadi, this classic wilderness camp offers excellent peace, privacy and is extremely remote.
- The camp overlooks a waterhole with good general wildlife sightings.
- Accessible by ordinary passenger vehicles.
- Getting there requires about a 7½ hour drive from Twee Rivieren.
- Must bring all food, water and wood.
- No fences and wildlife passes freely through the camp.
- No children under 12 allowed.

Lioness and cubs

GHARAGAB WILDERNESS CAMP

If you are an adventurous 4×4 traveller and enjoy dune driving and tranquillity, Gharagab is an ideal destination.

- Great dune-road access and classic Kalahari scenery.
- Comfortable canvas tents and basic self-catering facilities.
- Wild, unfenced, peaceful environment with occasional predators visiting camp.
- Fun 4x4 drive into and out of camp over red dunes.
- Strict 4x4 access only and long driving distances from other camps.
- Bring your own supplies; no shops, fuel or reception.
- Remote location means less flexibility for short visits.
- No children under 12 allowed.

BITTERPAN WILDERNESS CAMP

If you are an experienced 4x4 driver who enjoys exploring the central dune belt and unseen tracks, Bitterpan will be a good destination for you.

- The camp is elevated above the dunes with views and a nearby waterhole.
- As the camp is central in the dune wilderness, it provides a base for extended dune routes
- The camp provides a different corridor of wildlife movement, especially predators.
- Strictly 4x4 access only via sandy, one-way tracks from Nossob.
- Very little driving opportunity once at camp aside from the one-way loop.
- Bring all supplies and water; no shops or fuel close by.
- No fences and basic facilities; children under 12 not allowed.

URIKARUUS WILDERNESS CAMP

If you want remote riverbed wildlife viewing in a slightly more comfortable setting, you will love Urikaruus.

- A popular wilderness camp with attractive stilted riverside cabins overlooking the Auob riverbed.
- Great position for game viewing; animal movement along the riverbed is frequent.
- Slightly more comfortable cabin style with kitchen and deck.
- Large fridge-freezer and self-catering conveniences.
- Book well in advance; one of the most popular wilderness camps.
- Bring all food, water and wood; unfenced with no phone reception.
- Still remote, which requires self-drive and careful planning.

KIELIEKRANKIE WILDERNESS CAMP

If it is your first visit to a wilderness camp and you are fascinated by beautiful dune vistas without deep 4x4 travel, Kieliekrankie is the best choice.

- Spectacular dune location with panoramic red sand views and a nearby waterhole.
- Highly rated by travellers for tranquillity and natural setting.
- Accessible by ordinary passenger vehicles.
- Great camp for a first night in the wilderness before deeper exploration.
- Books out quickly; reserve early.
- Must supply own water and wood; unfenced.
- Set slightly closer to Twee Rivieren, so less remote than Gharagab or Bitterpan.

KALAHARI TENTED CAMP

If you want a mix of wilderness and a slightly larger camp with good routes nearby, you will enjoy staying at the Kalahari Tented Camp.

- Largest wilderness camp with more units; slightly higher chance of availability.
- Spacious canvas tents on stilts overlooking a waterhole in the Auob valley.
- Comfortable self-catering layout with kitchen equipment and storage.
- Good base for exploring both north and south dune roads.
- Unfenced and remote; supply your own food, water and wood.
- Long drive from Twee Rivieren or Nossob.
- Less intimate than smaller camps simply because it has more units.

Private lodges

The three privately operated lodges within the Kgalagadi Transfrontier Park offer a distinctive way to experience this vast semi-desert, combining exceptional remoteness with the ease of fully catered stays and expert guidance. Located deep within the park and accessible only by four-wheel-drive vehicles or lodge transfer, these lodges provide access to areas rarely reached by self-drive visitors. While each lodge has its own character and setting, they share a commitment to low-impact operations, unfenced wilderness living and close encounters with wildlife at waterholes and pans. For travellers who value solitude, interpretation and comfort, these lodges offer an immersive and rewarding alternative to self-catering camps.

!XAUS LODGE (SAN AND MIER)

- If you seek deep cultural engagement, peace, silence, stargazing and authentic Kalahari wilderness experiences, visiting this lodge is a 'must' for you.
- Here you will experience a meaningful connection to the Khomani San and Mier communities, offering storytelling, craft demonstrations, guided walks and cultural interpretation that you will not find at other lodges.
- Perched on a dune overlooking the vast heart-shaped !Xaus Pan, it brings you deep into Kalahari silence and space.
- A water trough is visible from the decks of the rooms, which draws wildlife such as gemsbok, predators and smaller mammals.
- The lodge is small and personal with strong emphasis on storytelling, interpretation and experiential immersion.
- 4x4 access only; deep sand driving from Kamqua picnic site. Transfers and timings must be pre-arranged.
- No fuel, cellphone reception, Wi-Fi or TV; electricity is generated only at set times.
- Low-key facilities reflect wilderness immersion rather than comfort luxury.

TA SHEBUBE ROOIPUTS LODGE (BOTSWANA)

If you prefer comfortable lodge amenities, great waterhole wildlife viewing and accessible game drives, with less emphasis on extreme remoteness, then Rooiputs Lodge is perfect.

- Overlooking dunes and a well-used waterhole, it is often a magnet for predators and grazing.
- While 4x4 is recommended on the last sandy stretch, sedan travellers can park at Twee Rivieren and obtain transfers.
- Spacious chalets on wooden decks with quality beds, bathrooms and a thatched lounge/dining area.
- Lodge with bar/restaurant, pool and communal spaces.
- Close enough to the park entrance for convenient day game drives.
- Being closer to the park gate (≈25 km from Twee Rivieren), it is busier and does not feel as remote as Polentswa or !Xaus.
- Electricity is by solar and backup generator; reliable but more basic than full-service lodges.
- No fuel or extensive facilities nearby.

TA SHEBUBE POLENTSWA LODGE (BOTSWANA)

If you seek maximum remoteness, quiet solitude, uninterrupted pan views and deep wilderness immersion, there is no better place than Polentswa Lodge.

- This is one of the most remote lodges in the entire Kgalagadi, located beside a sweeping dry pan deep in the Botswana wilderness.

Three sub-adult cheetahs

Myburgh du Plessis

Myburgh du Plessis

Springbok are the preferred prey for cheetah

- The pan attracts predators and antelope across wide vistas, and the isolation often means minimal other vehicles or lodges nearby.
- The lodge works on solar energy and backup generators. Has borehole water purification.
- Waterhole and pan views regularly produce sightings without long drives.
- Requires 4x4 access and is very remote; guests with sedan vehicles must generally park at Nossob and obtain a transfer.
- Nearest fuel is at Nossob/Twee Rivieren; plan well in advance.
- Only emergency satellite contact; no cellphone reception or guest Wi-Fi.
- Long drive to the lodge means careful itinerary planning (often via a stop at Rooiputs).

Myburgh du Plessis

Playfulness is part of growing up

Camping in Botswana

Camping in the Botswana section of the Kgalagadi Transfrontier Park is a true wilderness experience, reserved for those who value solitude, self-reliance and unfiltered immersion in the desert landscape. This vast eastern portion of the park is remote, lightly visited and deliberately undeveloped, offering a sense of space and silence that is increasingly rare. Campsites are simple, unfenced and set beside expansive pans or fossil riverbeds, where wildlife moves freely and nature dictates the pace of each day. There are no shops, fuel stations or modern comforts here, only sand, sky, wind and the beauty of the Kalahari. For well-prepared travellers, Botswana camping delivers one of southern Africa's most authentic and rewarding wilderness adventures.

Keep in mind:

- 4x4 access is essential; high-clearance vehicles with good sand tyres are recommended.
- Botswana camps are unfenced, offering true wilderness immersion. Predators move through camps at night.
- Facilities are basic; campers must be self-sufficient with water, fuel, food and gear.
- Camps are booked through the Botswana Department of Wildlife and National Parks (DWNP) and often limited to one night per site to preserve solitude.
- No shops, fuel or cellphone coverage in the Mabuasehube area; plan accordingly.

BOTSWANA CAMPSITES OFF THE NOSSOB ROAD

ROOIPUTS CAMPSITE

- Exceptionally scenic setting overlooking a productive waterhole, with frequent predator activity close to camp.
- Small, exclusive campsite with only a few stands.
- Located relatively close to Twee Rivieren, making it one of the most accessible wilderness-style camps.
- Excellent for photography, especially early morning and late afternoon when animals visit the waterhole.

POLENTSWA CAMPSITE

- One of the most remote and wild campsites set beside the vast Polentswa Pan, offering immense space, silence and a true sense of isolation.
- Outstanding predator sightings, particularly lion, leopard, cheetah and brown hyena around the pan and waterhole.
- Superb night skies and an unrivalled wilderness atmosphere for experienced, self-reliant travellers.
- Very long driving distances from Nossob or Twee Rivieren; fuel planning is critical.

MABUASEHUBE CAMPSITES (BOTSWANA)

- The Mabuasehube sector is one of the most remote and wild parts of the park, with several pans and sites clustered around them.

Serious fighting for supremacy

Peter Hall

- Immense wilderness feel; little traffic, big skies, deep silence.
- Excellent solitude and stargazing; no light pollution, minimal other visitors.
- Diverse habitats: clay-pan edges, dune fringes, thornveld and savanna.
- Wildlife across the board; predators, antelope, birds, reptiles; tracks abound.
- Waterhole views; many sites overlook pans and troughs that attract game.
- Very basic facilities; long-drop toilets and simple shade structures only (some sites have water; others do not).
- No fencing; wildlife is always close. Night walks are unsafe.
- Dust, heat, wind; exposed open country can be harsh, especially in summer.
- Fuel and supplies: none in the Mabuasehube area. The nearest dependable sources are at Nossob or Twee Rivieren.
- Navigation and route planning; roads are sandy and remote, Vehicle preparation is critical (spares, tools, recovery gear).

Daniel Wipf
African hoopoe

INDIVIDUAL SITE NOTES

- **Mabuasehube Pan** (Sites 1–4): Sweeping panoramas and solitude. Site 1: most secluded with dramatic views, but no water or facilities. Sites 2–4: share basic amenities; all overlook the pan.
- **Mpayathutlwa Pan:** Two well-spaced sites with shade and a long-drop toilet; excellent for photography and sunrise views.
- **Bosobogolo Pan:** Both sites have shade and long-drop toilets; Site 1 has a tap and shower enclosure.
- **Khiding Pan:** Bushier and more unpredictable for wildlife; close views but less open scenery.
- **Lesholoage Pan:** Two sites; Site 2 has water and a shower enclosure; a good balance of comfort and remoteness.
- **Monamodi Depression (East Gate):** Three sites near a more established area: full ablution facilities and drinking water. Good for entry/exit nights.

OTHER BOTSWANA CAMPS OUTSIDE MABUASEHUBE

SWARTPAN CAMPSITES

- Often have drinkable water in troughs near the pan.
- Shaded trees and open pan views make for pleasant camps.
- Water sources attract diverse wildlife in dry seasons.
- Can be busier because they are easier to reach.
- Shade and water are great but this also concentrates predators near camp.
- Very basic infrastructure (shade, long-drop toilets only).

GNUS GNUS AND THUPAPEDI (KHANDU)

- Quieter than Swartpan; closer to water sources in some seasons.
- Less obstructed views in many directions.
- Limited shade and fewer amenities.
- Water is less predictable; animals may move elsewhere after rain.

KAA PAN SITES

- Fantastic dune country feel and panoramic views.
- Often attract antelope, small carnivores and birds in early morning.
- Very deep sand approaching them; challenging access.
- Almost no shade; heat can be intense.

4x4 Trails

Typical 4x4 trail in the park

Gareth Salvage

Swartpan 1
Swartpan 2
Sizatswe
KAA GATE
Kaa
Thupapedi (Khandu Pan)
Kaa Game Viewing 4x4 Trail
Kannaguass/Kaa 4x4 Access Route
Polentswa Wilderness 4x4 Trail
Sesatswe
Polentswa Wilderness 4x4 Trail
Gnus Gnus
Mabua Kaa 4x4 Trail
Lang Rambuka
BOTSWANA
Unie-end
Union's End Picnic Site
Nossob
Geinab
Grootkolk
GROOTKOLK CAMP
Kannaguass
Gharagab
GHARAGAB CAMP
Gharagab 4x4 Trail
Dankbaar
Lijersdraai Picnic Site
Lijersdraai
TA SHEBUBE POLENTSWA LODGE
Polentswa
Polentswa Camp
Nossob
Kousant
Mabuasehube Wilderness 4x4 Trail
Mosomane
Langklaas
Bedinkt
Bedinkt Picnic Site
Kwang
Matopi 1
Matopi 2
Nossob/Mabuasehube 4x4 Access Route
SOUTH AFRICA
Swartbas
Cubitje Quap
NOSSOB REST CAMP
Nossob camp waterhole
Ratel
Marie se gat
Bitterpan 4x4 Trail
Rooikop
Marie's Loop
Klein Stofpan
Nossob 4x4 Ecotrail
Kaspersdraai
Cheleka
Nossob Road
BOTSWANA
BITTERPAN CAMP
MATA-MATA REST CAMP
MATA-MATA GATE
KALAHARI TENTED CAMP
Nu-Quap
Rosyntjiebos
Dikbaardskolk
Eland
Dikbaardskolk Picnic Site
Upper Dune Road
Sitsas
CRAIG LOCKHART CAMP
Strathmore
Moravet
Kameelsleep
Craig Lockhart
Dalkeith
Vaalpan
Jan se draai
14th borehole
13th borehole
Urikaruus
Auob
Witgat
Kamqua
Kamqua Picnic Site
Kransbrak
URIKARUUS CAMP
Rooibrak
Montrose
Nossob 4x4 Ecotrail
!Xaus Road
Gunong
!XAUS LODGE
Batulama
Gemsbokplein
Kij Gamies
Melkvlei Picnic Site
Melkvlei
Lower Dune Road
Auchterlonie Picnic Site
KIELIEKRANKIE CAMP
Tierkop
Auchterlonie
Kamfersboom
KijKij
Auob Road
Nossob Road
Munro
Rooiputs
TA SHEBUBE ROOIPUTS LODGE
Houmoed
Leeudril 4x4 Trail
Rooiputs Camp
DAWID KRUIPER CAMP
(under construction)
Leeudril
Samevloeiing (Confluence)
Twee Rivieren
TWEE RIVIEREN REST CAMP
Two Rivers Camp
TWEE RIVIEREN GATE

SANParks and Botswana 4x4 trails

Four-wheel-drive vehicles are increasingly popular, even among people who rarely need their capability in urban life. But for nature lovers and adventurers, a 4x4 is the key to slipping away from the crowds, breathing fresh Kalahari air and rediscovering silence. The park offers several opportunities for responsible, low-impact wilderness travel far from mainstream tourist routes. If you have a passion for wild places and an appetite for adventure, few experiences rival the Kgalagadi Transfrontier Park's 4x4 eco trails.

Eco trails in the Kgalagadi include **guided walks**, **self-drive off-road routes** and **SANParks-guided 4x4 trails**. If self-drive is not for you, several SATSA-bonded **safari operators offer guided off-road tours**. All options promise a wilderness experience of the highest order.

The Kgalagadi dune field is spectacular but **ecologically fragile**. Your aim should be to leave as little trace as possible, ideally nothing but tyre tracks. For this reason, access is controlled, numbers are limited and strict rules apply to vehicles and conduct.

Once you have booked a trail, careful preparation is essential. You will be entering true wilderness: **no shops**, **no water points**, **no fuel**, and **no cell reception**. You must be **completely self-sufficient**.

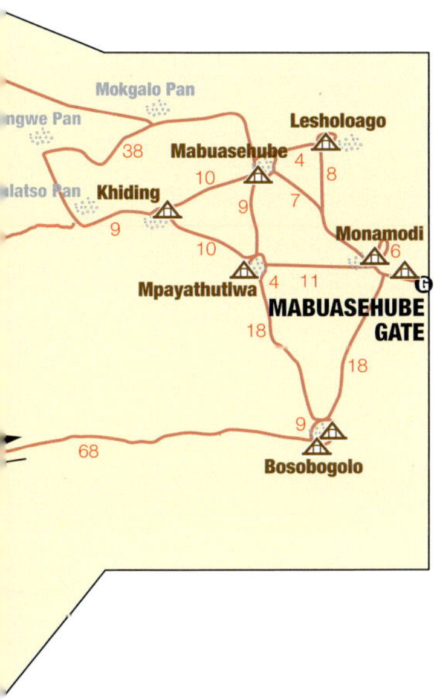

- Controlled entry
- No entry/exit
- Entrance gate
- Picnic site
- Camp site
- Camp site (A-frame)
- Rest camp
- Wilderness camp
- Lodge
- Borehole (sweet water)
- Borehole (medium water)
- Borehole (brackish water)
- Pan
- River
- Main road
- Main road (Five-star)
- 4x4 roads and trails
- Direction
- 3 Distance

Yellow devil's thorn after rains

WILDERNESS TRAIL CHECKLIST

For all Kgalagadi 4x4 eco trails

Essentials

- Valid permits and booking confirmation
- Fully serviced 4x4 with low range and high ground clearance
- Tyre compressor and tyre repair kit
- Two good spare wheels (if possible)
- Toolkit and basic spares (fan belts, fuses, hoses)
- Recovery gear: snatch strap, shovel, jack, wooden base plate
- Satellite-capable phone (recommended)

Water and food

- **Minimum 15 litres of water per person per day** (drinking and washing)
- Food for all days on the trail
- Gas stove (firewood cannot be collected in the park)
- Braai grid, firelighters and matches
- Cooler or fridge; sealed snack containers
- Basin and biodegradable soap

Camping gear

- Tent and groundsheet
- Sleeping bags and bedding
- Shade shelter for daytime meals
- Black bags for rubbish (take everything out)
- Toilet paper (burn after use)

Clothing and personal items

- Closed shoes (thorns, scorpions, snakes)
- Warm clothing for cold desert nights
- Broad-brimmed hat and long-sleeved shirt
- Sunscreen, sunglasses, lip balm
- Personal medications and first-aid kit

Navigation and safety

- Maps and GPS
- Headlamp/torch with spare batteries
- Binoculars and camera (protected from dust)
- Keep to designated tracks only
- Never travel alone unless allowed
- Reduce tyre pressure to ±1.6 bar (or lower for dunes)

Environmental care

- Leave **no trace** except tyre tracks
- Burn toilet paper; bury coals deeply
- Take all rubbish out with you
- Do not disturb wildlife or vegetation

Rules for visitor safety and park protection

- Register at entrance gate and carry permits for your booked trails
- Camp is restricted to designated, pre-booked sites
- Light fires only in provided fireplaces
- Drive only during prescribed hours
- No off-road driving
- Do not remove, damage, harass or feed any fauna or flora
- Remain in your vehicle except at designated spots
- No riding on roof-racks or any exterior part of a vehicle
- No pets are allowed in the park

Dune trails can be challenging

Gareth Salvage

Kalahari sand snake catching a tree skink

Elsie Potgieter

DRIVING ON SAND – QUICK REFERENCE GUIDE

For dune roads and 4×4 trails in the Kgalagadi

Tyres and traction

- **Deflate tyres** before entering deep sand (± **1.6 bar**; lower if needed).
- Lower pressures increase the tyre's **footprint**, improving grip and reducing track damage.
- Always **reinflate** when back on hard surfaces.

Stay on track

- Keep to **existing wheel tracks**. The sand is already compacted and the vegetation fragile.
- Avoid driving over grasses or shrubs at all times.

Use the right gears

- Engage **low range** for soft or steep dunes.
- Make **slow, smooth gear changes** at slightly higher revs.
- Momentum matters: keep it steady but controlled.

Dune safety

- Always drive **straight up or straight down** dunes.
- If a climb fails:
  - » **Reverse straight down in gear**
  - » Never turn on a slope
  - » Never coast downhill
- Crest sand is loose; be prepared for sudden loss of traction.

Stopping and pulling away

- **Coast to a stop** rather than braking hard.
- Hard braking builds sand ridges that trap wheels.
- If bogging down, **do not accelerate hard** as it only digs deeper.

If you get stuck

1. **Reverse gently** along your own compacted tracks.
2. Deflate tyres even further if needed.
3. Clear sand from behind and under the wheels; check if the chassis is resting on sand.
4. Repeat the reverse–forward manoeuvre patiently.
5. If still stuck:
   - » Use a **snatch strap** (if another vehicle is present)
   - » **Winch** or **jack** yourself out if travelling alone

Heat and hazard awareness

- Sand can exceed **60–70 °C** in midsummer.
- Avoid handling sand with bare hands; keep shoes on to prevent burns.
- Engines overheat more easily in loose, hot sand; drive gently and avoid over-revving.

Essential gear checklist

- Tyre compressor and tyre repair kit
- Shovel and recovery board (optional but helpful)
- Snatch strap/tow rope
- Basic tools and spare parts
- At least **15 litres of water per person per day** on remote trails
- Shade, hats, closed shoes, long sleeves
- Satellite messaging device if travelling alone

SANParks 4x4 trails

The following trails are within the SANParks section of the park and must be booked through SANParks.

- Leeudril 4×4 eco trail (short route)
- Nossob 4×4 eco trail
- Polentswa 4×4 eco trail
- Gharagab 4x4 trail (*See section on Wilderness Camps*)
- Bitterpan 4x4 trail (*See section on Wilderness Camps*)

LEEUDRIL 4X4 LOOP

Short route

- **Type:** Self-drive, one-way
- **Length:** ±14 km
- **Starts:** 2 km north of Leeudril waterhole
- **Ends:** Houmoed waterhole
- **Notes:** Easy, scenic dune-driving; ideal introduction to sand driving; book at Twee Rivieren
- **Booking:** SANParks permit is required

This short but rewarding route offers a gentle introduction to dune driving and the solitude of the Kalahari's interior.

Winding through soft red sand and low dune streets, the trail reveals the subtle beauty of dune-veld life; from shepherd's trees and dune grasses to larks, korhaans and the tracks of nocturnal wanderers pressed into the morning sand.

Though not technically demanding, a 4x4 is essential to protect the fragile dunes. Drive slowly, reduce tyre pressures and take time to appreciate the small wonders that flourish in this arid landscape. Booking is required at Twee Rivieren, and you must report back on completion.

NOSSOB 4X4 GUIDED ECO TRAIL

SANParks-guided

- **Type:** Guided wilderness trail (SANParks ranger accompanies the group)
- **Length:** 214 km
- **Duration:** 4 days/3 nights
- **Route:** From Twee Rivieren to Kousant and return
- **Nights:** Witgat, Rosyntjiebos and Swartbas camps
- **Notes:** Deep dune wilderness
- **Facilities:** No facilities except dry camps; fully self-sufficient
- **Booking:** Book with SANParks long in advance

This fully guided wilderness trail is a deep dive into the heart of the Kgalagadi dune field. Travelling far beyond the tourist roads, the route follows a series of long, parallel dunes between Nossob and the remote interior. Nights are spent at simple wilderness camps where the silence is profound and the stars overwhelming.

The Nossob eco trail is a guided 4x4 adventure across the Kgalagadi's dune wilderness, linking Twee Rivieren and Nossob along a remote, one-way route through the red sands. A SANParks guide leads the convoy, provides interpretation via two-way radios (supplied), and advises on driving, dune crossings and safety. A proper 4x4 with low range is essential, differential lock alone will not suffice.

The direction alternates monthly: in even months, the trail runs **Twee Rivieren** – **Nossob**, and in odd months, **Nossob** – **Twee Rivieren**. Groups depart at 09:00 on Mondays and finish on Thursdays. Bookings are essential, ideally 6–11 months ahead.

A minimum of two and a maximum of five guest vehicles are allowed (plus the guide vehicle). Trailers are not permitted. Children under 12 may not join.

Three rustic, unfenced wilderness camps – **Witgat**, **Rosyntjiebos** and **Swartbas** – offer long-drop toilets, simple shower cubicles and a braai area (bring your own grid and wood/charcoal). You must be completely self-sufficient: all food, water, shade, sleeping gear and rubbish bags must be carried in. Expect dazzling stars, nocturnal sounds and the thrill of predators passing in the dark.

Distances are considerable: ±300 km between start and next refuelling. In winter, guests finishing at Nossob are required to overnight there, as daylight hours are short.

Temperatures are extreme: **40–45 °C in summer**, with dune sand exceeding **70 °C**; winter nights may drop to **–11 °C**. Bring closed shoes, warm layers, sun protection and shade for lunch stops.

The trail winds through dune valleys and over small to medium dune belts. A few crossings require technique, but the guide will brief inexperienced drivers. You will be expected to repair any ruts you leave behind, which is part of the trail's low-impact ethic. After rains, tall grasses may clog radiators, so bring radiator protection.

Wildlife along the dunes includes bat-eared foxes, Cape foxes, jackals, Brant's whistling rats, korhaans, secretarybirds, ostrich, finches and – if luck is with you – a cheetah, leopard or lion moving between dunes.

Each vehicle receives a handheld radio to keep the group in contact, share sightings and warn of deep sand or obstacles. Interpretive stops highlight geology, dune ecology, spoor and desert adaptations.

Mating dragonfly pair

Botswana (DWNP) 4x4 trails and camping

MABUASEHUBE SOUTH ENTRANCE GATE

The **Mabuasehube South Gate** is the most commonly used entrance into the Mabuasehube sector of the Kgalagadi from inside Botswana. It lies on the eastern side of the park and is reached via long stretches of remote gravel and sand roads. This gate may be small and quiet, but it is the threshold to one of southern Africa's wildest and least disturbed protected landscapes.

How to get there

You can access Mabuasehube South Gate primarily from two directions:

1. From the town of Tsabong (Botswana)

- Tsabong is the closest supply town.
- From Tsabong, the road is initially gravel, then becomes deep sand as you approach the park.
- A **4x4 vehicle is essential** and towing is recommended only for very experienced off-roaders.
- Fuel and basic supplies are available in Tsabong but do not rely on it for everything, stock up thoroughly.

2. From South Africa via McCarthy's Rest border post

- Cross into Botswana, then continue through Tsabong to the park.
- This is a popular approach for self-drive visitors.

There is **no fuel, shop, tyre repair service or mobile phone signal** anywhere near the gate or within the Mabuasehube section, so **self-reliance is mandatory**.

What to expect at the gate

The South Entrance Gate is **very small, basic and functional**.

TYPICAL FEATURES INCLUDE:

- A small office or ranger post for **registration and permit checks**
- Limited or no water
- No fuel or workshop services
- No shop or supplies
- No formal accommodation at the gate itself
- Often **no cell signal**

You simply **check in, confirm itinerary and proceed into the wilderness**.

Swallow-tailed bee-eater

A different face of the Kgalagadi

Sabine Locher

ABOUT MABUASEHUBE (BOTSWANA)

The **Mabuasehube area** forms the remote eastern arm of the Kgalagadi and is one of the most pristine semi-desert wilderness areas in southern Africa. It is known for its **vast pans, huge horizons, sparse visitor numbers and intense solitude**.

LANDSCAPE AND HABITAT

- A network of **large salt-rich pans**, each surrounded by semi-arid savanna.
- **Low, rolling dunes** and heavy red sand.
- Vegetation is dominated by **camelthorn**, **blackthorn** and **silver cluster-leaf**, with wide open grasslands around the pans.

Wildlife

Although wildlife densities are lower than in the riverbeds near Nossob and Twee Rivieren, sightings can be exceptional because of the openness and isolation.

SPECIES YOU MAY ENCOUNTER:

- **Black-maned lions** (well-known residents, often at campsites)
- **Cheetah**, **leopard**, **brown hyena**, **bat-eared fox**, **honey badger**
- **Eland**, **kudu**, **gemsbok**, **springbok**, **wildebeest**
- **Meerkat** and **aardwolf**, especially near pans

The animals here are **wilder and less habituated** than those around busy tourist zones. Expect limited sightings.

Camping

ALL CAMPSITES IN MABUASEHUBE ARE:

- Unfenced
- Widely spaced
- Very private
- Rustic with minimal facilities

TYPICAL CAMPSITE FACILITIES:

- A-frame shade shelter
- Long-drop toilet
- Occasional bucket-shower enclosure
- Some sites have water, others do not
- No electricity, no cell service, no fencing

Who should go

MABUASEHUBE IS PERFECT FOR:

- Self-reliant overlanders
- Photographers drawn to minimalism and silence
- Travellers seeking **deep solitude**
- Naturalists and trackers
- Those with **true 4x4 and desert-camping competence**

It is **not ideal** for travellers who require daily comforts, regular sightings or easy logistics.

Booking is essential

Department of Wildlife & National Parks (DWNP)
PO Box 131, Gaborone, Botswana
Tel: +267 318 0774
Email: dwnp@gov.bw

The **Mabuasehube area** has seven camp clusters, each with two to four individual sites, totalling 17 campsites. Camps are named after the pans they overlook (except *Entrance Gate*). Two camps, **Mpayathutlwa** and **Mabuasehube**, are privately managed by the *Inter-Tourism Group* (Email: traveloptions@inter-tourismgroup.com).

WILDERNESS TRACKS LINKING THE MABUA PANS

Main circular route

- Mpayathutlwa – Monamodi
- Monamodi – Khiding
- Khiding – Lesholoago
- Various interlinking dune tracks between pans
- Mostly self-drive, deep sand
- Booking with Botswana DWNP required

The Mabuasehube section of the Kgalagadi Transfrontier Park comprises a series of large, striking pans that form the main focus of this remote wilderness. Campsites are positioned around the edges of these pans, many on slight rises with near-uninterrupted views that are ideal for quiet game viewing straight from camp. A network of 4x4 sand tracks links the pans, offering access to one of the most isolated areas of the park, far beyond the reach of mainstream tourism.

A main circular route connects the three largest pans – **Bosobogolo, Mpayathutlwa and Mabuasehube** – while **Lesholoage, Khiding** and the **Monamodi fossil valley** lie off the loop via sandy spurs. The terrain is gently undulating, dunes are modest in height, and the substrate is heavy Kalahari sand. Vegetation is classic arid savanna: open grassland interspersed with camelthorn, raisin bush and other hardy shrubs.

All major predators occur here, including **Kalahari black-maned lion, cheetah, leopard, brown hyena, caracal** and **bat-eared fox**. Smaller nocturnal mammals such as **Cape fox, aardwolf** and **black-footed cat** may appear after sunset, and **wild dog** are occasionally reported. Although visitors may not drive before sunrise or after dark, unfenced campsites overlooking the pans allow wildlife to pass silently through during the night. Lion frequently rest in shaded camping areas, and groups of two or three are often encountered rather than full prides. These lions are truly wild and unhabituated. Always remain alert.

Game is widespread and not guaranteed. For wildlife density, the **Nossob and Auob fossil riverbeds** remain the most productive areas. For solitude and wilderness, **Mabuasehube is unmatched**.

Travelling on the Botswana side requires complete self-sufficiency. The roads are narrow, soft and often grassed in summer. Deep sand driving dramatically increases fuel consumption, and **Nossob – ±8 hours away – is the only semi-reliable fuel source**. Carry at least double the capacity of your vehicle's main tank. Ample drinking water, recovery gear and spare tyres are essential.

Each pan is distinct. Mabuasehube Pan – clay floor rich in salts attracting wildlife for mineral licking. **Bosobogolo Pan** – short, shrubby grassland grazed by antelope and predators. **Mpayathutlwa Pan** – open views across grass-covered calcrete; scenic and rewarding after rain.

Campsites are unfenced and vary from **very basic** to **simple bush-style facilities** (A-frame shelters, long-drop toilets, occasional water points and shower enclosures). Bring **all drinking water**. Sites overlooking Mabuasehube Pan are especially recommended, with Site 1 offering the greatest privacy and views but **no facilities**. Other sites have shared rudimentary amenities. Some are close to the access road while others are more secluded.

With no light pollution, night skies are exceptional, particularly in winter when the Milky Way stretches overhead in a dense, shimmering band.

These trails require careful planning and bookings with Botswana's DWNP.

Sabine Locher

Sunsets are often dramatic

MABUASEHUBE CAMPSITE COMPARISON TABLE

Facilities in Botswana's wilderness camps may change over time; always confirm before travelling.

PAN/ CAMPSITE	NUMBER OF SITES	FACILITIES	SHADE	WATER	VIEW	NOTES AND CHARACTER
Mabuasehube Pan (Sites 1–4)	4	A-frames, long-drops, some shower enclosures	Good	Limited/ variable	Excellent	Site 1 very private and wild; 2 and 3 share facilities; 4 central and scenic
Mpayathutlwa Pan	2	A-frames, long-drops	Good	None/ varies	Superb	Big sky views; favoured for photography
Bosobogolo Pan	2	A-frames, long-drops; site 1 has shower enclosure and tap	Moderate	Site 1 only	Wide and open	Classic pan ambience
Khiding Pan	2	A-frames, long-drops	Moderate	None	Limited from camp	Bushier, predators may appear close and quietly
Lesholoage Pan	2	A-frames, long-drops; site 2 has water and shower enclosure	Moderate	Site 2 only	Good	Remote and little-visited
Monamodi Depression (East Gate)	3	A-frames, long-drops, full ablution block with water	Moderate	Yes	Limited	Closest to gate, useful for arrivals and departures
Matopi 1 and 2 (Transit Route)	2	No facilities at all	Limited	None	None	For en route overnighting exclusively

- **Most private:** *Mabuasehube Pan Site 1*
- **Best photography foreground:** *Mpayathutlwa Pan and Bosobogolo Pan*
- **Most useful for first/last night:** *Monamodi*

The campsites are unfenced – beware of the resident predators

Daniel Wipf

Daniel Wipf

A typical campsite scene at Mabuasehube

Predator-safety awareness notes

Mabuasehube is completely unfenced and lions are known to **sleep, hunt, vocalise, scent mark and raise cubs** around campsites. Most incidents occur due to **food, water or human scent rewards**.

Golden rules

- **Never** walk far from camp or into bushes, especially at dawn, dusk and night.
- **Do not leave food, braai grids, dishes or grey water** outside; lions and hyenas investigate smells.
- **Sleep inside a tent or rooftop tent**, not in an open shelter.
- **Sit with a view**; always keep a headlamp and torch within reach.
- **Do not run** if a predator approaches; move slowly to a safe position.
- **Teach children** rules before arrival; do not let them wander.
- **Use red light at night** to protect night vision and reduce attraction.
- **Never throw bones or leftovers into the bush**; it habituates predators.

Subtle warning signs to watch for

- A sudden silence in bird or jackal calls
- Dust clouds or oxpeckers on the move
- Fresh tracks around camp on arrival
- Repeated hyena circling behaviour
- Lion scent-marking structures or vehicle tyres

Most common visitors

- Lion, brown hyena, honey badger, black-backed jackal, African wild cat, leopard (rare but possible).

NOSSOB TO AND FROM BOSOBOGOLO AND MABUA GATE

Direct access road to the Mabuasehube area (public road)

- **Route type:** Two-way transfer road
- **Permit:** Get permission (permit) to drive this road
- **GPS:** S25°25'15" E20°35'49" (Nossob) S25°14'37" E22°02'60" (Bosobogolo)
- **Distance:** 160 km (Nossob to Bosobogolo) + 26 km to Mabua Gate
- **Travel:** Two-way, singletrack, **4x4 only**
- **Overnight:** Matopi 1 or Matopi 2 camp
- **Notes:** Crosses deep dune fields and long stretches of grassy sand track

This road is used primarily by travellers moving between Mabuasehube and Nossob without joining the guided trail, this remote route crosses deep dune fields and long stretches of grassy sand track. Camping at the two Matopi sites is completely primitive; no water, no facilities and no protection from wildlife. Perfect for seasoned travellers seeking authentic wilderness solitude.

The road linking Nossob with the Mabuasehube East Gate is a **183 km**, two-way direct access route. Although often referred to as a public road, you **must** have the necessary **park permissions** and **confirmed campsite bookings** on either side before travelling.

A **proper 4x4** is required, but the road can be driven solo with adequate preparation. The first **30–40 km** from the Nossob side are sandy with several dune crossings; thereafter, the road is generally firm but **heavily corrugated**.

Reducing tyre pressure to ±1.2 bar will improve traction and comfort. As it is a **singletrack**, remain alert for oncoming vehicles and use passing points where necessary.

Trailers are **not recommended**, especially when travelling **eastwards from Nossob**, where soft sand, tight turns and dune ascents can lead to **jackknifing** or mechanical damage. Experienced off-roaders have towed trailers and off-road caravans here, but conditions vary and caution is essential.

The **160 km** between Nossob and Bosobogolo typically takes **6–8 hours**. Two rustic overnight stops – **Matopi 1** and **Matopi 2** – are positioned midway. Both have **no facilities**, just a level patch beneath a **shepherd's tree** or **camelthorn** for shade.

These campsites offer **utter solitude**, unpolluted air and **true wilderness atmosphere**, where nights are marked by silence, stars and the distant (or not-so-distant) **roar of lions**. Camps are **unfenced** and visitors must take full responsibility for their own safety.

Typical campsite

Daniel Wipf

Daniel Wipf

Vultures are ever-present at kills

MABUASEHUBE WILDERNESS 4X4 TRAIL (GUIDED)

Often simply called the Mabuasehube 4x4 trail

- **Type:** Guided transboundary wilderness trail
- **Distance:** ±155 km
- **Route:** From Mabuasehube Khiding (Botswana side) – Nossob (SA side)
- **Nights:** Mosomane camp GPS: S25°07'94" E21°24'80"
- **Notes:** Crosses the wildest, most remote dune country; one-way (east to west) owing to dune orientation; advanced sand driving required
- **Duration:** 2 days/1 night
- **Vehicle:** High-clearance 4x4 with low-range only; **no trailers**
- **Bookings: DWNP advance booking required** for trail access and campsites

If you wish to get off the beaten track and explore areas few visitors ever see, this trail is an excellent choice. It is more than a wildlife-viewing opportunity. It offers rare access to remote parts of the park that remain largely untouched. The route runs east to west across the Kgalagadi, starting in Botswana and ending in South Africa on the western bank of the Nossob River.

There is a single overnight stop at **Mosomane Pan**, where **no facilities exist whatsoever**. To maintain a true sense of isolation, only one group may book the trail at a time (minimum two four-wheel-drive vehicles travelling together). This solitude is a major part of its appeal. Technically it is not a difficult drive; the route consists of sandy tracks with a few low dune crossings, but **no trailers are permitted**.

Travel must be in convoy, with a compulsory overnight stop at the designated campsite. There are **no camp markers**, so a GPS is essential.

Wildlife sightings may include **eland, kudu, meerkats and brown hyena**, with attractive stands of **silver cluster-leaf** (*Terminalia*) along parts of the route.

On arrival at Nossob, report to reception to confirm your safe completion of the trail. If you intend exiting at Twee Rivieren, you must check in there for immigration clearance (open 07:00–16:00). Alternatively, if you wish to remain in Botswana, you may return via the public access road to Mabuasehube and exit at Mabuasehube (south) Gate, or continue south to Two Rivers and exit into Botswana before travelling towards Tsabong (first section is untarred).

If your planned exit is into Namibia, **all immigration formalities must first be completed at Twee Rivieren**, even if you intend crossing at Mata-Mata.

It is one of the **most memorable experiences** in the Kalahari; challenging, remote and deeply rewarding.

POLENTSWA WILDERNESS 4X4 TRAIL INTO BOTSWANA

Self-drive circle route starting from Polentswa and ending at Lijersdraai

- **Route:** Polentswa – Sesatswe – Kaa – Lang Rambuka – Lijersdraai – Polentswa
- **Start:** S25°06'18" E20°24'37" (Polentswa)
- **End:** Re-enters Nossob valley at S24°59'32" E20°18'98" (Lijersdraai)
- **Distance:** ±257 km
- **Duration:** 3 days, 2 nights
- **Difficulty:** Moderate–difficult (deep sand, dune crests, encroaching thorn scrub)
- **Vehicles:** Minimum **two fully equipped 4x4s**, **no trailers**

The Polentswa Wilderness trail is one of the most remote overlanding experiences in the Kgalagadi, offering a three-day, two-night journey through wild Botswana dune country.

Starting at Polentswa, the route loops east and north toward **Sesatswe** and **Kaa**, before returning southwest via **Lang Rambuka** to re-enter the Nossob valley near Lijersdraai. This is a **self-drive trail only**. No guide accompanies you and **self-reliance is essential**.

The track is sandy, narrow and often overgrown with **three-thorn and black-thorn**, which scrape vehicles for long distances. A **protective body film** for your vehicle is strongly recommended. Dune crests can be difficult in hot months when the sand is loose and powder-soft. After good rains, **long grass may clog the radiator**, so check frequently.

Facilities at overnight stops are **non-existent**; no water, no firewood, no toilets, no showers no cell signal. Campfires must be kept minimal and only in existing hearths; **gas is preferable**, and firewood must be brought in. As with all Botswana wilderness trails, **you carry everything you will need**, including at least **40 litres of extra fuel per vehicle** and **10–15 litres of water per person per day**.

The trail follows part of a historic 1908 German patrol route. Sesatswe Pan is thought to be close to where final clashes occurred with a fleeing Khoekhoe band. Today, mere tracks, wind and distant horizons remain.

Wildlife is never guaranteed but **brown hyena**, **leopard**, **lion**, **eland** and **springbok** may patrol the pans, and the silence is profound.

Advance booking through **DWNP** is mandatory, with **strict limits** on group size and nights per campsite to protect wilderness quality. All travellers must **check in and out at Twee Rivieren**, even if remaining in Botswana, for safety monitoring and border-control purposes.

Most travellers book **Polentswa or Nossob** the night before and **Nossob** the night after completing the trail, as Twee Rivieren is usually too far to reach before gate closure.

Campers need to be self-sufficient

Daniel Wipf

Daniel Wipf

KAA GAME-VIEWING 4X4 TRAIL

Self-drive and self-sufficient circle route

- **Type:** Remote wilderness loop, deep sand; self-sufficient 4x4 only
- **Length:** ±197 km round trip from Kaa
- **Communication:** No cell signal; **satellite phone strongly advised**
- **Route:** No fixed direction; travel either clockwise or anti-clockwise
- **Nights:** Four camp sites to choose from
- **Notes:** Moderate technical sand driving, overgrown sections, no recovery support
- **Vehicle:** High-clearance 4x4 with low-range only; **no trailers**
- **Fuel planning:** Fill to maximum before entry; **minimum double-tank range**; nearest semi-reliable fuel **Nossob (± 8 hrs away)**
- **Driving skills:** Experienced off-roaders strongly recommended
- **Water:** Fully self-sufficient: **no water, food, or firewood supply** (exception: drinkable trough water at Swartpan)
- **Navigation:** GPS essential. Signage limited; carry maps and backup system
- **Bookings: DWNP advance booking required** for trail access and campsites

Kaa means 'nothing'. An apt name for a landscape where, at first glance, there appears to be very little. Yet with patience and awareness, it becomes clear this is a place where nothing is an illusion, and everything survives by quiet brilliance.

Pans north of the Nossob fossil riverbed lie in long, parallel chains; likely remnants of ancient north–south drainage lines that once emptied into the Nossob basin. Positioned between low, vegetated dunes, these pans attract animals searching for grazing, scarce water and natural mineral licks. The Botswana side of the Kgalagadi feels far wilder, emptier and more rugged than the South African side, and this trail is best suited to seasoned 4x4 travellers seeking true remoteness.

The route begins at **Kaa North Gate** (S24°21'91" E20°37'137"), then continues to **Sizatswe**, **Swartpan**, **Gnus Gnus**, **Thupapedi** and back to **Kaa**; a loop of nearly 200 km with no restriction on direction of travel. Expect to rough it. Facilities are minimal, weather can be extreme and water for wildlife is scarce outside a few troughs. This is genuine thirstland country.

The track as far as Sizatswe Pan is frequently overgrown with **three-thorn** and **black-thorn**, and vehicles are likely to be scratched. Trail maintenance is limited. All bookings must be made in advance through the **Botswana Department of Wildlife**, as strict limits apply to the number of vehicles, people and nights allowed at each campsite to protect wilderness conditions.

Travellers must be entirely **self-sufficient**: water, food, fuel, tools, spare wheels or repair kit, recovery gear, firewood, and preferably a satellite phone with emergency contact details.

Campsites are unfenced and extremely basic

- **Kaa Gate** – two sites with cold-water showers and water
- **Swartpan** – two shaded sites overlooking the pan; a nearby trough may hold the only drinkable water within ±100 km
- **Gnus Gnus** – limited shade, otherwise pleasant but basic
- **Thupapedi (Khandu)** – good shade near the pan; no facilities

Wildlife movements are unpredictable but remarkably diverse for such arid terrain. Nights are alive with sound – distant **lion**, **cheetah**, **leopard**, **brown hyena** and **jackal** – while spoor across the sands reads like a daily diary. During wet years, **tsamma melons**, **gemsbok melons**, and **annual grasses** flourish, drawing **herbivores**, followed by raptors such as **goshawks**, **falcons** and **snake eagles**.

Stargazing and night photography are outstanding thanks to the absence of light pollution and the clean desert air.

End of rainy season (January–April) is the best time for a visit as this is when its greener with higher wildlife activity. The worst conditions are experienced in mid-summer because of the heat, post-rain mud and overgrown thorn scrub.

A relatively new access route via **Kaa Gate** has made reaching this wilderness easier. From the **Trans-Kalahari Highway at Kang**, travel via **Hukuntsi** and **Zutshwa** towards the gate. Note that signage can be poor and travellers must navigate carefully.

KAA PUBLIC ACCESS ROUTE (4X4 ONLY)

Transit self-drive to and from Kannaguass to Kaa

- **GPS:** S24°53'51" E20°12'04" – S24°21'50" E20°37'53"
- **Distance:** 85 km (Kannaguass to Kaa)
- **Route type:** Singletrack access road, **not** a designated wilderness trail
- **Direction:** Two-way; travel permitted in either direction
- **Vehicle requirement**: **4x4 only** (no trailers)
- **Difficulty:** Moderate due to overgrowth and corrugations
- **Bookings: DWNP permit is required** for trail access

The direct access route between Kannaguass and Kaa is a basic service track rather than a wilderness trail, used primarily by park staff and government vehicles.

Travelling from the Nossob valley, the turn-off is 37 km north of Polentswa waterhole, just past Kannaguass waterhole on the right-hand side.

The track is narrow, sandy, corrugated and often overgrown, making progress slow and bumpy. Expect a travel time of **3–4 hours** to cover the 85 km. Although no permit is currently required, it is advisable to inform authorities of your travel intentions and estimated arrival time.

The route may be driven solo but breakdowns in this area can quickly become serious owing to the lack of passing traffic, signal and support. A **satellite phone** is strongly recommended.

All standard 4x4 rules apply. Deflate tyres to ±1.2 bar, avoid speeding, drive with care on uneven surfaces and **no trailers**.

While game viewing is limited, particularly outside dry periods, the scenery is classically beautiful and offers a rewarding sense of isolation for experienced off-road travellers.

Public road to Kaa

Daniel Wipf

MABUA TO KAA 4X4 DIRECT ROUTE

Public access road

- **Route type:** Service road
- **GPS:** S25°04'97" E22°09'29" (Mabuasehube) – S24°21'50" E20°37'53" (Kaa)
- **Distance:** 162 km
- **Vehicle:** 4×4 only, no trailers
- **Condition:** Overgrown, rough and slow-going
- **Bookings: DWNP permit is required** for trail access

The public access track between Mabuasehube and Kaa Gate is not an official wilderness trail. It is a basic service road, used mainly by park staff and government vehicles, and is open to visitors who are booked on either side.

This **singletrack route** can be driven in both directions but requires a capable 4x4 and a driver comfortable with remote, overgrown terrain.

The road is **narrow, scratchy, corrugated** and often slow to travel. It is suitable only for those who enjoy **extreme isolation** and do not mind the likelihood of **paintwork damage**. Many visitors prefer to exit the park and travel outside along the **cut-line** road (the unfenced boundary track), which offers almost identical wildlife potential. Game moves freely between the park and the northern buffer zone, so sightings can be similar.

The cut-line is generally easier driving, although the final ±40 km approaching Kaa can be **very sandy** and slow. Conditions change frequently, so **recent local advice** from the Botswana Department of Wildlife is strongly recommended. While experienced drivers have occasionally towed trailers on the cut-line, this is **not advised** without up-to-date information.

Kaa entrance gate

Daniel Wipf

Fauna and Flora

Hannes Lochner

Plants

The Kgalagadi is an **off-the-beaten-track destination** with immense wilderness appeal. Game viewing can be superb, birding is rewarding – especially for raptor enthusiasts – and its stark landscapes offer outstanding photographic opportunities.

However, it is worth remembering that from the game-drive roads, we see just a **fraction of what unfolds in the surrounding veld**. Sightings are influenced by time of day, weather, season and what we *expect* to find; our eyes are often tuned to large mammals, while countless smaller stories play out at ground level.

In this park, **roads and verges** form important wildlife **observation zones**. Predators frequently walk along the road or leave spoor, hair, scratching sites and resting patches. Tracks of beetles, rodents, millipedes, snakes, antelope and birds read like a daily diary of movement. After rain, everything from brown hyena to butterflies may drink from shallow puddles. When surface water is scarce, butterflies and other insects gather moisture from fresh dung. Ants build overnight mounds that attract chats and finches, searching for seeds, larvae and discarded fragments. Female agamas use the compact road edges to bury their eggs; ground squirrels and aardvark may dig more conspicuous burrows.

Road verges can be both useful and frustrating. Repeated grading forms high, **soft banks** that sometimes limit visibility, but these raised edges also become fertile seedbeds, ideal for grasses, herbs and shrubs that support rodents, reptiles, insects and nesting birds, while also providing cover for stalking predators.

Seasonal behaviour can be fascinating. Before heavy storms, tortoises frequently cross roads heading for higher ground; and female agamas climb into the tops of thorn bushes and face north … both well-known signs of imminent rain. Many birds use roadside perches as hunting platforms, including swallow-tailed bee-eaters, flycatchers, familiar chats, crimson-breasted shrikes and southern yellow-billed hornbills. Fiscal shrikes also use these lookout posts, though care should be taken not to confuse them with the similarly patterned fiscal flycatcher.

HOW TO TELL CAMELTHORNS APART

- **Camelthorn** – evergreen **dark green** leaves; **large, grey, sickle-shaped pods** forming carpets beneath mature trees
- **Grey camelthorn** – **silvery foliage**, partially deciduous; **thin, curved pods**
- **Hybrid** – **intermediate leaf colour**, **slender infertile pods**

Suricate during the season of plenty

Elsie Potgieter

Common Kgalagadi plants

The flora of the Kgalagadi is shaped by heat, wind, and unreliable rainfall, yet it is far richer than first impressions suggest. More than **400 plant species** have been recorded in the park, ranging from hardy dune grasses to deep-rooted trees along the fossil riverbeds. Prominent trees include **camelthorn** (*Vachellia erioloba*), **grey camelthorn** (*Vachellia haematoxylon*), **shepherd's tree** (Boscia albitrunca) and **silver cluster-leaf** (*Terminalia sericea*), which anchor the landscape and provide vital shade and forage. The dune systems are dominated by perennial grasses such as Stipagrostis species, while riverbeds support sweeter grazing after rain. Seasonal herbs and ephemeral wildflowers appear briefly after summer storms, transforming the red sands into a surprisingly delicate and colourful tapestry.

In the main text, both **common and scientific names** are provided for plant species, as common names often vary between regions and can be confusing or unreliable. For birds, reptiles and mammals, only common names are used, since these are generally well established and widely recognised. In the photographic gallery at the back of the book, the **English common name, Afrikaans name and scientific name** are all listed. The gallery highlights many of the commonly encountered species of the park, but it is not intended to serve as a complete species inventory.

Plants of the Kalahari must survive in an environment defined by **sand, heat, drought and intense sunlight**. While sunshine for photosynthesis is abundant, **water is the critical limiting factor**. Without sufficient moisture, plants cannot grow, reproduce or maintain vital cellular functions.

Some species survive by completing their life cycle rapidly after rain – germinating, flowering and setting seed within a few short weeks. Their seeds then remain dormant until the next favourable rainfall. To prevent premature germination or predation by seed-eaters, many plants produce hardened seed coats or require specific rainfall thresholds before sprouting.

Other plants endure through specialised root systems. Some spread wide, shallow roots to capture even minimal surface moisture, while others develop deep taproots to reach distant groundwater. Still others rely on underground storage organs such as bulbs, tubers or rhizomes, storing water and nutrients until conditions improve.

Limiting water loss is equally important. Many desert plants reduce transpiration through waxy coatings, fine hairs, fleshy leaves or stems, or very small foliage. Succulent tissues allow moisture storage while exposing minimal surface area to evaporation.

The very structure of Kalahari sand influences survival. Coarse red sands often retain water better than finer clay soils because they allow greater infiltration and less runoff. Their weaker capillary action also reduces upward evaporation. Surface temperatures may exceed 70 °C on open sand, yet just a few centimetres below, the temperature drops dramatically – a crucial thermal refuge for roots, bulbs and many small animals.

Most Kalahari trees develop deep, penetrating taproots that draw on subsurface moisture, especially along the dry riverbeds where occasional flows recharge the groundwater. On dune crests, where water lies deeper, trees are noticeably smaller and more stunted.

The most iconic tree of the Kgalagadi is the **camelthorn** (*Vachellia erioloba*, formerly *Acacia erioloba*). Its massive, sculptural form provides shade, nesting sites and food, creating a rich micro-ecosystem for birds, reptiles, insects and mammals. A close relative, the grey camelthorn (Vachellia haematoxylon), occurs mainly along the Auob River. Natural hybrids between the two species can be recognised by intermediate leaf colour and narrower, often infertile pods.

Carpets of devil's thorn blooms

Shepherd's tree (witgatboom)
Boscia albitrunca

Camelthorn (kameeldoring)
Vachellia erioloba

Grey camelthorn (vaalkameeldoring)
Vachellia haematoxylon

Silver cluster-leaf (sandgeelhout)
Terminalia sericea

Black thorn (swarthaak)
Senegalia mellifera

Candle thorn (trassiebos)
Vachellia hebeclada

Raisin bush (fluweelrosyntjiebos)
Grewia flava

Boshoff Steenekamp

Three thorn (driedoring)
Rhigozum trichotomum

Springbokopslag
Indigofera alternans

Buffalo thorn (blinkblaar wag-'n-bietjie)
Ziziphus mucronata

Doll's rose (duinerosie)
Hermannia burchellii

Doringviooltjie/kankerbos
Aptosimum spinescens

Dune bush (besembossie)
Crotalaria orientalis

Wild celery (wilde seldery)
Deverra denudata

Botterblom
Hirpicium gazanioides

Blue ganna (blouganna/netvetbossie)
Monechma incanum

Kalahari sour grass (Kalaharisuurgras)
Scmidtia kalahariensis

Dune Bushman grass (duinriet)
Stipagrostis amabilis

Blue Bushman grass (blouboesmangras)
Stipagrostis hirtigluma

Foxtail buffalo grass (bloubuffelgras)
Cenchrus ciliaris

Small Bushman grass (kortbeenboesmansgras)
Stipagrostis obtusa

Frutang (froetang)
Camptorrhiza strumosa

Osonanga (slangkop)
Lindneria clavata

Crinum lily (Crinumlelie)
Crinum foetidum

Plants

Nerine/vlei lily (vleilelie)
Nerine laticoma

Anja Denker

Aandblommetjie
Pancratium tenuifolium

Wild senna/eland's pea (swartstormbossie)
Senna italica

Devil's thorn (dubbeltjie)
Tribulus zeyheri

Devil's claw (duiwelsklou)
Harpagophytum procumbens

Karoo pumpkin/wild calabash (pampoenbossie) *Radyera urens*

Gemsbok cucumber (gemsbokkomkommer)
Acanthosicyos naudinianus

Tsamma melon (tsamma)
Citrullus lanatus

Cat's tail/cockscomb family (katstert)
Hermbstaedtia fleckii

Yellow mouse-whiskers (geel-cleome)
Cleome angustifolia

African cabbage (oorpeultjie)
Cleome gynandra

Sorrel (suring)
Oxalis semiloba

String of stars (hamelstertjie)
Heliotropium lineare

Wild sesame (brandboontjie)
Sesamum triphyllum

River cabbage/wild radish (rivierkool)
Platycarpha carlinoides

Hoodia (bitterghaap)
Hoodia gordonii

Ouheip (bitterkambro)
Adenium oleifolium

African milkweed (melkbos)
Gomphocarpus fruticosus

Cockscomb (katstert)
Hermbstaedtia fleckii

Dominique de Beer

Fights between rival male ground agamas can be aggressive, using powerful jaws and tail lashing

Hannes Lochner

Common Kgalagadi reptiles

The Kgalagadi hosts an impressive **55+ reptile species**, making reptiles one of the most diverse vertebrate groups in the park. This richness is largely thanks to their **excellent physiological and behavioural adaptations** to heat, drought and temperature fluctuations.

As ectotherms, reptiles **use the environment to regulate body temperature**, avoiding unnecessary water loss that challenges mammals and birds. Many species – such as **tortoises, geckos, agamas and sand lizards** can withstand extreme heat, reduce activity during the hottest periods, and rely on **efficient water conservation**, gaining moisture from food rather than drinking.

Their **burrowing habits**, heat-reflective scales and seasonal activity cycles further help them survive in a land of **scorching days, cold nights, scarce rainfall and sandy soils**, making reptiles some of the **best-adapted life forms** in the Kalahari.

Leopard tortoise (bergskilpad)
Stigmochelys pardalis

Kalahari tent tortoise (Kalahari-skilpad)
Psammobates oculifera

Ground agama (gewone grondkoggelmander)
Agama aculeata

Bibron's gecko (Bibron se geitjie/ reusegrondgeitjie)
Chondrodactylus bibroni

Common barking gecko (gewone blafgeitjie)
Ptenopus garrulus

Cape cobra (geelslang/Kaapse kobra)
Naja nivea

Puff adder (pofadder)
Bitis arietans

Horned adder (horingadder)
Bitis caudalis

Mole snake (molslang)
Pseudaspis cana

Common Kgalagadi birds

Although the semi-desert conditions of the Kalahari create a harsh environment for birds, the region supports a **surprisingly rich mix of resident and seasonal visitors**. The greatest challenges for birds here are **water scarcity** and **extreme heat**, yet many species have evolved remarkable strategies to cope. During dry periods, **overall bird density is low** but after good rains, there is a **rapid influx of nomadic and migratory species**, some of which remain only while conditions are favourable.

Life in the Kgalagadi is complex and birds must cope with **scarce water**, **extreme temperatures**, **limited shade**, **variable food supplies** and **highly unpredictable breeding conditions**. Yet birds have one great advantage: they can **move quickly across large distances**. Many species from surrounding regions take advantage of **good rains**, arriving to feed and breed while conditions are favourable and leaving again when resources dwindle.

More than **300 bird species** have been recorded in the park, but **over half** are **irregular or incidental visitors**. The latest census shows that **179 species** occur regularly, whether times are good or harsh. They survive through **adaptability**, despite the semi-arid environment. Among these, **86 species** are considered **true residents**, always present in the park. Other species are **nomads**, moving in response to shifting resources rather than season. **Almost 30 species** are **annual migrants**, making predictable journeys between breeding and non-breeding areas. **More than 160 species** are classified as **vagrants**, most of them **waterbirds** that visit **seasonal pans** during exceptional rainfall years. Others are **accidental arrivals**, such as the greater painted-snipe, simply blown or guided off course.

The Kalahari supports a **high density and diversity of raptors**, arguably more than many woodland reserves where you might expect richer prey availability. This may be owing to the **vast protected area**, minimal human disturbance and **large rodent populations**. Look for **pygmy falcons, pale chanting goshawks, tawny and martial eagles, bateleurs, lanner falcons** and **red-necked falcons**. After heavy summer rains, these are joined by **nomadic and migratory species** such as **yellow-billed kites, steppe buzzards, steppe eagles** and **black-shouldered kites**.

Nocturnal raptors are well represented, with **Verreaux's eagle-owl**, **spotted eagle-owl** and **pearl-spotted owlet** frequently seen along the riverbeds. Camps provide excellent night-time viewing. Nossob Rest Camp is renowned for hosting up to five owl species. Keep watch for **southern white-faced scops-owl** and **African scops-owl** in shade trees.

Many Kalahari birds are **insectivorous** and obtain most of their moisture from prey, reducing or eliminating the need to drink. These agile hunters forage among trees, shrubs and open ground, or from lookout perches.

Common and striking species include **chat and Marico flycatchers, fork-tailed drongos, lilac-breasted rollers, swallow-tailed bee-eaters, crimson-breasted shrikes, Kalahari scrub-robins, capped wheatears, black-chested prinias, ant-eating chats** and **common fiscals**. Summer brings **spotted flycatchers, lesser grey shrikes** and **red-backed shrikes**.

Many ground birds also rely heavily on insects. **Spotted thick-knees, crowned lapwings, double-banded coursers, Timminck's coursers, larks, northern black korhaans, kori bustards** and even **secretarybirds** include insects in their diet, particularly **harvester termites**, which drive feeding frenzies across the park. Following heavy rains, **white storks** and **Abdim's storks** may arrive in large numbers to exploit the abundance.

Seed-eating birds are often the **most numerous** but **highly nomadic**, moving to follow rainfall and fresh seeding grasses. Because seeds offer little moisture, these species must **drink regularly**. In mid-morning, flocks converge on waterholes, where they must drink quickly to avoid predators such as **lanner and red-necked falcons, black-backed jackals** and **African wild cats**.

Typical species include **Namaqua and Burchell's sandgrouse, Cape turtle doves, weavers, waxbills, whydahs, sociable weavers, white-browed sparrow-weavers, sparrowlarks, canaries, sparrows, buntings** and **finches**.

Sandgrouse are especially remarkable. **Daily round-trips of up to 160 km to water are possible**, and **males soak specialised belly feathers** to carry water back to chicks.

Most seed-eaters **switch to insects during breeding**, providing essential protein for growing young.

Common ostrich (volstruis)
Struthio camelus

White stork (witooievaar)
Ciconia ciconia

Abdim's stork (kleinswartooievaar)
Ciconia abdimii

Egyptian goose (kolgans)
Alopochen aegyptiaca

Secretarybird (sekretarisvoël)
Sagittarius serpentarius

White-backed vulture (witrugaasvoël)
Gyps africanus

Lappet-faced vulture (swartaasvoël)
Aegypius tracheliotos

Yellow-billed kite (geelbekwou)
Milvus aegyptius

Black-shouldered kite (blouvalk)
Elanus caerulens

Tawny eagle (roofarend)
Aquila rapax

Martial eagle (breëkoparend)
Polemaetus bellicosus

Brown snake eagle (bruinslangarend)
Circaetus cinereus

Black-chested snake eagle (swartborsslangarend)
Circaetus pectoralis

Bateleur (berghaan)
Terathopius ecaudatus

Steppe buzzard (bruinjakkalsvoël)
Buteo vulpinus

Gabar goshawk (kleinsingvalk)
Melierax gabar

Southern pale chanting goshawk (bleeksingvalk) *Melierax canorus*

African harrier-hawk (kaalwangvalk)
Polyboroides typus

Lanner falcon (edelvalk)
Falco biarmicus

Red-necked falcon (rooinekvalk)
Falco chicquera

Rock kestrel (kransvalk)
Falco rupicolus

Greater kestrel (grootrooivalk)
Falco rupicoloides

Pygmy falcon (dwergvalk)
Polihierax semitorquatus

Kori bustard (gompou)
Ardeotis kori

Ludwig's bustard (Ludwigse pou)
Neotis ludwigii

Red-crested korhaan (boskorhaan)
Lophotis ruficrista

Northern black korhaan (witvlerkkorhaan)
Afrotis afraoides

Three-banded plover (driebandstrandkiewiet)
Charadrius tricollaris

Crowned lapwing (kroonkiewiet)
Vanellus coronatus

Spotted thick-knee (gewone dikkop)
Burhinus capensis

Temminck's courser (trekdrawwertjie)
Cursorius temminckii

Double-banded courser (dubbelbanddrawwertjie)
Rhinoptilus africanus

Namaqua sandgrouse (kelkiewyn)
Pterocles namaqua

Burchell's sandgrouse (gevlekte sandpatrys)
Pterocles burchelli

Cape turtle-dove (gewone tortelduif)
Streptopelia capricola

Laughing dove (rooiborsduifie)
Streptopelia senegalensis

Namaqua dove (namakwaduifie)
Oena capensis

Barn owl (nonnetjie-uil)
Tyto alba

African scops-owl (skopsuil)
Otus senegalensis

Southern white-faced scops-owl (witwanguil)
Ptilopsis granti

Pearl-spotted owlet (witkoluil)
Glaucidium perlatum

Spotted eagle-owl (gevlekte ooruil)
Bubo africanus

Verreaux's eagle-owl (reuse-ooruil)
Bubo lacteus

White-backed mousebird (witkruismuisvoël)
Colius colius

Red-faced mousebird (rooiwagmuisvoël)
Urocolius indicus

Striped kingfisher (gestreepte visvanger)
Halcyon chelicuti

Eurasian bee-eater (Europese byvreter)
Merops apiaster

Swallow-tailed bee-eater (swaelstertbyvreter)
Merops hirundineus

Lilac-breasted roller (gewone troupant)
Coracias caudatus

African hoopoe (hoephoep)
Upupa africana

Green wood-hoopoe (rooibekkakelaar)
Phoeniculus purpureus

Common scimitarbill (swartbekkakelaar)
Rhinopomastus cyanomelas

Southern yellow-billed hornbill (geelbekneushoringvoël)
Tockus leucomelas

Acacia pied barbet (bonthoutkapper)
Tricholaema leucomelas

Cardinal woodpecker (karinaalspeg)
Dendropicos fuscescens

Golden-tailed woodpecker (goudstertspeg)
Campethera abingoni

Fawn-coloured lark (vaalbruinlewerik)
Calendulauda africanoides

Sabota lark (sabotalewerik)
Calendulauda sabota

Spike-heeled lark (vlaktelewerik)
Chersomanes albofasciata

Red-capped lark (rooikoplewerik)
Calandrella cinerea

Grey-backed sparrow-lark (grysruglewerik)
Eremopterix verticalis

Chestnut-backed sparrow-lark (rooruglewerik) *Eremopterix lecotis*

Cape crow (swartkraai)
Corvus capensis

Fork-tailed drongo (miksterbyvanger)
Dicrurus adsimilis

Ashy tit (akasiagrysmees)
Parus cinerascens

African red-eyed bulbul (rooioogtiptol)
Pycnonotus nigricans

Capped wheatear (Hoëveldskaapwagter)
Oenanthe pileata

Groundscraper thrush (gevlekte lyster)
Psophocichla litsitsirupa

Familiar chat (gewone spekvreter)
Cercomela familiaris

Ant-eating chat (swartpiek)
Myrmecocichla formicivora

Kalahari scrub-robin (Kalahariwipstert)
Cercotrichas paena

Black-chested prinia (swartbandlangstertjie)
Prinia flavicans

Rufous-eared warbler (rooioorlangstertjie)
Malcorus pectoralis

Spotted flycatcher (Europese vlieëvanger)
Muscicapa striata

Marico flycatcher (Maricovlieëvanger)
Bradornis mariquensis

Chat flycatcher (grootvlieëvanger) *Bradornis pallidus*

Lesser grey shrike (gryslaksman) *Lanius minor*

Common fiscal (fiskaallaksman) *Lanius collaris*

Red-backed shrike (rooiruglaksman) *Lanius collurio*

Crimson-breasted shrike (rooiborslaksman) *Laniarius atrococcineus*

Cape glossy starling (kleinglansspreeu) *Lamprotornis nitens*

Burchell's starling (grootglansspreeu) *Lamprotornis australis*

Wattled starling (lelspreeu) *Creatophora cinerea*

White-browed sparrow-weaver (koringvoël) *Plocepasser mahali*

Sociable weaver (versamelvoël) *Philetairus socius*

Cape sparrow (gewone mossie) *Passer melanurus*

Southern grey-headed sparrow (gryskopmossie) *Passer diffusus*

Scaly-feathered finch (baardmannetjie)
Sporopipes squamifrons

Southern masked weaver (swartkeelgeelvink)
Ploceus velatus

Red-billed quelea (rooibekkwelea)
Quelea quelea

Green-winged pytilia (gewone melba)
Pytilia melba

Violet-eared waxbill (koningblousysie)
Granatina granatina

Black-faced waxbill (swartwangsysie)
Estrilda erythronotos

Common waxbill (rooibeksysie)
Estrilda astrild

Red-headed finch (rooikopvink)
Amadina erythrocephala

Shaft-tailed whydah (pylstertroobekkie)
Vidua regia

Yellow canary (geelkanarie)
Crithagra flaviventris

Black-throated canary (bergkanarie)
Crithagra atrogularis

Lark-like bunting (vaalstreepkoppie)
Emberiza impetuani

Hannes Lochner

The lanner falcon's streamlined, muscular build is perfectly designed for speed and agility in flight

Myburgh du Plessis

Lanner falcon, a master bird hunter of the Kalahari skies

Common Kgalagadi mammals

The Kgalagadi supports a **remarkably rich mammal community**, with **around 58 recorded species** adapted to its semi-arid environment. While overall diversity is lower than in wetter savanna systems, the park is famous for its **large predators** – including **lion, leopard, cheetah, spotted and brown hyena, and African wild cat** – as well as **iconic antelope** such as **gemsbok, springbok, eland, red hartebeest and wildebeest**. Smaller mammals are abundant but often overlooked, ranging from **meerkats, Cape fox and bat-eared fox** to **aardwolf, aardvark and honey badger**. This specialised community reflects evolutionary adaptation to heat, drought, sparse vegetation and unpredictable resources, making mammal watching in the Kgalagadi a study in resilience and behaviour rather than sheer numbers.

In the Kalahari, a land known for extremes, a few conditions are truly essential for survival: **adequate food and water**, and the ability to **reproduce successfully** so that the species endures. Added to these are the challenges of **coping with intense heat**, avoiding excessive moisture loss through breathing, panting or excretion, and **regulating body temperature** well enough to avoid fatal heat stress.

With these fundamentals in mind, game viewing in the Kalahari takes on deeper meaning. Rather than simply ticking off species, contemplate **how** animals survive under such demanding circumstances: their **behaviour**, **physical adaptations**, and **reproductive strategies**. Behaviour in the Kalahari is rarely random.

Rainfall is **erratic**, ranging from about **150–500 mm per year**, and some years receive virtually none. Water is a scarce commodity in the Kgalagadi. Remarkably, many animals survive long periods **without drinking free water**. Some obtain moisture directly from **food** (herbivores with water-rich gut contents) while **predators** may rely on the **blood and body fluids** of their prey. Others drink only when necessary, sometimes travelling long distances. Some can store water in tissues (small mammals) and others reduce moisture loss through behaviour (shade-seeking, resting, nocturnal activity.

Temperatures swing to extremes: **summer days may exceed 40–50 °C**, winter nights can drop to **below 10 °C**, and **sand surface temperature** can surpass **70 °C**, while shaded areas may be **20 °C cooler**. A single day can see a change of more than **30 °C**. These conditions demand extraordinary physiological and behavioural adaptations. Animals deal with these adverse conditions in different ways. Most animals rest during hottest hours and feed or hunt at dawn, dusk or night. Others use burrows, shade trees, shrubs or abandoned nests as refuges; many desert-adapted species have light-coloured coats, while evaporative cooling is effective for others (panting).

Behaviour is a way of conserving energy. Slow, deliberate movements reduce heat load and energy waste. Seasonal or opportunistic breeding during favourable conditions helps offspring to survive. Some animals switch diets seasonally (e.g. insects, seeds, browse, graze) and others enter torpor or reduce metabolic rate in extreme drought or cold.

When food and water are scarce, **nomadic movements** are triggered. During good years, many animals favour the **Botswana side** of the park, where **savanna woodland** offers more browse and shelter. As drought intensifies, **pans dry**, vegetation becomes fibrous, and animals drift back towards the **riverbeds**, where even light rainfall promotes **grass growth** owing to a **shallower water table**. Historically, migration routes extended **as far as the Orange River**. Within the modern Transfrontier Park, a **broad, anti-clockwise seasonal movement** is still observed; **northeast in summer, southwest in winter**. Although the **spectacular mass springbok migrations** recorded over a century ago no longer occur – largely as a consequence of fencing and human barriers – smaller-scale, natural migrations still take place.

For protection against predation many animals have sand-coloured coats to help with concealment. In this way they can blend with their environment to avoid detection. Some use burrow systems to provide shelter from predators and temperature extremes.

Rain-triggered breeding cycles and rapid young rearing.

Lion (leeu)
Panthera leo

Leopard (luiperd)
Panthera pardus

Cheetah (jagluiperd)
Acinonyx jubatus

Caracal or desert lynx (rooikat)
Caracal caracal

African wild cat (vaalboskat)
Felis silvestris

Black-footed cat (klein gekolde kat)
Felis nigripes

Slender mongoose (swartkwasmuishond)
Galerella sanguinea

Yellow mongoose (witkwasmuishond)
Cynictis penicillata

Suricate (stokstertmeerkat)
Suricata suricatta

Black-backed jackal (rooijakkals)
Canis mesomelas

Bat-eared fox (bakoorjakkals)
Otocyon megaltis

Cape fox (silwerjakkals/silwervos)
Vulpes chama

Small-spotted genet (kleinkolmuskejaatkat)
Genetta genetta

Brown hyena (bruinhiëna)
Parahyaena brunnea

Spotted hyena (gevlekte hiëna)
Crocuta crocuta

Aardwolf (aardwolf)
Proteles cristatus

Cape porcupine (ystervark)
Hystrix africaeaustralis

Damaraland mole-rat (Damaraland blesmol)
Cryptomys damarensis

Springhare (springhaas)
Pedetes capensis

South African ground squirrel (grondeekhoring) *Xerus inauris*

Brant's whistling rat (Brant se fluitrot)
Parotomys brantsii

Black-tailed tree rat (swartstertboomrot)
Thallomys nigricauda

Four-striped grass mouse (streepmuis)
Rhabdomys pumilio

Pygmy mouse (dwergmuis)
Mus minutoides

Bushveld elephant shrew (bosveldklaasneus)
Elephantulus intufi

Cape hare (vlakhaas)
Lepus capensis

Ground pangolin (ietermagog)
Manis temminckii

Aardvark/antbear (erdvark)
Orycteropus afer

Common warthog (vlakvark)
Phacochoerus africanus

Giraffe (kameelperd)
Giraffa camelopardalis

Eland (eland)
Tragelaphus oryx

Greater kudu (koedoe)
Tragelaphus strepsiceros

Gemsbok/oryx (gemsbok)
Oryx gazella

Red hartebeest (rooihartebees)
Alcelaphus buselaphus

Blue wildebeest (blouwildebees)
Connochaetes taurinus

Springbok (springbok)
Antidorcas marsupialis

Honey badger (ratel)
Mellivora capensis

Common (grey) duiker (gewone duiker)
Sylvicapra grimmia

Steenbok (steenbok)
Raphicerus campestris

After the rains a rainbow

Geo Jooste

Index

MAP INDEX

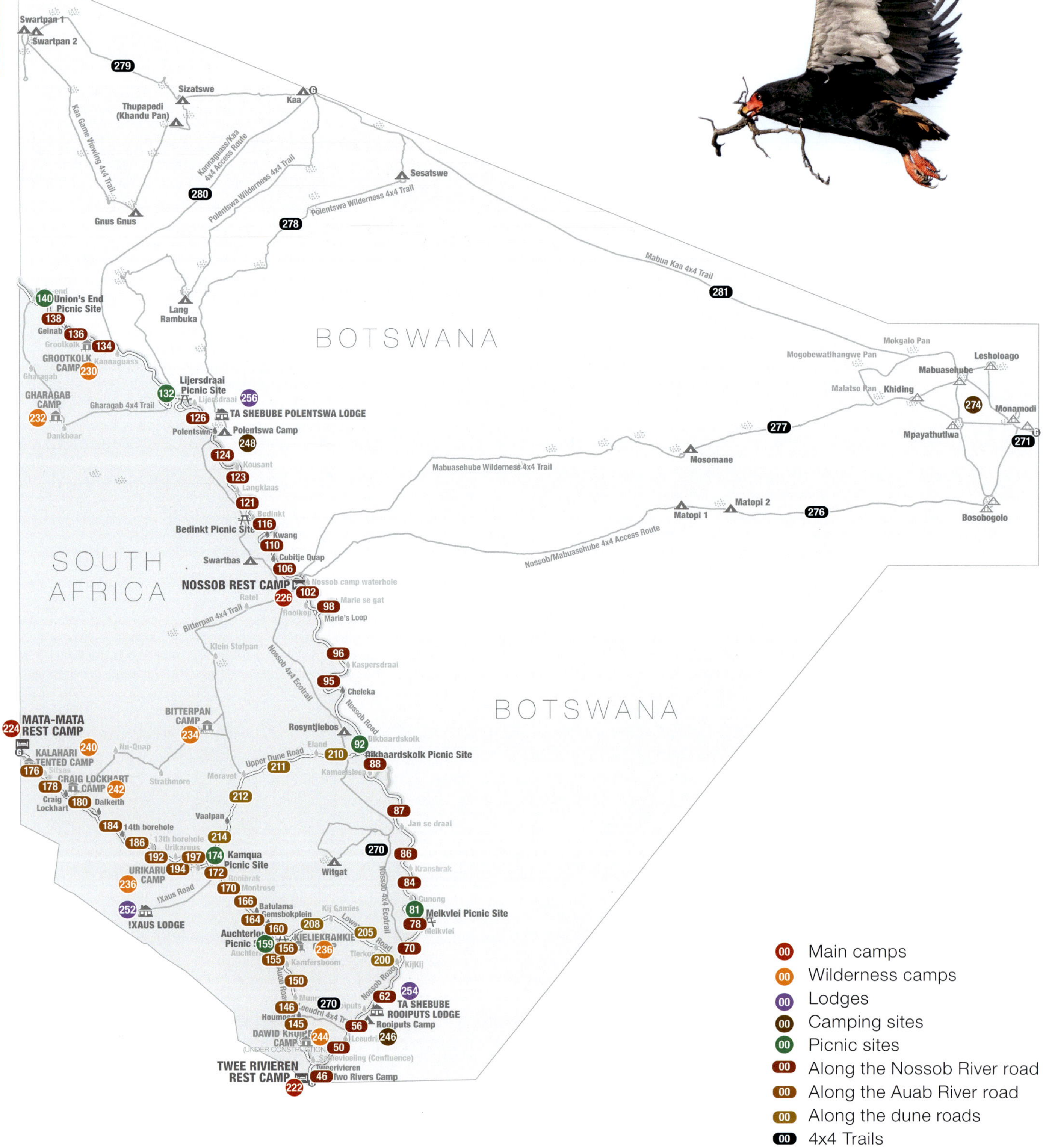

WATERHOLES

CAMPS

Lion

Male lion

Hannes Lochner

INDEX OF PHOTOGRAPHERS

The Kgalagadi Transfrontier Park is a haven for nature lovers and photographers alike. In this revised second edition of the Kgalagadi Self-drive, Routes, Roads and Ratings, **HPH Publishing** invited photographers to participate by supplying their best images for possible inclusion in the new edition. The response was overwhelming. From over 3 000 photo submissions, we had to select those images that best suited the text and the available spaces. This was extremely difficult since we received so many excellent images. The enthusiasm for capturing special moments in nature shows the deep appreciation and awareness of the natural world in the beloved Kgalagadi Transfrontier Park.

Photo images of the following photographers were selected:

Bushveld sengi and ground agama

Hannes Lochner

Gharagab memories in a cup

Brett Ellis

Helen Keller once said, *"Alone we can do so little; together we can do so much."* This book is the result of exceptional teamwork. At times we worked independently, at other times side by side, but always united by a shared vision. Each contributor brought creativity, insight, expertise and commitment … and together we shaped a long-held dream into reality. Over the years, every member of this team has developed something of a love affair with the Kgalagadi. It is a place we value deeply, respect profoundly, and feel privileged to interpret.

Philip and Ingrid have been regular visitors to the park since the early 1970s. They have seen green seasons and grey ones, witnessed the evolution of tourism, and observed how visitor expectations have shifted over time. Today, people want more than sightings; they seek context, meaning and connection. The rise of nature photography has made the Kgalagadi one of southern Africa's most sought-after destinations and travellers increasingly want to *understand* the bigger story behind the scenes.

Ingrid undertook the research and writing and was responsible for weaving the book's narrative. With a BSc (Hons) in Zoology, including botany and entomology, she was well prepared for the task. Both she and Philip contributed photography. Philip curated, edited and managed the image library while also applying his extensive natural history knowledge and experience in environmental education to review and strengthen the text.

For **Heinrich**, the Kgalagadi has always been a place of creative inspiration; a landscape that continually calls him back. With a degree in engineering, he chose instead to dedicate his career to raising awareness for conservation and promoting knowledge of our wildlife heritage. Working on this book was like reliving the wonders of the Kalahari and watching them evolve into something tangible and hopefully meaningful to readers. Heinrich directs **HPH Publishing** (*www.hphpublishing.co.za*), where he specialises in wildlife books, photography, filmmaking and creative storytelling.

Second Edition
ISBN 978-0-6398580-5-0
Text by Ingrid van den Berg
Photography by Philip & Ingrid van den Berg, Heinrich van den Berg and invited contributors
Cover image by Kathy Kay
Publisher: Heinrich van den Berg
Edited and proofread by Margy Gibson
Design, typesetting and reproduction by Heinrich van den Berg and Nicky Wenhold
Maps by Nicky Wenhold
All Geographical Information System (GIS) datasets were obtained from Scientific Services, South African National Parks, and have been utilised with permission and according to the requirements of the Data User Agreement

Printed and bound in China

First edition, first impression 2017
Published by **HPH Publishing**
50A Sixth Street, Linden, Johannesburg, 2195, South Africa
www.hphpublishing.co.za
info@hphpublishing.co.za